MW01052714

PETERS & KING

Thomas D. Schiffer

Published by

**krause
publications**

700 E. State Street • Iola, WI 54990-0001
Telephone: 715/445-2214
Web: www.krause.com

Please call or write for our free catalog.

Please call or write for our free catalog of pulications.
Our toll-free number to place an order or obtain a free catalog is 800-258-0929
or please use our regular business telephone 715-445-2214.

Library of Congress Catalog Number: 2001096279
ISBN: 0-87349-363-X

Dedication

This book is dedicated to my wife Carol. She read every word of it before anyone else, did the primary editing and commented on the content. It was she who wielded her schoolteacher's red pencil and went with me on countless trips to research, photograph, and interview; trips that we called "vacations." While I like to think all of that was interesting to her, and I'm sure that some of it was, there was always the interminable waiting while... "I take just one more picture...see just one more person...ask just one more question...copy just one more chapter...write just one more page...look in just one more book..."

As skinny as these lines are, I hope they have substance enough to adequately convey my true appreciation.

Tom Schiffer

Foreword

Memory doesn't serve me as to when exactly I first met Tom Schiffer. It just seems like I've known him forever. In fact, most people active in black powder shooting circles know him. What I didn't know about him was that he was such a dedicated and talented researcher. That is, until he forwarded a draft of this book for me to review.

Herein Tom brings forth a wealth of detail about the King Powder and Peters Cartridge companies. For instance, did you know that the many gun- and blasting-powder mills of the late 1800s usually sold their products from the backs of horse-drawn wagons during lengthy trips about their trade area? Beyond that, by interviewing people, or searching out the memoirs of those who lived nearby in the heyday of those companies, Tom actually gives the reader a feel for life in Kings Mills: a town centered around gunpowder and, later, firearm cartridge manufacturing. Here's another 'for instance': powder plant explosions were considered a way of life in such towns, and the plants themselves were designed for quick rebuilding after explosions. Of course this was long before the birth of OHSA. However, when Tom mentions as many as 3,000 windows being replaced after a powder plant explosion, I can't help but think that the most lucrative occupation around Kings Mills would have been that of a glazier!

As an avid black powder competitor myself, I must admit to having only a vague idea as to how gunpowder was manufactured in former times. This book goes into minute details of the process. I found it fascinating that mules and the horses used to pull the powder carts from the manufacturing plant to storage sheds were fitted with non-sparking bronze shoes held on with copper nails. Furthermore, all the tools used inside the plant—such as shovels, mallets, and chisels—were made of wood. Yet, occasionally a workman had to be fired because he was found carrying matches!

All of us modern shooters are familiar with the R-P headstamp of Remington ammunition, but sometimes we forget that the "P" stands for Peters—as in Peters Cartridge Company. Before reading Tom's manuscript I honestly did not realize that Peters ammunition was also manufactured in Kings Mills, Ohio. Nor did I realize that when Peters Cartridge Company was formed in 1887, it was first intended only for shotshell manufacture. Peters did not produce metallic cartridges until well into the 1890s, and advertised that nary a grain of black powder was used in their loading. The story of Peters Cartridge Company's output during two world wars, their acquisition by Remington in the 1930s, and their eventual move to Connecticut is detailed herein.

But, beyond the story of gunpowder and firearms cartridge manufacturing, Tom Schiffer has done considerable research into life in the town of Kings Mills—right down to gaining some insight into the social pecking order of a small mid-west industrial community. Furthermore, there are chapters on the exhibition shooters affiliated with Peters Cartridge Company through the decades, and even one on collectible artifacts left over from King Powder Company and Peters Cartridge Company. Who would have guessed that an *empty* Peters 12-gauge shotshell box could sell at auction for $275?

Of much interest are the Appendices in which are detailed the life stories of several people instrumental in the formation and running of both companies, and even some of the lawsuits that occurred between Peters and Winchester in the early 1900s. Today's Kings Island Amusement Park located near Cincinnati, Ohio, is well known, but I didn't realize that it sits upon the onetime site of Kings Mills, where so many tons of black powder had been manufactured.

And for one tidbit I will be forever grateful to Tom Schiffer. Often I have read in vintage accounts where old timers said things like "I didn't have a rifle with me, only a gun." That just didn't make sense to me, but in this book is the detail that in the late 1880s "gun" was not the generic word for firearm that it has become today. In that period, a "gun" is what we now call a shotgun. Now some of those old accounts make so much more sense to me.

From reading *Peters And King* I can see that this has been a lifetime's research project for Tom Schiffer. He quotes correspondence and trips made to the area around Kings Mills dating back many years. I am glad that he has put all these details on paper, and I think modern firearms enthusiasts will gain a deeper understanding of the industry by reading them.

Mike Venturino
Livingston, Montana

Contents

Preface

This book has been written for shooters, hunters and collectors. It is the story of the Peters Cartridge Company and its parent, the King Powder Company—and their products. It is the story of the people who made them, promoted them and used them.

These two companies enjoyed—or at least embraced—an importance and influence all out of proportion to their size and market share. This story is a study of the effect of strong personalities, invention and changing times on the powder and cartridge businesses. You will meet A. O. Fay, J. W. King (I and II), F. O. Kneeland, Lammot du Pont, J. Q. du Pont, Ahimaaz King, G. M. Peters, Milton F. Lindsley (I and II), Wanda Lindsley, Annie Oakley, Philip Quayle, Colonel George King and many others.

Among those people were to be found entrepreneurs, innovators, inventors, managers, leaders, chemists, powder makers, workers, in-laws, outlaws, a physicist and a preacher. The story is, by turns, one of ouster, rivalry, revenge, triumph, intrigue, success and disaster. The story is not always pretty, but it is always interesting. I sincerely hope you enjoy reading it as much as I have enjoyed bringing it to you.

Acknowledgments

A book about Peters and King could have been written without the input of others, but this one most assuredly was not. The input of others has taken this book to dimensions that I would never have hoped for in the beginning. The sheer number of people, the quality of their input and the enthusiasm with which it was given, was both staggering and gratifying.

While it is safe to say that without them the book would have been less than it is, there are those whose contribution deserves special recognition.

First on my list is Miss Edna Bowyer. She worked as secretary to the King Powder Company for 25 years, until it closed. She grew up in Kings Mills and her father was foreman of the shot tower at Peters. Her input was wide in scope, accurate, insightful and freely given.

Next is Sharon Cunningham, who edited my text. She waded through my rhetoric and weeded out redundancy and steered the text back into the main chanel when it wandered.

The collections of Bob and Betty Carter, Jim Eckler, Tom Rowe, James Claggett, George Kass, Dan Schlegel, Mick McLaughlin, Ted Bacyk, Mike Sayers, John Malloy and Ron Willoughby were thrown open to me.

Jim Sones, Doug Culver, Windy Klinect, Joe Baldwin, John Dutcher, Mike Beyer, Dave Spencer, Dale Hedlund, Jim Rodgers, Kenneth Lane, the late Tony Dunn, John Kuntz, John Pople-Crump, Lester Smith, Dick Baldwin, Bess Edwards, the late James Tillinghast, the late Phil Orem, Fred Pott and Merrill Deer sent me enough valuable material to more than fill a file drawer and a large box.

Randy Cochran, who guided me through the pitfalls of photographing most of the material shown in this book.

Arguably, the largest repository of King and Peters material is in the files and collections of the Warren County Historical Society. Much of it was donated by Edna Bowyer. I started there when Hazel Phillips was curator in about 1974; later, Tom Kuhn. Mary W. Payne is now curator and Mary Klei on the staff; Dixon Maple was, until recently, president of the Historical Society, he being succeeded by Jim Klei.

The Hagley Museum and Library in Wilmington, Delaware, which houses much information about the powder and explosives industry. Valuable information was supplied by Robert Howard, then engineering curator, John Rum, Mary Lou Neighbor (whose mother worked for Peters), Lynn Catanese, Dr. Nash, Lynn Joshi and Marjore McNinch.

Remington Arms Company, Richard Dietz, Public Relations, Wayland E. Hundley, Assistant General Counsel, Samual G. Grecco, Vice President Business Development and Vince Scarlotta, Production Engineer.

Library of Congress.

The Trapshooting Hall of Fame and Museum, Vandalia, Ohio, especially, but not limited to Dick Baldwin, Executive Director.

The Cincinnati Historical Society, Linda Bailey, David Conzett and Laura Chase.

The records of the Ordnance Department in the National Archives provided some material found nowhere else. Mich Yocleson was most helpful in that maze of paper, as were Mike Pynn, Andy Schiffer and my wife Carol.

National Rifle Association publications, *American Rifleman* staff, Ivan Inghraham, Associate Editor, Gregg Conner and Mark Keefe.

Little Miami, Incoporated, Eric Partee.

Mercantile Library (Cincinnati).

Warren County Engineer's Office, Jerry Stiles, Engineer.

The Smithsonian Institution, Harry Hunter.

Ohio Secretary of State.

Historical Society of Western Pennsylvania, Hines Regional Historical Center, Kay Moriarity.

The Greene County Library in Xenia, Ohio, Joan Baxter.

The Greenup County Library in Kentucky, Dorothy Griffith.

The Mason Historical Society, Lucy Gorsuch, curator.

Mason Public Library.

The Suffield (Conn.) Museum, Lester Smith, curator.

The Annie Oakley Foundation, Bess Edwards, President.

New Haven Free Public Library.

Greenup County Historical Society, Ruth Cummins, curator.

Broome County Public Library, Binghampton, N.Y., Gerald Smith.

Buffalo Bill Historical Center.

Carlisle Barracks, U.S. Army.

Institute of Makers of Explosives, Lon Smith.

International Ammunition Association, Inc, Dale Hedlund and Chris Punnett.

The Gun Report, John Kuntz.

Muzzle Blasts, Maxine Moss, Sharon Cunningham and Terri Trowbridge.

The Single Shot Rifle Journal, Rudi Prusok, who threw open the American Single Shot Rifle Association's vast archives to me.

The Cincinnati Railroad Club.

Bureau of Mines.

U.S. Geological Survey, Steven Bryce.

The following people also contributed in various ways to this project.

Don Adams, Emmor Baily, Pablo Ballentine, John Bivins, Jo Harris Brenner, John M. Browning, Kathy Caldwell, Jerry Cox, Bill Dibbern, Bill Dwire, Boyd Ellis, Frank Fahringer, Mick Fahringer, Stephen Farfaro, Ruth Fisher, Don Geary, John Grant, Noryl Hamilton, Russell Heath, Harold Himes, Charles Holden, Elmer Keith, Joseph Warren King (II), James Knott, Dr. Harry Lee, Howie McClanahan, George McCluney, Irene McCracken, Steve McDowell, Leonard Michael, Pat Miller, John Murphy, Charley Nunner, Mark Olding, Roger Peak, Harley Peck, Gary Quinlin, Jim Radley, Richard Rexraad, Bob Roberts, Lillian Sackett, Lon Santis, John Schiffer, Andy Schiffer, Tom R. Schiffer, George P. Schiffer Jr., Fred Schwietert, Stuart Shepherd, Walter Edward Smith, William Paul Smith, Gene Spicer, Mike Venturino, Otto Witt, Bill Woodin.

There were others, unnamed, who have asked for one reason or another to not be identified.

All of these contributions are sincerely appreciated. I hope they enjoy the fruits of our collective labors.

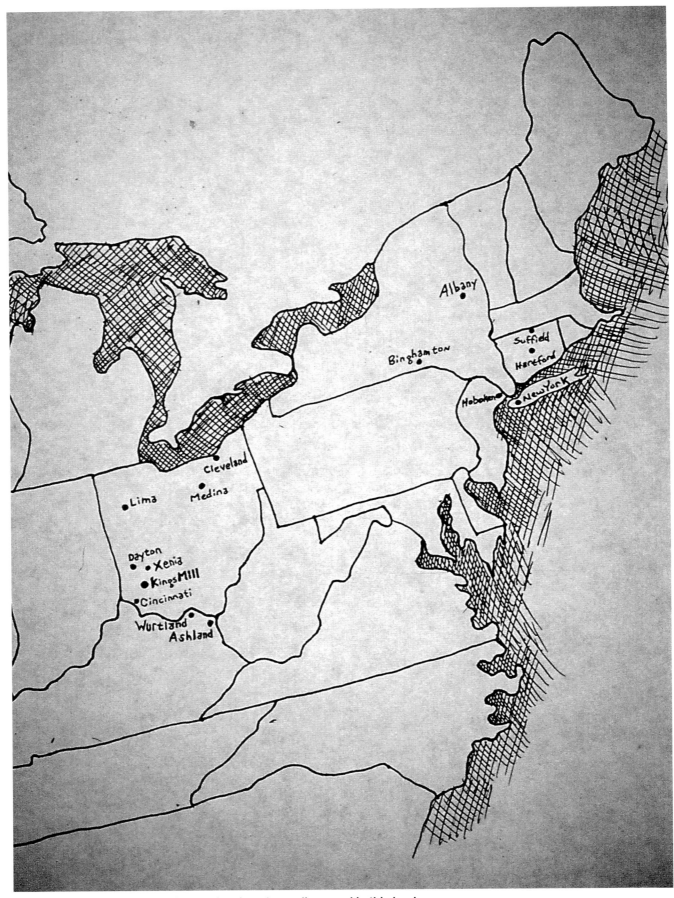

Map of the Eastern United States showing places discussed in this book.

Chapter 1

The Early Days

*T*HIS IS THE history of a frontier era powder manufacturer which evolved into a force in the industry, said to be the third largest in the country by 1890. It later founded another company to load cartridges which far outstripped the founder in size. They supplied this country with fine quality gunpowder and ammunition for sporting, military and industrial use. Thanks to their inventiveness, innovation, enterprise and vigorous promotion, Peters and King helped define and build much of the shooting sports activity we enjoy today.

Joseph Warren King is the person who brought the King name to the powder business in Ohio. King was from Suffield, Connecticut. Suffield is a contraction of South Field. Suffield is a sleepy New England town only two miles northeast of today's Hartford airport. Suffield was founded in 1670. There had been members of the King family associated with the town dating from 1674.

James King was born in 1647 in Devonshire, England. He married Elizabeth Fuller of Ipswich, Massachusetts, and they moved to Suffield in 1674. The lineage drops through Capt. Joseph King (1689-1756), Joseph King (1741-1814), John Bowker King (1779-1853), to Joseph Warren King (1814-1895). As far as can be determined, all of the

Portrait of Joseph Warren King (1814-1885) now hanging in the Greene County (Ohio) Historical Society, Xenia, Ohio.

above lived out their lives in Suffield except Joseph Warren King. (The genealogical information here and for Ahimaaz King is from a chart compiled by L. F. Erskine in 1971.)

Suffield boasts that it has the nicest main street in New England. Main Street is now Route 75. At least two old King family residences still stand on Main Street in Suffield: one on the south end of the street, the other on the north end a mile or so away. The King house on South Main was built in 1764 by Dr. Alexander King and is today the museum of the Suffield

Historical Society. Between these two King houses, it is nice indeed. The street features handsome houses on each side of north and south lanes divided by a grassy median with mature trees. Although the thoroughfare is not sullied by tacky commercial enterprises, the old houses here are abundant evidence that the early Suffield residents did not lack enterprise.

Lester Smith, curator of the Suffield Historical Society, reported that by 1764 Suffield had sawmills, gristmills, iron works, tanneries, ship building, distilleries, and a copper mine. The first cigar manufacturer in America was located here, the center of the Connecticut valley. This valley is, yet today, a producer of fine leaf tobacco for cigars.

Interestingly, a pamphlet given out by the Historical Society says Dr. Alexander King's diary gives a careful recipe for producing saltpeter for gunpowder. Dr. King's diary has enough entries seditious to the Crown as to have interested King George in testing the tensile strength of some hemp in that section of the Crown's Colonies!

Robinson's *History of Greene County* says Joseph Warren King was born in Suffield on August 30, 1814. He was descended from

Peter Brown, who came over on the Mayflower. He became a successful book agent when quite young. He ventured west into the Western Reserve part of Ohio while still a boy of 16. The Western Reserve is that peculiar part of Ohio that belonged to the State of Connecticut. It might explain why he chose that place to start out in life.

King met with some success in Ohio. He returned to Suffield in 1838 and was married to Betsey Kendall of his old hometown. The Kendall family was also a prominent one in Suffield. She was descended from Governor William Bradford, who also came over on the Mayflower. Their honeymoon trip was to their new home in Westerfield in Medina County, Ohio. At this place King opened a general store among pioneer conditions. Ohio was still a vast wilderness. Betsey Kendall King's narration of that trip, and her subsequent trip home with her first born some three years later, is found in the appendix of this book. Robinson also said that King later moved

to Lima, Ohio, where he became involved in pork packing, as well as general merchandising. He evidently met with success in these ventures.

History of the Explosives Industry tells us that Suffield, Connecticut, also produced a Baptist preacher by the name of Linus Austin. Linus is only the first of two Baptist preachers to figure in this narration. Linus Austin had five sons who went west as young men.

In 1833, the sons established a powder mill in Akron, Ohio. Akron was at that time the center of a coal-producing region that serviced Cleveland and other large cities. They made "blasting and a little rifle powder." In 1846, Alvin and Lorenzo Austin left their brothers and, with a man named Carlton, started a mill at Goes, Ohio. Goes was, and is, a tiny place a few miles north of Xenia.

In 1850, King bought Carlton's interest in the Goes Mill. The mill had operated under the name of Austin and Carlton. The mill then became Austin and

King. In 1855, the Austins left the Goes Mill and went back to Akron. The mill was again reorganized as the Miami Powder Company (also known as Frontier Mills) on May 26, 1855. J. W. King and a half dozen others were the incorporators. Sometime after 1856, J. W. took a nephew into the powder business. The nephew, Ahimaaz King, was born in Suffield on October 18, 1839. He traveled west when he was seventeen, and a bit later he joined his uncle in the powder business. Ahimaaz was probably the first King to be associated with the day-to-day operation of a powder mill.

Ahimaaz King was descended from James King (1675-1747), brother of Joseph Warren's ancestor Capt. Joseph King (1689-1756), down through Ebenezer King (1728-1816), Thomas King (1781-1808), Thomas King (1808-1849) to Ahimaaz King (1839-1909). As in the case of J. W. King, all of Ahimaaz King's ancestors after James King lived and died in Suffield.

Little Miami Railroad locomotive and crew *ca.* 1850. Both Miami Powder and King Powder were serviced by this early railroad, known in later years as the Pennsylvania. *Greene County (Ohio) Historical Society.*

Miami Powder Company, Frontier Mills. Joseph Warren King started in the powder business here about 1850.

Greene County (Ohio) Historical Society.

The Miami Powder Company, located at Goes Station on the Little Miami River and Little Miami Railroad, primarily produced rifle powder, since it was not near the coal fields where blasting powder would be in demand. Goes takes its name from an original settler who purchased the land from the Shawnee Indians for two horse blankets. The millrace had been constructed for the scythe factory located there in 1839.

The business was successful in spite of an uncertain waterpower supply and indifferent railroad service.

King augmented the waterpower from the river with a small steam engine. The Little Miami River is indeed little at this point, being hardly larger than a creek. King also introduced the first wheel mills used at the Frontier Mills.

The annual powder production under Austin and Carlton was 4,364 kegs of rifle powder and 1,303 of blasting. This rose to 6,211 and 6,383, respectively, by 1860 under Austin and King. According to the *History of the Explosives Industry in America*, during the Civil War a rate of 10,000 kegs

of rifle and 3,800 kegs of blasting was reached.

T. T. S. Laidley of the U.S. Ordnance Dept. rated a number of powder mills in the U.S. in a report to the Chief of Ordnance on January 2, 1864. Part of his report showed the following:

"Orange Powder Mills, Newburgh, N. Y., Smith & Rand owners and agents; 16 barrels capacity; some very good.

Du Pont's Powder Mills, Wilmington, Del. E. I. Dupont & Co., owners and agents; 175 barrels capacity; very good.

Frontier Mills, Xenia, Ohio, Miami Powder Co., J. W. King,

Ahimaaz King (1839-1909) and his road wagon for selling powder when he was associated with the Miami Powder Company. Ahimaaz later built the mills at Kings Mills and founded the town.

Greene County (Ohio) Historical Society.

Abandoned Miami Powder Company (1846-1925) buildings as they appeared in 1985. The Little Miami River and railroad were located behind the buildings. Hercules operated this plant in its later years, long after the Kings sold out.

President; 6 barrels capacity; inferior."

[Note on the above report: A keg of powder contains 25 pounds net, of powder. The barrels referred to in Laidley's report above may have contained 100 pounds. If so, the production rates listed above would make sense.]

Whether the above rating was typical of Miami's output or not, the mill's production was in good demand. Certainly the fact that the mill had, as yet, no local competition did help in that regard. In the early days, powder was sold largely from wagons throughout adjoining states. When J. W.'s nephew, Ahimaaz King, came to work there, it was not an uncommon occurrence for him to take a wagonload of the powder on a sales trip of several hundred miles and lasting perhaps a month.

In 1985, Joseph Warren King II (now deceased) was interviewed in the old King mansion in Kings Mills. This is the house that Ahimaaz King built for his family in about 1886. Joe stated that Ahimaaz met his future wife, Amanda Luck, on just such a powder-selling trip when he reached Medora, Indiana.

History of the Explosives Industry says that by 1870, the Frontier Mills of the Miami Powder Company's output of blasting powder increased from 9,572 kegs in 1866 to 29,540. By 1871 it had jumped to 36,655 kegs. This, to me, is a sure sign that the area was evolving from a frontier into a more civilized state. Blasting powder would be of little use on the frontier, but in great demand for mining, canal building, quarrying and other construction-oriented uses.

J. W. King became well established in Xenia. He was president of the local bank and during the Civil War built his family a fine home in the town. It was called "The Kingdom." It was this house which is said to have suffered the loss of its windows when a local group fired at it with a blank load of powder from a cannon.

This event was supposedly in retaliation for King's selling powder to the Confederacy. How, why, or if, King might have done this escapes me, but it is part of the legend. See Appendix 8 in this book for the narration of this story by best-selling author of *Ohio Town*,

Helen Hooven Santmyer. Ms. Santmyer played at "The Kingdom" as a child and tells stories relating to "The Kingdom" and King's daughters.

History of the Explosives Industry says that in 1872, Addison Orville Fay, president of the American Powder Company of Massachusetts, with a company of men, most of whom were financially interested in The American Mills, got control of the Miami Powder Company. They elected Fay president. J. W. King was no longer president, but Ahimaaz was still running the mills for a time. Then he was let go. Old J. W. did not take the ouster gracefully, as will be seen.

There is a letter in the files of the Hagley Museum that sheds some light on what was happening. The May 24, 1878, letter was from F. L. Kneeland, general agent for Du Pont in New York. It was written to Du Pont in regard to activities concerning the Gunpowder Trade Association (of which the above mentioned Fay was secretary). It said that: *"Fay turned young King out of Miami's Mills because he was old man King's nephew. There is no doubt of that and King knows it. King's plan is to get control of the Miami Co., put Fay out and his nephew in. There is no doubt of that in my mind."*

As will be seen, old J. W. did not regain control of the Miami Mills. However, the letter bears eloquent testimony to the high feelings between Fay and King. No doubt those feelings directly led King to start a new gunpowder mill only thirty some miles away and to vigorously conduct the economic warfare against the Miami Powder Company that ensued.

In 1877, both Kings disposed of their interests in the Miami Powder Company. The Goes plant would go on well after the Kings left, to suffer the explosion of 50,000 pounds of powder on March 26, 1886. Later, in 1891, Miami would be the first powder mill in the land to be electrified. Hercules Powder Company acquired these mills in 1921 and closed them in 1925.

In 1878, the Kings founded the King's Great Western Powder Company. They also bid on and acquired 832,000 pounds of surplus musket and cannon powder from the St. Louis Arsenal. Evidently King's plan was to erect a new powder mill and rework this cheap surplus powder. The cheap powder would then enable King to undercut Miami's prices and drive Miami out of business. In this way might old J. W. get his revenge.

Musket and especially cannon powder was not of the same proportions as good rifle or sporting powder. However, all were made from sulfur, charcoal and potassium nitrate. Put back under the wheel mills and sweetened up with enough of the short ingredients for making sporting powder, the powder could then be reworked. The wheels, press, corning and glaze operations could make excellent powder (assuming the surplus powder was not contaminated with foreign material).

This was quite a coup, but required considerable resources to accomplish. Suitable land had to be acquired, mills erected, machinery bought and installed, men trained, the surplus powder paid for and freighted to the new mill and stored, the powder reworked and packaged, and customers lined up.

The Gunpowder Trade Association had been founded on April 23, 1872, to fix prices in the gunpowder industry. Most of the powder industry was still reeling from the low prices created when the Civil War ended and there was much idle powder making capacity in the United States.

The government did not help that situation when they dumped surplus powder into the marketplace after the war. The Gunpowder Trade Association activity started before the Sherman Anti-Trust Act was passed into law and was, at the time, a legal pursuit. As might be expected, King's activity

Isaak Stubbs' old gristmill race was the basis for the construction of Kings Great Western Powder Company. The mill building itself was never used by the powder company for the manufacture of powder, but for maintenance facilities and storage.
The King Powder Company, Illustrated 1896. Courtesy Bob and Betty Carter.

caught the attention of the Gunpowder Trade Association.

King adamantly refused to join the Gunpowder Trade Association, nor would old J. W. agree to any of its pricing structure. There was considerable concern by the Miami Powder Company and other members of the GTA. It was not a peaceful time in the powder industry and King was considered the maverick.*

After divesting themselves of their interest in the Miami Powder Company at Goes Station north of Xenia, the two Kings, J. W. and Ahimaaz, looked for a place to erect powder-making facilities. At that time, the late 1870s, nearly all powder mills were run by water power, sometimes augmented with steam power. The Kings found a place some thirty miles south of Xenia on the Little Miami River and Little Miami Railroad, called the gorge. The name indicated a narrow river valley with steep hills on either side and a great drop in stream elevation per mile. Beers' *History of Warren*

County says there was already a race built there to run a gristmill. They bought the land from the estate of the late Isaak Stubbs, who had operated the mill. As early as 1799 there had been a mill at that location built by William Wood. George Hunt bought the mill and laid out the town of Gainsboro at the mill site. The town did not "take" and had practically disappeared by the time that the Kings arrived, in spite of having its own post office as early as 1822.

On August 8, 1878, the King's Great Western Powder Company was set up as a corporation having a manufactory at a place called King's Station. The incorporation papers from the Ohio secretary of state say the location was mid-way between South Lebanon and Foster's Crossing on the Little Miami River. The offices remained in Xenia, with additional offices at the mill and at Cincinnati. There has been some confusion due to the fact that King owned land in South Lebanon. One early letterhead actually stated: "*Mills*

One of the entrances to the King powder line in April of 1915. The men are probably Herb and Felix Koch who were not associated in any way with the King Powder Company. *Cincinnati Historical Society, Koch collection.*

at South Lebanon." A keg mill was operated there, but not a powder mill.

Saying the mills were at South Lebanon is consistent with their later saying the mills (and, later, Peters Cartridge) were in Cincinnati. Neither company

ever had any manufacturing facility in Cincinnati. The fact was, at first, nobody knew where King's Station was. The biggest nearby place that anybody knew of was South Lebanon. Therefore, the mills were said to be at South Lebanon in the early years.

South Lebanon was the "base camp" for Ahimaaz King as he directed the construction work. The old millrace had to be considerably enlarged. The mill building was across the river from King's Station and the dam was located about a mile upstream, midway between the mill and South Lebanon. The money, the ownership and the "home office" remained in Xenia where J. W. King was the main man in the operation. J. W. King retained his family, his residence "The Kingdom," and his other business interests in Xenia, where he continued to reside until his death in 1885.

It was Ahimaaz King, J. W. King's nephew, who was the ramrod in the building and subsequent operation of the King's Great Western Powder Company and the town of Kings Mills. Business contacts, direction and most importantly, money, flowed through and from Xenia. An 1896 company pamphlet credits J. W. with exerting energies in this, his new enterprise that, it also said, contributed to his death in 1885.

The King powder line at Kings Mills changed with the times. As the markets grew or were created, the line increased and decreased in size and capacity. As technology allowed on the one hand, and demanded on the other, changes were made. Some of these changes were dictated by enterprise, others resulted from forces beyond the control of the owners.

As might be expected, the original powder line was water powered. The first products of the King's Great Western Powder Company were the traditional black sporting powder and blasting powder. King deepened and widened the existing millrace that had powered the old Isaak Stubbs grist mill, erected a head gate and raised the level of the dam a bit to throw more water into the race. The race was well over one mile in length!

The millrace itself was parallel to the river on the west side

The millrace ran parallel to the river and supplied all the power for the King's mills until about 1894 or 1895, when it continued in existence for many years furnishing hydroelectric power. In later years, it was simply allowed to exist for whatever safety factor it provided. Most of it still exists as a big, empty ditch. *The King Powder Company, Illustrated 1896. Courtesy Bob and Betty Carter.*

(right bank, descending) and, of course, never very far from it. The over riding principle is that at a place where the river has a large natural gradient, the river is dammed and some of the water is diverted into a millrace. The millrace runs parallel to the river, but on a much flatter grade; just enough gradient to get the water to flow along it. It will be seen that the farther you get from the dam, the greater the differential in water elevation becomes (from race to the river surface). Let's say that the river falls 20 feet in a mile; the race one foot. There will therefore be a difference in elevation of 19 feet. It is this difference in elevation, through which the race water can be made to fall, that can be harnessed with water wheels to power the mills.

At intervals along the race, powder mills were constructed between the race and the river. Each mill had its own water wheel and utilized the force of the water to power the mill. Other than horses and mules and manpower, there was no other form of energy used, except in the dry house. Here steam from a remote boiler was used.

On February 20, 1889, King's Great Western Powder Company changed its name to simply, the King Powder Company. This is likely done in anticipation of increasing capitalization from $325,000 to $500,000 on January 22, 1890. Water power became, at times, insufficient to run all the mills at a rate equal to demand, particularly in the dry summer months. It is reasonable to assume the money was to be used to purchase a stationary steam engine. An engine was erected on the land side of the race about this time. The boiler to drive the engine was several hundred feet from the mills, for safety, and was located just downstream from the bridge.

Additional capital was also needed shortly to electrify the powder mills. As business grew, it was decided to discontinue the use of individual water wheels

A powder mill. Water from the millrace *(foreground)* flowed past the mill wheel on its way back into the river transferring some of its energy to the wheel. The wheel powered the machinery inside the mill building through a series of shafts and gears. Low water in the summer was as much of a problem as floods were in the spring. *Cincinnati Historical Society.*

for the mills. All the available water was taken across a single, much bigger wheel near the bridge. This bigger wheel turned a dynamo to generate electricity. Electric motors were then used to drive the individual mills. Sometimes long line shafting was used to drive more than one mill from the same motor. *The King Powder Company, Illustrated* booklet, and *Warren County*

Atlas of 1903, say that, in 1895, King's was one of the first powder mills in the country to be electrified. The old Miami Powder Company was first to be electrified, after the Kings left to found their own mill.

A steam-powered dynamo augmented the water-powered dynamo at Kings Mills. The combined horsepower (hydroelectric plus steam-

The power house of the King Powder Company in 1896, shortly after electrification. The mills were thereafter individually powered from a dynamo inside the power house, turned by a single big water wheel and/or a steam engine as the stage of the river dictated. Sometime after about 1917, power was imported from the big Peters power house across the river and this was abandoned. It was from here that the first electricity in the town of Kings Mills originated. *The King Powder Company, Illustrated 1896. Courtesy of Bob and Betty Carter.*

Dynamo for generating electricity could be powered by either steam or water wheel power.
The King Powder Company, Illustrated 1896. Courtesy of Bob and Betty Carter.

However, the powder line was still subject to visits from Old Man River in the spring.

Floods did shut the operations down, but not for as long as in waterpower days. In the old days, the river had to recede far enough from the level of the race to re-establish a head differential for the mills to operate.

The old millrace was retained for safety reasons. Edna Bowyer, long-time secretary of King Powder, said that employees near an explosion could dive into the race to escape the heat. Powder contamination on their clothes was a danger to them. Indeed they called themselves "powder monkeys" due to the black hue they took on from the charcoal in the powder dust.

Neither the electric or steam motor nor the internal combustion engine replaced the horse- and mule-powered railroad used to tie the various powder operations together. It wasn't pure sentiment that caused this. It was deemed safer to utilize the quadrupeds shod with bronze shoes and copper nails. Brass wheels were mounted on the cars (they were called buggies here) to minimize the chance of a spark. The buggies were about twelve feet long. At KICO in Kentucky, this narrow gauge railway was called a tram. Edna Bowyer said they were simply referred to as "the rails."

David Spencer was a maintenance foreman at the KICO plant (owned by King) in Kentucky. He noted that at the KICO mills, the crossties were located to match an easy stride for the draft animals. To do otherwise was to risk the horse (or mule) stepping too close to the edge of the crosstie. When this happened, the horse's shoe might hang on the edge of the tie and pull off as the horse raised its hoof. The horse would then be through doing any effective work until it had paid a visit to a farrier to have the shoe replaced.

There were certain mills along the tram system where the horse was not allowed to go. Here

powered dynamo) was said to be 1000. Electric power gave King a flexibility not known before. At some date after the turn of the century, water power was abandoned altogether.

By the time electrification occurred, the King Powder Company had created Peters Cartridge Company, then seven years old. Peters also tapped into this electric power source. Electric illumination was provided for the powder line and later the town. This allowed two and/or three shift operation. The mills were now powered by individual electric motors and low water in the summer was not likely to shut down operations.

"Powder Monkeys." Here is a shift going off duty, before getting washed up. Powder dust on their clothing and on their person was a danger to the worker.
The King Powder Company, Illustrated 1896. Courtesy of Bob and Betty Carter.

there was a planked section between the rails as a walkway for the teamster/operator himself to use in pushing the buggy on into the mill. The corning mill was such a location. Naturally, where the rails crossed the millrace, the crossties were planked over so the animals could walk without falling through. The teamster would ride on the front of the buggy from mill to mill.

Horses learn a routine quickly if it is repetitive. The powder mill animals soon learned where to go to wait when they were not being used. They also quickly learned how many total rounds to make in a day. The teamster had his work cut out for him if he wanted to extend the horse's day a bit. The animal would let him know about it!

Isaak Stubbs' original gristmill building was several stories high. King Powder utilized it for storage and as a repair shop. In its grain grinding days a water turbine, not the more picturesque water wheel, had powered it. The old gristmill took no direct part in the manufacture of powder.

Powder underwent several steps in its manufacture. Sulfur and potassium nitrate were purchased and shipped in by railroad. Willow and alder wood was bought locally from farmers and others and turned into charcoal on the grounds. In later years, at least by the 1930s, charcoal was purchased outright.

Noryl Hamilton, King's chief chemist, said charcoal made on the site had to be pulverized before taking it to the mill. The charring was done on site in little stone buildings made for the purpose. Some of these were located against the base of the hill, back from the river and the race.

Raw materials were warehoused and weighed out in the proper proportions into hoppers carried in or on the horse drawn buggies. These would be in lots totaling about 600 pounds in weight. The proportions were about 75 percent potassium nitrate (450 lbs.), 15 percent charcoal (90 lbs.) and 10 percent sulfur (60 lbs.). Once roughly mixed, the powder was referred to as "green" powder. It would burn vigorously but was not nearly as explosive as it would become after incorporation.

A horse or mule drew the buggy with the three raw materials to the wheel mill. These three materials altogether made up a 600-pound "wheel charge." The hoppers had wheels of their own and could be rolled from the horse drawn buggy into the mill building. No worker was allowed inside a mill building while the mill was in motion. The two giant ten-ton wheels were stopped with an external switch or clutch and the wheel charge was then distributed. The mill was restarted from outside the building.

In waterpower days, the mill could be stopped by shutting off the water supply to the wheel and started by reversing the procedure. This could be as simple as placing a board across the sluiceway leading to the wheel, blocking the water.

The wheel mill itself consisted of a horizontal round bedplate of steel perhaps ten feet in diameter. The plate was situated at a convenient height above the floor. Sticking up through a hole in the middle of the plate was a vertical shaft with a "tee" shaft fixed to it at the top. The "tee" shaft carried two ten-ton rollers, one on each side of the "tee." The rollers were perhaps eight feet in diameter and two feet wide and were made of cast iron.

The center shaft rotated slowly, under the influence of a very large bull gear under the floor and the bedplate. This caused the large wheels to run around the ten-foot diameter circular plate near the outer edge. The wheels rotated by being dragged around the plate by the "tee" axles of the rotating center shaft.

There was a wooden curb perhaps two feet high around the periphery of the steel plate. A similar one on the inside was to protect the hole in the middle, where the "tee" shaft came up through the plate. This kept the

The tramway wound its way through a wooded setting. Here you can see planking between the rails for the teamster to push the buggy where the horse and mule was not allowed to go and the shed roof over the place where he stopped to load and unload powder. Note the flimsy construction.
Cincinnati Historical Society.

powder confined to the steel bedplate. Wooden "plows" were hung off the center shaft in such a position as to follow the big rollers and throw the powder mashed to the sides of the heavy wheel back under the tread of the wheel following it.

Close scrutiny of the geometry involved revealed that when an eight-foot diameter wheel with a two-foot wide face was forced to run around the bedplate on a relatively tight four-foot radius from the center of the bedplate, it executed a more or less skidding motion over much of its face with respect to the bedplate itself. This skidding motion provided a real grinding motion to the powder not unlike the action of the pharmacist's mortar and pestle. Hamilton, chief chemist of the powder company until 1940, said that the wheels were free to contact the steel bedplate itself, with the face of the wheel and the bedplate being held apart only by the presence of the powder.

The raw "green" powder was shoveled onto the bedplate with a spark-free wooden shovel. After being spread out somewhat evenly, the mill was vacated and the power source activated. As stated, no employee was to enter a wheel mill building when the mill was under power. Illumination was provided by electric lights shining in windows at the ends of the mill house. Side windows also let light in during daylight hours.

Nearly all of the buildings were made of the flimsiest construction. This was for two purposes. First, the building was cheap and could be easily replaced, and secondly, it provided little resistance to any explosion, thus minimizing the effects thereof. Construction usually consisted of the lightest of wood framing with corrugated tin walls and roof. The mill buildings were all painted red. When an explosion did occur in a wheel mill, the wheel mill itself was often undamaged, but the building itself would be completely missing.

Care was taken to remove any foreign material from the wheel charge that might cause a spark. This included "clinkers" which formed sometimes as the mill wheels rotated. These clinkers were hardened material from the raw powder and may have been the result of too much moisture leaching out potassium nitrate, which solidified and formed a lump sticking to the bedplate. It may have been sulfur, which fused together to form the "clinker."

Edna Bowyer worked in the office a few hundred feet from the nearest wheel mill. She said she could hear or feel the *"clunk"* of a "clinker" on the bedplate all the way up in the office as the ten-ton wheels rolled over it. The

Wooden shovel used to move powder into and out of mills.
Courtesy of Edna Bowyer.

wheel mill would be shut down when this happened and the "clinker" very carefully removed from the bedplate using only a wooden mallet and wooden "chisel" or punch. Allowing the wheels to run over the clinker was considered dangerous.

The wheel mill incorporated the powder. That is to say it intimately mixed and ground the three ingredients together such that, ideally, any particle of one ingredient was able to "see" the other two. Wheel time varied with the kind and quality of powder being made. Rifle or sporting powder was given more wheel time than blasting powder. Fuse powder was a high grade of sporting powder.

The wheel time was measured in hours, sporting getting four to six hours and blasting, two to three hours. As the wheel time elapsed, the wheel charge became increasingly *(to a point)* explosive. It went into the wheel mill as a flammable solid that, at best, would sputter and burn like a firecracker fuse. It came out as a low explosive. Wheel mills were a great improvement over the stamping mills used in prior years.

Stamping mills were obsolete and therefore not used at the King's operation. A stamping mill consisted of a great many logs held vertically, each having its bottom end in its own individual hole, or shallow pocket, in a horizontal wooden bed. The logs were lifted a short distance vertically and allowed to fall back into the hole. The action was from mechanical cams actuated by *(usually)* a water wheel. A handful of powder placed in each hole in the wooden bed would be more-or-less incorporated as the stamping progressed.

Getting back to the wheel mills, when the wheel time was almost elapsed, an empty powder buggy and driver would appear. The wheels were stopped and the horse and powder buggy waited patiently under the shed roof "porch" in front of the mill. The driver and the wheelman then shoveled the incorporated powder into wheeled bins and rolled the bins back onto the buggy. The incorporated powder was now an explosive. No women were ever allowed to work on the powder line.

The buggy was pulled by the horse along the rail track to the press. A buggy with a fresh charge would arrive in time to reload the mill.

A wheelman might run two mills, unloading and loading one mill while the other mill was doing its wheel time. Unlike many jobs on the line, there was sometimes time to sit and wait for the incorporation to be completed. This time was to be spent in the little "dog houses" built for the purpose some distance from the mills. The slack time was an attractive feature for some wheelmen, although their job was one of the most hazardous on the line.

At the press house, the incorporated powder was dumped and shoveled into the press by the operator, assisted by the buggy driver. The press was usually a horizontal affair with a series of aluminum plates spaced about three inches apart. The plates were about two feet square and maybe an eighth of an inch thick. When loaded, this formed a multi-layered *sandwich* of plates and powder.

When the above 600 pounds of incorporated powder was placed between the plates, hydraulic pressure was used to compress the plates. A pressure of 10,000 pounds to the square inch was employed. This compressed the three inches of powder into little over one inch!

When the press was opened, the two-foot square by one-inch thick press cake was separated for the aluminum plates. Said cake was more than hard enough to retain its shape. The cakes were loaded onto a different buggy and the horse or mule pulled it to the next operation in the powder line, the corning mill.

This next mill consisted of a hopper feeding the press cake to a pair of rotating wheels having brass teeth. The teeth were intermeshed so that the press cake was ground into grains of various sizes. The granulated powder was then pulled by buggy to the dry house where it was dried from three percent moisture to about one percent, with steam-heated air.

It was, perhaps, the cozy warmth of the dry house that tempted workers to linger there on a cold day. If the dry house suffered an explosion, it would be far more powerful, usually, than blowing a wheel mill. This was due, primarily, to the fact that there was likely to be far more powder involved; workers present in the dry house during an explosion would not likely survive. After the powder was dried, it was then taken by buggy to the glaze mill.

The glazing mill consisted of a large wooden barrel in which the powder was placed. There was one operator here. The barrel was rotated about its long horizontal axis and the individual powder grains were tumbled. This did several things. The powder, rolling incessantly over itself, picked up mechanical heat. This heat *(too hot to put your hand in!)* fused the low melting temperature sulfur on the outside of each powder grain.

The glaze, thus formed, protected the powder somewhat against the pickup of moisture in storage. During the last part of the glazing process, a bit of graphite—maybe one to two pounds—was added to the barrel. The added polish may have added to the ability of the glaze to resist moisture, flow more freely and resist the buildup of a static electric charge. It also looked better—more sales appeal!

The now nearly-finished powder was drawn by rail to the separator where it was classified into the various granulation sizes of commerce. This was done by successively passing the powder through screening of the required

sizes. There was no official granulation size uniformity except that required by the military. It was, however, generally understood at all mills that fffg powder was finer than ffg, etc.

Granulation size determined, to a large extent, the burning rate of the finished powder. In sporting powders, the finer grades like fffg were suitable for pistol and small caliber rifles. The larger granulations were for shotguns, large rifles and muskets.

At most stages of production, more or less powder dust accumulated. This was cleaned up and recycled into the wheel mill charge so as not to be wasted.

The classified powder, of various grades, was then pulled by horse to the pack house where it was packaged. Two men worked in the pack house. In early days, the powder kegs were of wood at the King's Great Western Powder Company. However, King soon put powder up in tins of various sizes. These sizes ranged from two-ounce salesman's samples up through half pound, one pound, two pound, six and a quarter pound (quarter keg), twelve and a half pound (half keg) and twenty-five pound (keg) sizes.

In the sporting powder, granulations ranged from ffffg (fine priming powder), to fffg (rifle and pistol powder), ffg (shotgun and musket powder), and fg (musket powder). Fuze powder was yet another grade. Powder was also made on the sporting line for the fireworks trade. This had its own set of granulations. In the infrequent event of some off-specification sporting powder production, a local fireworks manufacturer was called in and a sweeter than normal price named. After sifting it between his fingers and looking at it thoughtfully, he always bought it.

Blasting powder manufacture was very similar to that of sporting powder. The main difference was that blasting powder was made with sodium nitrate and not potassium nitrate. There was a small difference in percentages of the ingredients used since sodium nitrate is a more efficient oxidizer than potassium nitrate.

"B" powder, as Lammot du Pont who developed it in 1857 named it, was a more powerful explosive than powder made with potassium nitrate and was much cheaper. King Powder's chief chemist Noryl Hamilton said

potassium nitrate cost about $0.14 per pound against $0.02 for sodium nitrate in the 1930s. Since the nitrate made up about three fourths of the ingredients, it can be readily seen that this was an important cost factor.

The big disadvantage of sodium nitrate that prevented its use for sporting purposes was that it contained nearly inseparable impurities. Either the impurities, or the sodium nitrate itself, were very hygroscopic, taking on moisture

rapidly from the air. Blasting powder, which could be kept sealed in the keg until needed, was relatively unaffected. Blasting powder, if kept in a storage horn or flask like sporting powder, for any length of time, would take on enough moisture to weaken it or render it useless.

Blasting powder was made on the same kinds of mills as sporting powder and the sequence was the same. Blasting powder granulations were generally larger so corning and sifting would be a bit different, but for the most part, the operation was very much the same. For reasons of cross contamination, the equipment was dedicated to its use, either sporting or blasting. That is to say that sporting or rifle powder was made on one line or set of equipment and blasting powder was made on an entirely separate line. In the 1930s, these were known as the "A" Line for sporting powder and the "B" Line for blasting Powder.

During later years, the upper end (nearer the race head gate) was dedicated to the "B" Line. The "A" Line was a half-mile down the river from the bridge. The "B" Line pretty much occupied the land that was originally used for water-powered mills. The "A" Line used in later years was constructed on the hillside of the road to Foster, not next to the river. In other words, on the right side of the road leading to Foster, not the left side. The race itself did not extend down this far. The powder line snaked back and forth up the face of the hill ending up on the plateau at the top. There was a barn for draft animals for the "A" Line and another about a mile away for the "B" Line.

G. M. Peters was married to Mary Elizabeth King, Joseph Warren King's daughter. In spite of his background as an ordained Baptist minister, he resigned his pastorate to fulfill "filial duties," and joined King's Great Western

Blasting powder granulations of the King Powder Company.
The King Powder Company, Illustrated 1896. Courtesy of Bob and Betty Carter.

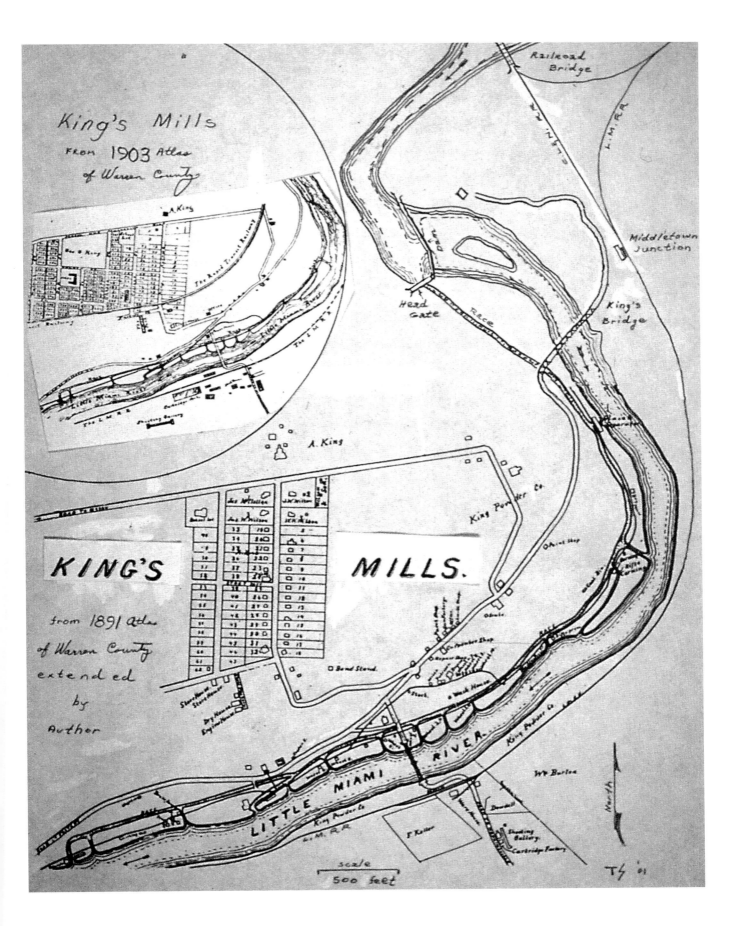

King's Mills

FROM 1903 Atlas
of Warren County

A. King

KING'S

from 1891 Atlas
of Warren County
extended
by
Author

MILLS.

Railroad
Bridge

Middletown
Junction

King's
Bridge

Head
Gate

Race

A. King

King Powder Co.

LITTLE MIAMI RIVER

scale
500 feet

North

Powder Company in 1881 as vice president. He became president when J. W. King died in 1885. Peters invented a cartridge-loading machine and patented it. It was decided that a "captive" cartridge loading plant would be a good outlet for some of their sporting powders. Accordingly, investors in the King Powder Company organized the Peters Cartridge Company and built a cartridge-loading facility on the opposite bank of the river from the powder works in 1887. See Chapter 2 for details of that operation.

On July 1, 1895, Milton F. Lindsley was hired to put the King Powder Company in the smokeless powder business. As will be learned elsewhere in this book, Lindsley was an experienced powder manufacturer who had worked for Dittmar in New York and, later, New Jersey. Construction was started on the smokeless powder line right away. It was located roughly at the lower end of the "A" line. In the smokeless production, wood pulp was nitrated, neutralized, and dried. The facilities for doing this were constructed on the side of the hill using the change in elevation to facilitate material flow through the processes. This latter was a factor liberally utilized in the set-up of much of the King equipment and processes.

The sulfuric and nitric acids used in the nitration process were most likely purchased and sent back to the vendor as spent acid to be reworked. King's Smokeless Powder manufacture was discontinued before 1913 when the company said: *"The old form of King's Smokeless has been abandoned. A new smokeless powder is now in process of development by this Company along the lines of modern requirements, which promise well and will doubtless soon make its appearance on the market. But word of this announcement will be made later."* The above is from the *Handy Book for Trap Shooters and Sportsmen*, August 1913. I have not learned of any replacement smokeless ever being introduced. King's Smokeless Powder was a single-based powder. Milton F. Lindsley always bragged that no high explosives (picric acid, nitroglycerine etc.) were used in making his powders.

Canister lots of King's Smokeless were likely discontinued when the King Mercantile Co. was formed at the

Collectors would love to poke around this Peters and King trade show booth. A Smokeless Powder poster tells us it was at least 1895. The fact that there is no Semi-Smokeless in sight may mean it was '95 or early 1896. The seated woman, Etta Butts Lindsley, was perhaps better known by her shooting name of "Wanda." That is her husband Milt behind her. Seated to the right is a youthful George G. King. The two other gentlemen are unknown. At collector prices today there is a small fortune within reach of them all. Note the "busted duck" posters, the Peters 100-shell boxes, a picture of old J. W. King as well as one of the works and a selection of now rare powder cans. *Courtesy of J. W. King (II).*

turn of the century. Noryl Hamilton was chief chemist there in the 1930s and knows nothing of its manufacture. Perhaps it was pushed aside by the powders made by Du Pont and others on a grand scale after the turn of the century. Noryl Hamilton was chief chemist at the King Powder Company from about 1933 until 1940. In 1940, he entered the United States Army. He became an officer in the Ordnance Department and had about 100 explosives plants (mostly making TNT) reporting to him.

King's celebrated Semi-Smokeless Powder was made into the early 1930s. Noryl Hamilton reports King made at least one batch when he was first there. He reports they bought smokeless powder left over from WWI, or powder from Du Pont, to manufacture their Semi-Smokeless since King no longer made smokeless powder. In the late 1920s, Peters advertised they were using a new "improved" Semi-Smokeless powder in loading some of their cartridges. This may well have been when the change was made.

Semi-Smokeless powder was sold in cannister lots for muzzle-loading firearms for many years after the early 1930s, but it was likely all stock from their magazines. By WWII, Remington (after 1934, Peters was a division of Remington) said the cartridges previously loaded with King's Semi-Smokeless would henceforth be loaded with either Semi-Smokeless *or* Lesmok powder. Lesmok was Du Pont's answer to King's Semi-Smokeless powder. Both Peters and Remington were at that time owned by Du Pont.

Semi-Smokeless Powder *was* a combination of smokeless and black powders incorporated under the wheel mills. King's advertising claims that it was neither smokeless nor black nor a combination thereof are at odds

Milton Lindsley and an assistant stirring experimental powder in the laboratory.
The King Powder Company, Illustrated 1896. Courtesy of Bob and Betty Carter.

with the patent papers. The Semi-Smokeless powder I have used and examined *(not much)* is of a bluish cast and the individual grains are much rounded in contrast to the angular grains of most black powders. In the early 1930s when Noryl Hamilton was there, Semi-Smokeless was made on the "A," or Sporting Line.

Semi-Smokeless Powder was arguably King's most significant contribution to accuracy-minded shooters. It was used at one time or another by many of the finest shots in the country. This usage started shortly after its introduction in 1896. It was a cannister powder (sold in small tins and kegs) used by schuetzen shooters like Harry Pope and Charles Rowland, and muzzleloaders. The early days of the National Muzzle Loading Rifle Association were full of reports of its successful use in their matches. It was loaded into many of Peters cartridges up to WWII. It was perhaps most widely known in 22 long rifle match cartridges. By 1942, Red Farris reported that stocks of the cannister Semi-Smokeless were depleted until there was only CG granulation left, suitable for the larger-caliber rifles. It is not known if any was made after the war, but stocks of it were sold,

probably up until the plant closed in 1958.

In 1933, Milton F. Lindsley Jr. patented an explosive that was to be used for blasting. It was a big seller for the King Powder Company. It was called Detonite. It consisted of mostly ammonium nitrate, sugar and sulfur. It was manufactured on the hill above the "A" Line where Kings Island amusement park is now located. Detonite was not a "permissible," but it was very safe to use and store and was a very inexpensive explosive. According to a U.S. Bureau of Mines bulletin, King had marketed a permissible explosive as early as 1911 or 1912. The above was either an improvement thereon or a cheaper explosive.

Permissible dynamite was available earlier, but Lindsley developed a permissible version of Detonite called Red Crown Permissible. This was a cheaper explosive than dynamite. See the KICO chapter for definitions and more information on permissible, dynamite and Detonite.

So stable was Detonite that dynamite had to be used to set it off! Ordinary dynamite caps would not do it. This is true of most any explosive based on ammonium nitrate. Detonite was also put up in cartridges for

The test gallery was in a wooden "tunnel" located behind the King and Peters office on the hill. It was part of their laboratory.
The King Powder Company, Illustrated 1896. Courtesy of Bob and Betty Carter.

specialized usage, just as King's other explosives were. Detonite was relatively safe to manufacture and handle.

King had a controlling interest in the Illinois Powder Company. The Illinois Powder Company made King's dynamite that was sold under the trade name Rex Dynamite. All of the original dynamites were based on nitroglycerine. No nitroglycerine-based explosives were commercially made at Kings Mills or at the subsidiary, KICO, in Wurtland, Kentucky.

Finished powder and incoming raw materials had to be tested for strength and purity, respectively.

Noryl Hamilton said that as Chief Chemist at King Powder, he worked in the laboratory behind the King's office building. This building was erected about 1895 as an office for both the King Powder Company and the Peters Cartridge Company. Peters moved out, probably in 1917 when their large Building No.1 was completed. The older building burned in 1950.

Judging by surviving evidence, the shooting range associated with King's lab was about 60 feet long. Incoming raw materials were tested in the lab for purity and charcoal was tested for volatile matter and BTU content. Finished goods were tested for strength. The most commonly used test was to load a 45/70 cartridge with blackpowder and shoot a bullet through a chronograph on the range. The test "vehicle" was the ubiquitous Trapdoor Springfield.

At other times, explosives were tested by other means. In later years, there were periodic reports throughout the day from whatever explosive was being tested. Dave Spencer says that Detonite was tested at KICO by shooting a 30-caliber high-powered rifle into a standard eight-inch cartridge from some little distance. Dave was the chief mechanic on the "White Line" as they called the Detonite Line at KICO. The Detonite cartridge was not supposed to explode when so tested. To his knowledge, none ever went off when so tested.

The powder lines at Kings Mills had a park-like appearance. An aerial photo of the Peters Cartridge plant across the river does not reveal any of the details of the King Powder Company because a canopy of trees screens the powder line. Edna Bowyer reports that vegetation on the line was controlled by grazing sheep. The company narrow-gauge railroad with its quaint bridges across the millrace and openings for the water wheels wended its way back and forth over and along the lazy millrace.

Edna also reported the trees were sometimes a hazard after

Milton Lindsley operating chronograph equipment in the 1890s.
The King Powder Company, Illustrated 1896. Courtesy of Bob and Betty Carter.

an explosion. It seems the leaves collected unburned powder after some explosions. That is, if said tree had any leaves remaining after the explosion. Attempts were made to remove this powder lest it become a hazard.

The roadway surfaces were of crushed stone and, no doubt, cinders from the boiler house. Here and there rose a chimney from a washhouse or boiler house. Horse- or mule-drawn vehicles were slowly pulled from mill to mill. It was said the King management expected employees to do a day's work but that nobody was expected to kill themselves.

Life-long Kings Mills resident Edna Bowyer as well as her mother and father, loved to fish. While Edna was the most active at this, her mother was the acknowledged expert. There was a "hole" in the Little Miami River below the dam spillway where large shovelhead catfish lurked. There was the "Dry House Hole",

not too far away, which was said to be 30 feet deep.

There was the "Rock Hole" where the railroad had discarded large rocks on the Peters side down near the island below the bridge. It was this latter place where Edna fell in one day and could not get out anywhere near where she fell in due to the large rocks and steep banks at this location. Mental images of snakes did not slow her in seeking an exit!

Bass, perch and bluegills were found in these holes. Then there was the little bridge across the race, near the dry house. Catfish and shiners could be had from the race. The attraction here was easy access and a bridge to fish from; the banks could be slippery and steep elsewhere and the brush discouraging. At lunchtime, Edna would often leave the King Powder Company office, with a lady friend, to fish. The dry house was about a half mile upstream from the office

and she would often have to scurry back at the expiration of the hour.

During wartime, especially, there were guards at the gates and rounds were made as frequently as every twenty minutes. Explosions were investigated by the FBI on the chance that an enemy agent had caused them. There was an incident in the Spanish-American War where a stranger was severely burned in an explosion on the line. He was discovered in a nearby barn after the blast. It was said in a newspaper account that he spoke in a foreign language! The fate of the "agent" and his probability of guilt, are unknown.

At one time, there were three successive events where live primers were found in the unfinished powder. None caused any explosion although, in the last event, the corning mill set off one of the primers. By some miracle, the powder did not

Edna Bowyer, secretary to King Powder, in fishing togs. Photo was taken on the King powder line at the bridge over the millrace leading to the larger bridge beyond spanning the Little Miami River itself. These bridges were the property of the King Powder Company. The "dry house" fishing hole was located nearby in the river.

"Old" Milt Lindsley was superintendent of the King Powder Company from 1895 to 1930.
The King Powder Company, Illustrated 1896.
Courtesy of Bob and Betty Carter.

Milton Fletcher Lindsley Jr., shown here in his retirement years, was superintendent from 1930 until King closed their doors for good in 1958. Milt subsequently ran the large Charlestown Arsenal near Louisville until retirement.
Courtesy of Edna Bowyer.

ignite. It was felt that disgruntled employees deliberately put these in the powder. No primers were found in the powder where these employees worked. They were arrested, jailed and arraigned: their fate is unknown– probably thrown out of court for lack of evidence. As far as I have been able to learn, none of the more recent events were discovered to be sabotage.

During times when additional employees were needed, employees for the King Powder Line were recruited from Indiana and Kentucky, eastern Kentucky mostly. A few of the workers could not read or write and were of a "rough character." This was, I believe, not true of most of them. Surviving workers from eastern Kentucky, when interviewed, did not prove to be so.

Any employee would be instantly dismissed if found with matches near the powder line. Their shoes had to be made with wooden pegs, not steel nails. Edna Bowyer reports there were,

over the years she worked there, a few scuffles among the powder line employees over some alleged social infraction while visiting the office on payday. None involved the King management staff.

It has been said that "Old" Milt Lindsley, when he was Superintendent of King Powder Company, would invite any miscreant up to the office, where they would put on the *(boxing)* gloves with Milt. It was strongly implied that dissension from that employee ceased thereafter! Another invitation was not anticipated with any enthusiasm! Old Milt was Superintendent from July 1, 1895 to 1930 when he died. The job of superintendent was then taken over by Milton Lindsley, Junior, who served until King closed in 1958.

During WWI there was an explosion at the King Powder Company. The newspaper account listed the names of

those involved, and where they were from. None of the five were from Ohio, Kentucky or Indiana. This was, of course, at a time when manpower was badly needed.

About 1935, the United Mine Workers organized the plant. There were no strikes or overtly nasty events, but these were some tenuous times, according to Noryl Hamilton. There was no little apprehension as to what might happen. Nothing did! The plant remained organized until it was shut down in 1958.

After WWI was over, the company turned their hand to relieving the congestion that had been the rule for some years at Kings Mills. This was done by seeking out and purchasing an additional site away from Kings Mills. The ultimate site chosen was nearer the coalfields and a good labor market. Wurtland, near Ashland, Kentucky, was chosen (see chapter on KICO).

Construction was started in 1919 and the new plant was put on line in 1922. This did not shut down the Kings Mills operation at all, but certainly there was not the growth at Kings Mills that had occurred before that time. The new plant was called KICO, which was a contraction of the words King Company.

In the new KICO plant, no sporting powder was made, but both sporting powder and dynamite were distributed through the KICO powder storage magazines to appropriate markets. KICO did make blasting powder ("black line") and Detonite ("white line"). Details will be covered in the chapter on KICO.

During WWII, King had contracts with the government for practice bombs and flares. Temporary production facilities were set up in what had been Zentmeyer's old livery stable in the lower end of Kings Mills near the Cliff House. Women sewed powder bags there for one of the contracts. The practice bombs were less than a foot and a half long and could be easily launched from an aircraft by hand. They were constructed of sheet metal and contained a paper shotshell with a live primer. Sand was added to make it weigh the requisite amount and the bomb contained enough black powder to mark the place where it struck the earth with white smoke.

During this war period, women workers were still not utilized on the powder line. They were, however, employed to load powder into bombs and flares. There was at least one incident during the war in which some ladies were burned, some quite badly. Some of the loading activity took place at Middletown Junction and some over near the "A" Line on the top of the hill.

During the 1930s and on through WWII to 1958, much of the repair work where outside

Zentmeyer's old livery stable was pressed into service during WWII as a place for women to sew powder bags. No powder was involved at this point.

people were needed was done by Leonard Michael of Michael's Machine Shop located in nearby Maineville.

When WWII ended, there was a period of readjustment. Cancellation of wartime contracts necessitated some

Leonard Michael, founder of Michaels' Machine Shop in nearby Maineville, Ohio, got his start as a machine shop by doing work for King Powder. Here he leans on his first lathe, bought for work on King projects. Leonard took the aerial photo of the plant shown elsewhere in this book from his private open-cockpit International biplane in 1935. He was in charge of the local Civil Air Patrol during WWII.

layoffs as production was refocused on peacetime needs in the explosives industry.

After WWII, the Korean "Police Action" claimed a good deal of attention from King with a similar mix of products to those made in WWII. Women were again pulled into the work force but, again, not on the powder line. The truce with North Korea was signed in June of 1953 and this work was phased out.

After the Korean Police Action, normal business resumed for a few short years. In about 1957, it was generally discovered that ammonium nitrate and fuel oil (ANFO) could be used as a cheap, effective blasting agent. This soon put many blasting agent manufacturing plants out of business. The King Powder Company was one of them.

The death of Col. George King was probably a factor, too. In June of 1958 a letter was circulated stating the doors would close for good when business could be wound up. The King's Powder line employed about 400 at peak times; about 200 or so in peacetime. Employment had dwindled to about 20 by 1958.

There were many loose ends to tie up. The powder buildings were all destroyed to prevent injury by casual entry. There was much land to sell and assets to dismantle and dispose of. A junk man was called in to scrap out the metallic equipment. Probably a fortune by today's collector's prices–in powder cans alone–was consigned to the scrap yard!

The houses owned by King Powder were offered for sale to the employees first. The powder manufacturing property was sold off. Taft Broadcasting erected King's Island Amusement Park on part of the property. The Detonite line was only a short distance from where stands today the reproduction of the Eiffel Tower.

A few employees of the King powder line survive. They generally have fond memories of both the Kings and of their own employment there.

* G. M. Peters, when he became president of King, reluctantly joined the Gunpowder Trade Association (GTA). The GTA controlled pricing in the powder industry until after 1900 when DuPont was sued under the 1889 Sherman Antitrust Act for fixing prices. King then withdrew from the GTA and was not prosecuted. For a more comprehensive history of this, see *History of the Exposives Industry*.

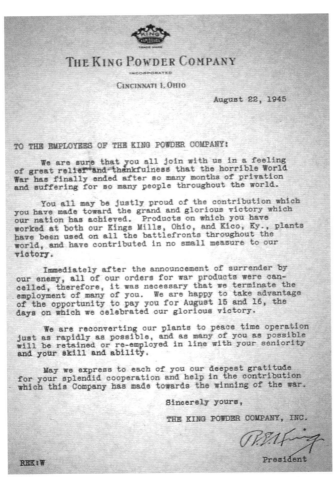

The end of WWII was good news, but meant layoffs for some of the 400-500 employees said to work at King Powder during the height of the war effort.
Courtesy of Bob and Betty Carter.

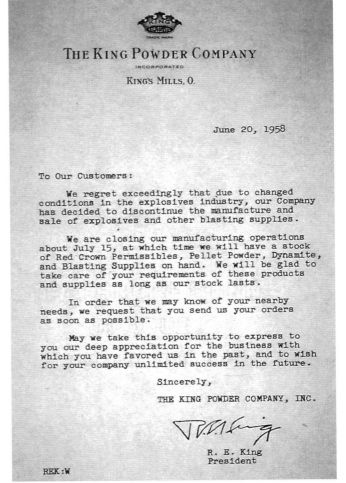

Saying goodbye to good customers as the plant shut down in 1958. *Courtesy of Bob and Betty Carter.*

Chapter 2

The Peters Cartridge Company

THE PETERS CARTRIDGE Company was organized on January 24, 1887. This is confirmed by the Secretary of State in the Peters Articles of Incorporation. It was founded by Gershom Moore Peters, his brother O. E. Peters, and others. Gershom Peters was the son-in-law of J. W. King who founded the parent company of the Peters Cartridge Company, the King Powder Company. *History of the Explosives Industry* says G. M. Peters went to work for King in 1881. He was vice president, succeeding to the office of president upon the death of J. W. King in 1885.

In this chapter we will trace the growth and development of the Peters Cartridge Company from loading paper shells manufactured by others, to becoming a full-fledged cartridge works which claimed to be the most self-contained cartridge plant on the globe. We will trace it through three wars and at least two economic depressions, one of them the most serious in United States history.

This chapter is written with both the historian and the

Gershom Moore Peters (1843-1919) was a Baptist minister who married Joseph Warren King's daughter, Mary. He invented a cartridge-loading machine that introduced a "new article of commerce," the sale of automatic machine-loaded shells. He is shown here as president of the King Powder Company.
The King Powder Company, Illustrated 1896. *Courtesy of Bob and Betty Carter.*

cartridge collector in mind. I want to make known at the outset what was meant when the Peters Cartridge Company said that they [Peters] had introduced a "new article of commerce." In plain terms, Peters claimed there was no commerce in *automatic machine-loaded* shotgun cartridges before Peters introduced them.

Peters clearly differentiated their *automatic* machine-loaded shells from any produced by a *hand*-actuated machine. Differences will be noted later.

The reader and researcher will do well to carefully note the difference between *making* (empty) shotshells (also called "paper shells") and *loading* shotshells. The two operations were very different, yet the terms have been used interchangeably (as will be seen) and, sometimes, incorrectly. The term *making* shotshells means fabricating, or manufacturing empty paper shells; *loading* means to load empty paper shells with primer, powder, shot and wads to produce the finished shotshell ready to shoot. (You will see the terms shotshells, shotgun shells and shotgun cartridges. All refer to paper shells loaded with shot; ammunition used in a breech-loading shotgun.)

We will talk of metallic cartridges later, for rifles and pistols, where the entire cartridge case is made of copper or brass. The paper shells mentioned above were a composite of brass and paper.

We also need to consider what Peters meant by automatic machine-loaded cartridges. Any loading press, however crude, can be correctly called a machine.

Franklin L. Chamberlin of Cleveland, Ohio patented an automatic loading machine on April 17, 1884. This was nearly three years before the Peters Cartridge Company was founded and by 1888, Chamberlin had commercialized machine-loaded shotgun cartridges in 16, 12 and 10 gauges. The Chamberlin press, like the Peters machine, was a dial face device, but the Chamberlin press was hand operated and individual components were placed in the cartridges by hand. The Peters machine was power-driven (by steam engine-powered line shaft) and no individual hand insertions were necessary. Chamberlin and Peters bought paper shells from members of the Ammunition Manufacturers Association, UMC, Winchester and United States Cartridge Co. The true significance of the Peters automatic machine was that three people could tend a machine that spit out some sixty cartridges per minute, hour after hour. Labor costs were greatly reduced which put the operators of such a machine in an extremely competitive position.

Gershom Moore Peters stated the following in his Letters Patent, No.360,043, filed March 6, 1887: "...My invention relates to improvements on machines for loading cartridge shells....

"...The object of my device is to readily and rapidly fill and cap [prime] cartridge shells by continuous and automatic movements....

"There have been devices heretofore used in which shells have been loaded from receptacles containing powder, shot and wads. In these devices the wads have been first cut and then placed in receptacles, and then fed into the shells from the said receptacles. In my device the pasteboard, felt, or wad material is fed from a strip wound on rollers, and automatically cut and rammed or pressed into the shell, thus saving time and labor in their replacement and economy in first cost of material."

Peters continued, stating that his machine automatically introduces empty paper shells, caps them, meters powder into them, cuts wads from rolls of felt and rams them into the shells, meters in the shot, cuts, places, seats and crimps the finished shell and ejects it for inspection and packing; all automatically! This was way ahead of the Chamberlin operation.

I will take several citations from Harold F. Williamson's book *Winchester, the Gun that Won the West*. Williamson touches on things relevant to the Peters operation, and the scholarly nature of the book and documentation Williamson provided invites a confidence found all too rarely in books of this type. He had access to records in the Winchester archives that make me positively green with envy. The Peters company records (before 1944)–if any still exist–have not been found.

Both Dick Dietz, Public Relations Director of Remington in 1974 and Wayland E. Hundley, Assistant General Council of Remington as this is written, have offered their services to find any records relating to "old Peters." Hundley said: "*I am unable to locate information at the corporate headquarters or within the company that would assist you further. If I do run across this information, I will let you know.*" Dietz wrote me essentially the same thing a quarter of a century ago. This chapter has not been constructed from "whole cloth" but rather has been painstakingly put together from bits and pieces. Documented and thoughtful dissent is invited.

City directories, advertising, company literature, price lists, catalogs, cartridges and cartridge boxes, company publications such as *The Primer* and *Peters Informer*, interviews with surviving employees, their relatives, associates, contract workers, regional history books, gun books, loading books, patent

files, newspapers, magazines, photographs and depictions of the works, customers and cartridge company engineering drawings, Remington archives, Remington's historian, historical societies, libraries, manuscript collections, local history interviews, gun writers such as Elmer Keith and Harold McFarland, the H. P. White laboratory, the National Archives, the Library of Congress, the Hagley Museum, Ohio Secretary of State's office, the Carlisle Barracks, County Clerks' offices, The U. S. Department of Commerce, cartridge collectors, powder can collectors, U.S. census records and personal examination of the surviving Peters manufacturing facilities, artifacts and more, have been "mined" to produce this chapter and this book.

Not all of the above sources bore fruit. As has been aptly said: Experience is what you get when you were looking for something else! A good deal of experience was acquired on this project!

Williamson, in his book, noted: "*For the first few years following 1880 there was little change in the Winchester line of shotshells. Production was **confined** to primed and unprimed brass and paper shotshells, wads and primers, which were sold to **users who loaded them** [emphasis the writer's] according to their preference in respect to powder and shot combinations.*" This statement supports the opening thesis and sets the stage for the story that is to follow. Winchester was one of the Big Three cartridge loading companies at the time.

F. C. Tuttle, in an article titled *Ammunition by Peters* sent me by cartridge collector Dale Hedlund, said that: "*... [G. M. Peters] was a natural inventor. Even before going to college he invented and subsequently sold a ball-bearing axle and a revolving rake reaper.... His first conception of a loading machine was what is known as the endless chain type. But he never used his drawings to*

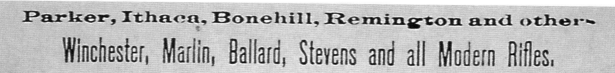

Here is an early (1888) advertisement for Peters indented shells. Note there are three indentations. The very earliest had but two indentations. This was a patented feature of Peters' shells. *Jim Sones collection.*

build this machine, having decided that wear on the chain links would, in time, impair its usefulness. He therefore abandoned the project and developed the round table (dial face) machine, which was a success from the start."

The standard company line was that Peters entered the shotshell loading business in 1887, G. M. Peters having invented the first shotshell **loading** machine (Patent No 360043, March 29, 1887, copy in author's collection). Gardner stated Peters produced the first machine-loaded cartridges in the world. As noted earlier, depending on the construction the reader cares to place on the term "machine-loaded," Chamberlain did or did not precede Peters in this.

The 1887 Cincinnati City Directory listed: "Peters Cartridge Company, Machine Loaded Shotshells." Cincinnati was chosen to be the seat of the Peters' general offices although no manufacturing of ammunition ever took place there. Early

cartridge boxes, until 1934, proclaimed: "Manufactured by The Peters Cartridge Company, Cincinnati, Ohio."

The above fiction was no doubt perpetrated in order to list a place of manufacture familiar to most buyers. It may also have been done to trade on whatever prestige Cincinnati may have had, at that time, as a manufacturing area of precision machine tools. Certainly few of their prospective customers would have heard of Kings Mills.

Cincinnati was, at the time, rising rapidly as a precision tool center. Indeed, one of the first firms Peters did business with was the Cincinnati Screw and Tap Company. This firm later became known as the Cincinnati Milling Machine Company; still later Cincinnati Milacron.

Cincinnati Screw and Tap may have fabricated the first loading machines for Peters. They were certainly involved in rebuilding them later as will be seen. Cartridge collector William Paul Smith says that Robinson constructed the first loading

machines for Peters. This would have been the J. M. Robinson & Company at 229 W. 2nd St. Cincinnati, Ohio. It is certain that subsequent tinkering of a serious nature was required to make them function reliably. It is likely that this is where Cincinnati Screw and Tap entered the picture.

The *Cincinnati Enquirer* of October 6, 1919, noted in G. M. Peters' obituary that he moved to Cincinnati from Xenia in 1887, when King's offices were moved to Cincinnati from Xenia.

Williamson mentions that Peters, during the first few years, "*purchased its empty shells from the members of the Ammunition Manufacturers' Association. By agreement, with the association these loaded shells were not to be sold below Association prices and Peters was not to purchase empty shells from any other source.*" According to Williamson, the Ammunition Manufacturers' Association was formed September 27, 1883, by Winchester Repeating Arms

Company, Union Metallic Cartridge Company, U. S. Cartridge Company and Phoenix Cartridge Company.

Williamson notes in his book that [the Ammunition Manufacturers' Association] sales of ammunition expanded over two and a half times from 1887 to 1901; there was a nearly seven-fold increase in shotshell sales in the same time period. It can be readily seen that Peters entered the trade at a fortuitous time.

Williamson went on to say: *"During this period, the members of the [Ammunition Manufacturers'] Association produced a considerable volume of ammunition components which were loaded or "assembled" [quotes added by Williamson] by others.... From a competitive standpoint, the most important of the loading companies were those sponsored by the powder companies who were attracted by the opportunity of developing a controlled or assured market for a portion of their [powder] output....*

"A loading Company might handle metallic cartridges or shotshells, but most of them appear to have concentrated on the latter. The principle reason for this was the comparative simplicity of the operations; the machines [I feel these are the simple hand loading machines, not sophisticated automatic machines] for loading shotshells being less complicated and easier to operate than the equipment for metallic ammunition; because 10- and 12-gauge shotguns were the most widely used, production could be concentrated on one or two sizes of shotshells, whereas metallic ammunition involved a larger number of different calibers. There was also the attraction to the powder companies of a larger use of powder in a given number of shotshells than in the equivalent amount of ordinary calibered metallic ammunition.

*"...While the Association members were willing to sell ammunition components, they were highly sensitive to any move by other concerns to engage in the **manufacture** of such components. This is shown by the activities of Winchester and UMC during the 1890s. In 1892, the Creedmore Cartridge Company, of Barberton, Ohio, a concern that had been established by the Diamond Match Company interests to produce metallic ammunition, was acquired. The factory was operated for a time by the Association, after which it was dismantled and the machinery distributed among the members."*

A cartridge collector, the late Roland Koepke, in a December 1970 issue of *The Gun Report,*

This ad shows Peters' indented cartridges as well as roll-crimped cartridges in April 1889. Note the introduction of "Blank Shotgun Cartridges" which were loaded without shot to save freight. The customer could add it after purchase.
Advertisement in Forest and Stream *issue of April 11, 1889. Courtesy of Trap Shooting Hall of Fame and Library.*

noted he had seen an advertisement in the Jenny and Grahm Gun Company Catalog (Chicago, 1890) for Peters Cartridges. Shown in the ad were cartridges with the headstamp WRA CO Star and UMC Star. These shells should be pretty easy to identify because of the Peters method of holding the top wad in place, (G. M. Peters Patent No. 299162, May 27, 1884).

In this innovation, thought to be unique to Peters, a triangular stab indentation was made at two places around - and through - the periphery of the muzzle end of the shell. This indentation projected a triangular piece of the paper tube sidewall into the cylinder of the shell. This kept the top wad from being pushed back out by the compression stored in the wads during loading.

Wad pressure, retained through the cartridges' shelf life, was very desirable in causing the powder to burn efficiently and cleanly. A bit later in Peters' production, the twin indentations were changed to a similar, but less severe, version that had no sharp angle in the middle but featured indentations located 120 degrees apart around the periphery of the shell muzzle (three indentations) instead of the two original at 180 degrees apart. This was yet another of G. M. Peters' inventions (April 10, 1888, No 380689, according to Jim Sones in the November-December issue of the *International Ammunition Association Journal* issue No. 392). An advertisement as early as July, 1888, offers the newer configuration.

Thus, the earliest of Peters production were in Winchester or UMC "Star" brand cases and had either the unique top wad retention (known as "indented" cartridges) or the standard roll crimp. The roll crimp shells can be real sleepers in that the casual observer might well think them Winchester or UMC loadings. Examination of the top wad will reveal the difference. Don't rule out their having used shells made with U.S. Cartridge cases.

A September 25, 1889, Peters Cartridge Company letterhead shows a cartridge with the three indentations of the 1888 patent. Underneath the shotshell, it proclaims *"Crimped or indented as desired."* And, *"Sole controllers in the U.S. of Peters' Patent fastenings for cartridges and Peters' patent Cartridge Loading Machine."* And, *"The most accurate & scientific cartridge loader in existence. Each machine loading 4000 cartridges per hour."*

The unique indentations evidently did not last but a year or two, so Peters shells made in this way should be considered quite rare. Peters advertisements for shells with this indentation were claimed to have *"wonderful pattern and penetration. Light recoil and a clean gun. Used consistently by many of the most successful expert and amateur Trap Shooters."*

How much of this efficiency Peters thought was because of the indentations instead of the usual roll crimp of that day was not stated in their claim for excellence. The above claims notwithstanding, Peters soon turned exclusively to the standard roll crimp used by the rest of the industry at the time. It looks like the indentation system used the mouth of the paper case pretty severely and would have discouraged those who wanted to reload the shells more than once (if that) after they were fired.

I strongly suspect that the "light recoil" claimed was due to light wad pressure. Therefore, there was not as much velocity as with more wad pressure and a good roll crimp to hold it in place.

F. C. Tuttle noted in an article in 1932 that: *"...Depending for its empty shells upon manufacturers who were also marketing loaded shotgun shells, the company was in an exposed position. By advancing the price of "empties" and cutting the price of their* *loaded shells, competitors had the young company at their mercy. Peters escaped eventually by acquiring patent rights to manufacture empty shotgun shells."*

I wonder to what extent Peters' competitors did squeeze them, or whether Peters perceived this potential problem and moved to meet it. I also wonder to what extent Peter's offer to sell automatic machinery to other loading companies may have brought on the actions mentioned.

Williamson's book is quoted concerning the acquisition of shell manufacturing machinery as follows:

*"In 1889, just before it sold its cartridge business to Winchester, the American Buckle and Cartridge Company of New Haven had begun negotiations with Peters to have shotshells **loaded** by machines recently designed and built by American Buckle.* [Emphasis is mine; I believe the word Williamson intended to use here was *made*. Peters already *had* a viable automatic loading machine, what Peters needed was a way to *make* the empty paper shells needed for loading.] *Immediately following the sale of its cartridge business, American Buckle wrote Peters '...we have just... sold out our paper shell machinery and stock of shells to the Winchester Repeating Arms Company. ...Our patents are still our own property. ...It will not be possible for any one to successfully enter the paper shell business unless they come into the possession of the patent or invent an entirely new process and machinery, and it is certain that the last named alternative would be very difficult, if not altogether impossible.'*

"The following month Peters purchased the patent rights and two sets of machinery and tools for the manufacture of paper shotshells from the American Buckle and Cartridge Company. [A Peters Cartridge Company letter dated December 2, 1891,

Peters' first shot tower was built in 1895. It stood near where the present tower is located in an almost direct line with the axis of the river bridge. The present tower succeeded it during WWI.
Warren County Historical Society.

written on letterhead that exhibits no shotshell but mentions *"Manufacturers of PRIZE paper shells."* It appears, then, that the first Peters manufactured and loaded shells were head stamped PRIZE].

"On March 18, 1892, Winchester brought suit against Peters Cartridge Company alleging patent infringement on one of the machines sold to Peters by the American Buckle and Cartridge Company. The case, which dragged on for a number of years, was bitterly fought. Winchester finally won the case in March 1900, and was

subsequently paid damages of $1,000. By this time, the patent under controversy had run out and there was no question about Peters' right to the use of machinery under dispute.

"While this was being carried on Peters had been able to continue its manufacture of [loaded] shotshells using machinery which did not infringe any existing patents. The Company [Peters] had an exclusive agreement with its paper supplier, made its own shot [starting 1895], and developed its own facilities for the manufacture of primers and wads.

"Peters seems to have built up its sales outlets during the period when it was loading empty shells purchased from the Association. These outlets remained with the concern after its break with that organization."

Peters introduced shotgun shells loaded with powder and wads, but without shot in them. Peters felt that home loaders of shotshells would like to add their own locally made shot since much of the shell weight, and hence freight cost, was due to the shot. Peters used the trademarked terms *Shotless* and *Shot Gun Blanks* to represent this feature on the labels.

In their trademark application for *Shotless* and *Shot Gun Blanks*, Peters claimed usage since August 1, 1888. A price list from Jim Sones of about that date states: *"Loaded in Star, Rival, Club, or Climax Shells... The boxes bear beautiful and appropriate labels; the "Popular" being designated by yellow, the "Quick-shot" by Blue and the "Ducking" by Red; making most attractive shelf goods."*

The color refers to the box. It is this latter feature–attractive shelf goods–that is a big reason Peters Cartridges, along with their boxes and advertising, is so collectable. I have not seen a *Shotless* shell.

The Peters factory was founded on the south side of the Little Miami River and occupied

This map shows the location of Peters after the explosion of July 15, 1890. Note there is a "shell factory" (1) at the lower end of town, and a "cartridge factory" (2) along the "road to Hopkinsville" *(later called Grandin Road).* Taken literally, the shells were at that time (1891) made in town and loaded near the site of the explosion. Peters in future years would build their main plant on the plot marked "F. Keller" and beyond. *Warren County Atlas, 1891.*

land leased from the King Powder Company. The main works, the entire production facility, of the King Powder Company was located on the north, or opposite, side of the river. The Little Miami River flows generally from north to south to the Ohio River. You could make a case for Peters being on the east side and King on the west: however, for this book, Peters will be on the south side, King on the north. This is the way most of the locals viewed it.

Initially the King Powder Company office (along with Peters' office), warehousing and magazines were located on the south side of the river where the fledgling Peters Cartridge works was situated. These buildings and a few residences were clustered along the side of the Little Miami Railroad and around the Kings Mills railroad depot. The surrounding steep hills hemmed the buildings into a fairly close proximity to each other, to the railroad and the river.

An iron bridge near the depot connected the two sides of the river. Grandin Road, on the south side, connected at its north end across the bridge with the not-so-lazy switchbacks that elevated the roadway to a connection with King Avenue up in the town of Kings Mills itself. Kings Mills is situated nearly two hundred feet above the river and a scant 500 feet horizontally from the water to the near edge of town. This is a steep road.

The Peters business was evidently doing well with some forty women working in the factory when the great explosion of July 15, 1890, occurred (see Chapter 3 on the July 15, 1890, explosion). This explosion destroyed all buildings and residences, including a boarding house on the Peters side of the river. The depot, a paper shell factory, cartridge factory, office, residences, warehouse, etc., were all destroyed either by the initial and subsequent explosions or the resulting fire.

Herculean fire fighting efforts by employees kept the fire from the magazines or more lives would have been lost. Other than shipping facilities and the office, which were destroyed, The King Powder Company production buildings and machinery were not affected, all being located on the opposite side of the river.

The entire Peters operation, on the other hand, was destroyed rather completely. Perhaps some of the steam engine and/or boiler facilities were salvable, but little else was. It is on record that Peters had their loading machinery rebuilt by Cincinnati Screw and Tap. The fact that there was an immediate attempt to put Peters back into business speaks eloquently that the business had thus far been successful.

The Peters letterhead of late 1891 included this terse comment: "*UNAVOIDABLE ACCIDENTS AND HINDRANCES EXCEPTED IN ALL ARRANGEMENTS*." This statement was no doubt due to a reaction to the events of 1890!

The blame for the explosion was placed on the carelessness or recklessness of a railroad freight crew. Damages were said to be $150,000. Peters and King filed suit against the Pennsylvania Railroad, for by then, the Little Miami Railroad had become a division of the Pennsylvania Railroad system. Rather than wait for a settlement, Peters decided to set up a temporary factory in the lower end of the Kings Mills town. Settlement with the railroad was not made until 1900. See the chapter on the explosion of July 1890 for details of the settlement.

Kings Mill native, Alice Curran Pelle, remembered that her "*... father and grandfather were employed by the company in New Haven, Connecticut which made the machinery for the rebuilding of a new plant to be built this time on top of Kings Mill hill at the far end of town [actually the nearest end of town to the destroyed cartridge factory]. The buildings were made of some sort of tin. My father was sent to Kings Mills with the new machinery to oversee the setting up of it. It was very inconvenient there for shipping, etc., and it was again moved to its original location across the Pennsylvania Railroad tracks. ...While there he met and fell in love with Dorthea Ludeke and after a short time they were married. ...my father became superintendent of the Paper Shell Department of the (Peters) Company....*" The Peters Informer* printed this obituary on May 16, 1940: "*W. J. Curran started in October 1890 just after* [the] *business* [was] *getting underway. Manufacture of* **paper shells** [not loaded shells; shell loading had already started in 1887] *had begun only a short time before the disaster* [July 15, 1890, explosion]. *His early experience in the manufacture of shotshells was acquired in plants in New Haven and Bridgeport. He came to work under Mr. B. W. Place, the first superintendent of the paper shell department...*"

Speculation here favors American Buckle being the source of the machinery to replace that lost in the fire. The American Buckle and Cartridge Company, where Peters originally obtained their paper shell machinery and patents, was located in West Haven, not New Haven, Connecticut. However, the two towns were (and are) close enough for a West Haven person to say they were from the better-known New Haven.

According to Robert Pelle, a Curran descendent, Curran and his father had been, or at that time continued to be, employees of American Buckle and Cartridge. American Buckle did say in their 1889 proposal to Peters "*...our patents are still our own property*" following the sale of American Buckle's paper shell

The Park Department Store at the lower end of town. I believe this occupied the shell factory building known locally as "the tin whistle" that was vacated upon moving that operation back down the hill and across the river. The move was made to eliminate the considerable burden of freighting shell components up and down the steep hill. The building has been gone for many years.   *Cline postcard. Courtesy of Joseph Warren King II.*

business to Winchester. Therefore Peters simply returned to the well and got more paper shell manufacturing machinery from, or through, American Buckle. Remember that there were two classes of machinery damaged or lost in the fire. This refers to the paper shell manufacturing machinery only, not the loading machines.

Winchester was sensitive to other companies competing with them at this time. It is extremely unlikely that Winchester would have been amenable to such a deal; and definitely was not the source of the machinery [Winchester **was,** however, in both New Haven and, prior to April 1871, in Bridgeport]. Curran was sent by A. B. & C. with the machinery to oversee its setup, and elected to stay on at Kings Mills.

The following information about Bill Schneider, taken from the February, 1942 issue of *The*

Primer, reveals the approximate date that the factory was moved back to its pre-explosion site. It also reveals several things about the factory in its early years that I've seen nowhere else: *"...Bill [Schneider], who resides in Hopkinsville, first saw the light of day in 1877.... At the age of 15 [1892 or 1893], Bill entered the employ of the Peters Cartridge Company. His starting rate was $3.50 a week, a rate that was soon raised to $4. Because of shipping difficulties encountered* [because the cartridge factory was then located in Kings Mills; across the railroad, across the river and away up the hill]*, the factory was moved* [back] *down the hill* [and across the river] *into what is* [in 1942] *known as Building No.6. The office was at the entrance to the building. The machine shop and metallic department occupied the remainder of the first floor. Waterproofing and*

tube rolling operations were conducted in a smaller building on the hill in back of what now is known as the powder room.

"Bill's first job was filling fountains [these were very likely powder and shot hoppers] *on the assembly line.... The entire operation at the time was hand fed, so it is apparent that Bill has progressed with the Peters Cartridge Company through a long period of machine operation progression. He has witnessed the advent of automatic feeds and high R.P.M.s."*

If the above is to be taken literally, there **might** have been metallic cartridge activity at Peters as early as 1892 or 1893! The earliest source, independent of a catalog, I have seen which positively mentions metallic cartridges appeared in the December, 1943, issue of *The Primer.* It states, *"Joe Mills of South Lebanon, a native of Indiana, started* [with Peters]

management, it has gained a worldwide reputation. Its growth and success, in the face of unusual obstacles, have been the marvel and admiration of all conversant with its history. It may be regarded as a pioneer in the manufacture of shotgun ammunition by mechanical processes. It literally created a new article of commerce and established a trade before unknown or thought possible, thus benefiting many and opening a field of operation whose advantages other manufacturers have been quick to seize [this would refer to the loading machine, not paper shell manufacture].

"Its loading machine is without an equal in the world. It loads with great rapidity and with far greater accuracy and uniformity than can be had by the most careful and expert hand-loading. It is entirely automatic and each operation is so guarded by testing and telltale devices that a mistake in loading is practically impossible. Numerous patents, covering this and other machines connected with the business, have been obtained by this company and triumphantly fought through the courts to the full establishment of its exclusive rights.

"The factories of this company are among the largest and certainly comprise the most complete ammunition plant in the world. Its various buildings aggregate a floor space of over 150,000 square feet, which would make one building about a mile in length with thirty feet in width. New buildings and extensions are constantly being added. These factories are crowded with machinery of the latest improvements and all running in charge of men of large experience and great success in their special lines. The output in all kinds of shells and ammunition amounts to hundreds of millions annually.

"The Company started originally with the single purpose of loading shells, but the attitude of its competitors and the

exigencies of its trade forced it into the manufacture of every thing pertaining to the ammunition business. Its printed list today embraces 165 different styles of metallic cartridges, and more are being constantly added. It is regularly putting out 634 different styles and loads of shotgun ammunition; and this number can be doubled and almost trebled by adding chilled shot loads and loads of various nitro powders. It produces the greatest variety of goods of any cartridge concern in the world, and does what no other concern attempts, makes practically everything entering into the completed shell or cartridge of whatever kind except some of the rawest parts of the raw material and some of the nitro powders [Obviously, this latter statement refers to Peters' mother corporation the King Powder Company; Peters Cartridge Company itself never made powder.] The result is this Company not only obtains everything at first hand, but is able to watch over every detail of the process and to know that it is right.

"Take for instance the **Primer**. This Company not only constructs its own primers, but makes every particle of fulminate entering into same. ...

"Take again the **Wads**. All wads used or sold by this Company are of its own manufacture. It has in connection with its works, one of the most complete felt factories anywhere to be found. It makes felt wholly for wads and with a view to securing the best results in loading. ...

"The same may be said of the **Shot**. This company does not buy shot from the different towers, each peculiar in its methods and somewhat varying in size though having the same designations. It makes its own shot, having for this purpose a tower of the latest pattern. The shot can, therefore, be always counted on as the same, which is a very important matter in securing accuracy and uniformity of results.

"So one and another article might be enumerated as made by this Company and tending to insure the perfection of its ammunition. Let us refer to the completed goods.

LOADED SHELLS

"LEAGUE. This is a capital shell for all ordinary purposes, strong and a sure killer. It is of a manila color and is loaded with black powder made especially for this Company, and in such a way as to secure results highly satisfactory to shooters of this powder.

"REFEREE. A handsome purple, and loaded with King's celebrated Semi-Smokeless, for which this Company has the exclusive right among all loading companies. The Referee is therefore without a competitor, and is pre-eminent because of its quality. It has a velocity equaling the best nitro powders, with low breech pressure; has greatly lessened smoke; is very clean, quick and strong; is splendid for field or trap, and moreover can be had at a trifle above the price of black powder shells.

"But the favorites for Trap Shooters are the following:

"IDEAL. This is a cherry color with a high polished brass and Peters No. 3 Battery Cup Primer. This is loaded with any and all standard makes of bulk Smokeless powder, and develops these powders to their highest efficiency.

"NEW VICTOR. Green, medium brass. This is also loaded with bulk smokeless powder. While it is medium in price, it is of very high quality and a great favorite at the trap.

"PREMIER. Orange color, high polished brass, Peters No.3 Battery Cup Primer. This is loaded with dense smokeless powders, and gives the highest results in these powders.

"HIGH GUN. Bright blue, medium brass, Peters No.3 battery cup primer. Also loaded with dense smokeless. Medium price but high in quality.

METALLIC AMMUNITION

As made by this Company, it consists of all the numerous styles of rim and central fire cartridges demanded by the trade. All the regular metallic goods are loaded exclusively with King's Semi-Smokeless powder. **Not a grain of black powder is put behind a bullet**. However good Semi-smokeless may be for shot gun ammunition, it is even better for rifle and revolver cartridges. There never was a powder like it for this purpose. It is exceedingly quick, clean, of high velocity, great power, low breech pressure, and very safe. It does not strip the ordinary lead bullet or cause the leading of the gun, and therefore gives an accuracy and uniformity never before equaled. It generates very little smoke and no unpleasant gas. These features combined with its accuracy and cleanliness, have caused its adoption by first-class shooting galleries throughout the country. It admits of almost continuous shooting without cleaning the gun, obscuring the vision, or affecting the accuracy-points especially appreciated in target practice, extended hunts or in closely confined galleries. It is equally adapted to small and large calibers, pistol and rifle, big game and small, long range and short. [These statements meant a lot more to the shooters of that day. It is almost impossible for the shooter in our day and time to realize that a .22 rifle would often "coke up" with powder fouling to the extent a bullet would lodge in the barrel after shooting less than a box of cartridges! In light of this you can imagine that accuracy would have become history long before the bullet lodged in the barrel.]

"Hundreds of successful contests can be cited to prove these statements. This powder and these cartridges have won first place and repeatedly in all the great shoots, State, National and International of recent years. They hold the world's record.

"This Company also loads in its metallic goods the various standard smokeless powders, so far as these powders have been perfected for rifle purposes.

"Especial success has been attained in the production of the Sporting and Military cartridges using regular and high pressure smokeless powder, with full jacket and soft point bullets."

Bill Fenton reported in the May, 1962, issue of *The Gun Report* that: "[Peters] *brought out one of the gems in the world of the shotgun shell collector. This item is known as the stripe or candy stripe which may be encountered, but only rarely, in 10, 12, and 16 gauge with red stripes or blue green stripes on a light manila case, vintage 1896 to 98.*"

O. E. PETERS, TREASURER.

O. E. Peters, brother of G. M. Peters, was treasurer of the King Powder Company and president of Peters Cartridge Company for many years.
The King Powder Company, Illustrated 1896. *Courtesy of Bob and Betty Carter.*

This is a good place to look at the men who guided Peters' efforts and took the company through the critical formative years. The original Articles of Incorporation for the Peters Cartridge Company was signed by: G. M. Peters, O. E. Peters, A. King, W. K. McKibben and J. H. McKibben.

O. E. Peters was the first president and general manager. In 1932, F. C. Tuttle, vice president and treasurer of Peters stated:...*O. E. Peters* [previously a successful merchant at Lancaster, Ohio]...*was a man of tireless energy. Quick and brusque in business, he was easily touched by another's mischance or distress; he performed many unobtrusive kindly acts. He was intellectually quick; it would be difficult to elaborate on any proposition to him, for he would cut through to the conclusion and give his answer quickly.... [he] was a tower of strength in all the early struggles of the company.*"

By 1900, the tail was certainly wagging the dog. The Peters Cartridge Company had become much larger than its parent the King Powder Company. In yet another of the strange quirks that seemed to hover about these two companies, Ahimaaz King managed the Peters Cartridge Company, and Gershom Moore Peters was president of the King Powder Company. The two companies worked closely on many matters. This was especially true in the early days of the cartridge company. Among joint ventures was advertising, as noted in several previous quotations and in some early advertisements shown in the advertising chapter.

The invention, development, loading and promotion of Semi-Smokeless Powder was a good example of

Babcock and Wilcox water tube boilers with extensive coal conveyors to facilitate the influx of coal. There were elaborate boiler feed-water treating facilities to ameliorate the native hardness of the local water.

The engine room next to the boilers housed one fair-sized Corliss reciprocating steam engine and two High Speed Buckeye reciprocating engines. No turbines were used. These engines turned generators that provided electrical energy for the cartridge plant and the powder plant across the river (the powder plant had at one time supplied power to the cartridge plant). At a later date, this same facility had sufficient capacity to provide steam for the Kings Mills Ordnance Plant as well.

This is in contrast to the way in which the original Peters plant was powered. Steam engines in an earlier day directly drove line shafting which, in turn, powered machinery off the line shafting with large, flat, continuous belts. An engine (and engineer and perhaps another boiler and boiler operator) was required for each line shaft, which was at any distance removed. Any attempt to chronicle the various locations of steam engines and boilers prior to 1895 on both sides of the river would soon exhaust the reader and, to be sure, the writer. It very likely would be a lifetime's work and to little benefit.

For a rapidly growing, sprawling plant, many scattered discrete sources of power became intolerable; hence the centralized generation of electricity. Line shafting was still utilized, but line shafts could now be located anywhere wiring could be pulled. The localized shafting would then be powered by one large electric motor per shaft. The shaft, in turn, would run any number of machines, each one having its own flat belt, running from the line shaft, hanging off the ceiling, to the machine.

The Peters plant management shared this quaint office with The King Powder Company until Peters' new R-1 Building was complete, about 1916. After Peters moved out, King occupied it until it was destroyed by fire in 1950. Shown here in its early days, it was later doubled in size.
The King Powder Company, Illustrated 1896. *Courtesy of Bob and Betty Carter.*

The Peters/King office in later years. *Steve McDowell.*

In earlier days, the original central power plant was located at the King Powder Company and electricity was generated by both water and steam power, said to have a combined capacity of 1,000 horsepower.

The advantage of having electric lighting throughout the plant is obvious. It made winter hours the same as

The King Powder Company powerhouse supplied power, or at least electrical energy for lighting, to the Peters Cartridge Company until 1901 when Peters erected their own powerhouse. This structure was on the King Powder Company side of the river. *Steve McDowell.*

summer hours, rainy days as productive as sunny days, and allowed the workday to be prolonged for overtime to meet sudden extra production requirements. It also allowed the flexibility of doubling–even tripling–plant size by the simple expedient of going to a second or third shift of the same machinery (if additional workers could be found).

There had previously been a smaller centralized power plant on the Peters side. Joe Weine went to work for Peters in 1900

These workers proudly pose with their work. The chimney is marked with the date 1901 and represents the genesis of electrical power generated on the Peters side of the river.

Warren County Historical Society.

and remembered they were getting power from the King facility at that time. It was shortly after 1900 that a power plant was brought on-line on the Peters side. The original King powerhouse supplied illumination for the town of Kings Mills. When this started and ended is not known.

It would have been something to see the Peters engine room in action in its heyday. The engines had large flywheels which were rotated by the relatively slow, rhythmic and nearly silent extension and contraction impulses of shiny piston rods. The senses would not be assaulted by the roar of exhaust and squeal of tortured rubber or the high-pitched whine of turbines that set one's teeth on edge.

The Peters engine room would have provided a more subtle and quiet experience. Normal conversation could be held over the subdued, but powerful, piston pulsations more sensed than felt. Together with the quiet breathing of the engines and gentle drone of the engine-driven generators, the smells of hot oil and live steam would combine to give the observer a real sense of the power being channeled into useful work.

The flashing of connecting rods, crossheads and the monkey motion of the valve gear would be enough to excite the "little boy" that still lurks in many of us.

Turbines are more efficient, lower in cost and easier to maintain than the reciprocating engines at Peters. Turbines also do not commit the sin of allowing their lubricating oil to foul their condensate. However, the predictable–even mesmerizing–repetitive motion surrounding the connecting rods, reach rods, crank pins, bell cranks, dash pots, reversing gear, lubricators and governors of a reciprocating steam engine will claim and excite your curiosity long after it is sated from staring at a closed turbine casing that reveals none of its secrets.

The Peters engine room, with its chief engineer's office in the corner, and electrical switch gear and steam meters on the south wall, has long since grown cold. It has given way to the cold hand of those who would profit from the salvage of the considerable tonnage of metal involved. They left behind a jumble of conduit, a chaos of rusting pipes, vacant anchor bolts, holes in the floor and walls and broken windows. The structure remains, but I do not go there any more.

This "new" [in 1917] boiler house replaced two earlier boiler houses which were located together more or less between the new boiler house and the machine shop. The abandoned boiler houses, Buildings R-58 and R-34, were allowed to remain as host to Dove Rock (clay target) manufacture; a hot, dirty and altogether onerous operation. These buildings are completely gone now but were still there in 1973.

The primer building R-9 was constructed in 1919. It is predictably somewhat remote from the rest of the facility, and of very substantial construction. The old tramways connecting to bunkers built into Magazine Hill are yet in evidence as this is written. The building itself was used by Columbia records to press discs in the mid-1940s. It has fairly recently been refurbished and used by a local industry.

As mentioned earlier, some of the wooden buildings did remain to the end of the Peters Cartridge days. The biggest was the Richmond Building. It was here that the paper shells were loaded. Why this building escaped modernization or replacement can only be speculated upon. I believe that the function of the building was probably too important to take off line if there was not another good place for its relocation. Then too, during a slack period of any magnitude, there may not have been the cash flow to cover its replacement.

Another reason might have been that the Richmond building was constructed at the base of, and part way up, a steep hillside—which does not appear to be very stable. A rigid monolith of a building is less accommodating to small shifting of the footers than is a post and beam frame structure. Take your choice or supply your own theory. Whatever the reason, it survived its Peters Cartridge days to serve as a whisky warehouse for Seagrams Distilling Company Ltd., that had—and still has—a distilling facility in Lawrenceburg, Indiana, fifty or so miles away. R-21 was not razed until after the mid-1970s.

There were several long wooden buildings between the railroad and the river which were used to make felt for the cushion wads in the shotgun shells and perhaps to do some cupping or drawing of shell heads or cartridge cases.

Another wooden structure was Building R-6, which was connected to Building R-1 by an elevated passageway, and housed the bullet-making equipment.

The buildings were for the most part connected by being built contiguous to one another or as above, connected by an elevated passageway. By this means personnel and material could be moved from department to department without regard to weather.

The WWI period was one of almost frantic activity. One may remember that WWI started without the participation of the United States, in 1914. In spite of this, there were large orders from both the Russians (reported) and the British. It was these contracts that provided the cash flow to enlarge the plant and to replace most frame buildings with buildings featuring reinforced concrete and brick.

Peters' officer Tuttle, wrote about 1932 that the primary items produced in these war years were the Mark VII British (.303), .45 Automatic (ACP), 7mm(?), and 7.65 (he probably meant the 7.62 Russian), and .30-caliber 1906 U.S. government cartridges.

Foreign contracts deserve notice here. They provided revenue for the company, and perhaps more importantly, they provided a real basis for fulfilling American contracts after the United States entered the war.

John Pople-Crump of Colefors, Gloucestershire, UK, kindly researched the matter in the Public Record Office (PRO).

John found the following:

First- all British munitions contracts were negotiated via J. P. Morgan's New York office and Morgan Grenfell in London, which brings me to the first item of interest - a couple of telegram messages where Peters are first mentioned as a possible source of .303-inch Mark VII ammo. (After deals were already in progress between Rem-UMC and US Cartridge Co.; the British government intentionally did not approach Winchester at this stage because they wanted to keep a clear stage for the Russian govt. to get 7.62mm ammo from Winchester - who were being wooed by the French govt. for 8mm Lebel).

Copy of telegram received 1st March, 1915 at 7:45 PM, Morgan Grenfell, London to J. P. Morgan, New York:

2352 In view close relations understood to exist between US Cartridge Co & Peters Co & fact former is familiar with difficulties manufacturing Mark VII, War Office suggest best plan might be to make contract with US Cartridge Co allowing them to sub-contract with Peters Co thus contracting with more substantial Co and benefiting by their technical knowledge.

Copy of telegram received 4th March 1915 at 10 AM, J. P. Morgan & Co, New York to Morgan Grenfell & Co., London:

163 (your 2352) Peters Cartridge Co unwilling to accept order Mark VII in view of difficulties manufacture and prospects securing large orders simpler cartridges. Stop. U. S. Cartridge say no connection Peters Co. and decline consider contract with a view to letting Peters Co. as sub-contractors as in that event would feel compelled to devote time and attention improvement plant & organization Peters Co. which would be difficult. Would feel disposed apply extension their facility. Stop.

The same file as these telegrams (MUN7/55) also contained a table of SAA promised to be delivered by U.S. and British manufacturers, and this chart indicated that Peters promised delivery of .303 Mark VII from July 1915, starting at 2 million per week and building to 4 million per week. No contract record on file.

I [Pople-Crump] was unable to determine which U.S. ctgs. were condemned as practice only, but did find file(MUN 4/6263) which referred to Government of South Africa receiving 12 million Mark VII from Britain in 1924 to replace 12m rds of .303 received 1916-1918 via British Govt. File contained reference to U.S. 303 being condemned for machine-gun use in British Service- which is interesting re your comment about testing Savage MGs [machine guns] with NZ [nitro cellulose] powder loads from Peters, when the NZ loads were expected to operate standard Vickers MGs.

Lastly - found in MUN5/190/1440/6 "Output of SAA [small arms ammunition] from USA":

.303	Total 1915	Total 1916
Natl.	Nil	Nil
Conduit		
and Cable		
Peters	17, 800,000	156,000,000
Rem-UMC	18,3000,000	125,962,000
U.S.	54,200,000	284,400,000
Cart Co.		
Winchester	11,600,000	19,954,000

I have only ever seen P15 VII & P16 VII headstamps.

From the pages of *Supply of Ammunition,* printed by H. M. Stationery Office Press, Harrow, which Pople-Crump also kindly sent, we have this from pp 38:

IV Cancellation of American Contracts:

While the output in the United Kingdom was rising steadily, the requirements of the War Office were reduced. So much capacity was freed by the reduction of July 1916, that the Supply Department raised the question of canceling the American Contracts. This step was desirable from the point of view of economy alone, the price of American Ammunition being roughly 8 pounds, 10 shillings per 1,000 compared with 6 pounds, 10 shillings for British Ammunition. It was even more desirable from the point of view of the quantity and quality of the supply. The ammunition produced by the U. S. Cartridge Company (more than 50% of the whole) was regarded by the War Office as suitable for emergency use only. And much of it was sentenced for practice at home. The American contracts were also greatly in arrears. On 15 July, 1916, the Remington Arms Union [Metallic Cartridge] was nearly 209,000,000 behind, the National Cable And Conduit Company 118,000,000, and Peters Cartridge Company 96,000,000. ...On 17 October the Minister sanctioned the cancellation of all the American contracts, and supply from this source entirely ceased by April 1917.

The United States entered WWI on April 6, 1917 and added to Peters orders government contracts for great quantities of .30-06 and .45 ACP ammunition. Peters had to go to extra shifts and add considerably to the workforce to accommodate these orders. There was recruiting in Kentucky and Indiana for additional workers. The town of Kings Mills could not handle the extra personnel although the residents were encouraged to take in boarders if at all possible. Temporary housing was set up in the Homestead Hotel attic and elsewhere.

Williamson reported that the contract costs of ammunition for the government were set on a base cost, plus 10%. The "fair cost of production" was predicated on base prices of essential raw material, including copper, zinc, lead and powder. If the contractor achieved a cost lower that the normal, in addition to his 10%, he was given 20% of the cost saving. Conversely, if the contractor's cost was above the base cost, it cost him 20% of the overage. There was no adjustment for wage increases.

According to Williamson, at Winchester, weekly wages increased from $16.22 in September 1917 to $19.50 in November 1918. This was about a 20% increase. There was no method of compensating for the increase in wages in the base cost of the contract. This was obviously costly to the contractor and caused him to resist pay raises. How much this affected Peters is not known.

During this period it was said some workers would, at the end of their shifts, enter bedding so recently vacated by the next shift's workers that it was still warm!

At this time, the Interurban Railway and Terminal (I.R.&T. Rapid Division) line ran through Kings Mills. From 1903 to 1922, the interurban ran from Cincinnati to Lebanon with

Workers trooping down the hill from Kings Mills to work. This is probably early in WWI.
Cline post card photo.
Courtesy of Joseph Warren King II.

Interurban Railway and Terminal (IR&T) was a big factor in bringing workers to both the King and Peters operations during WWI. It was out of business by 1923 and was thus not a factor in WWII operations. This line ran from Fountain Square in Cincinnati to Lebanon, Ohio, and ran right through the lower end of Kings Mills town. This trestle was located just a few hundred feet from the King Powder Company dam on the river.
Cline post card photo. Courtesy of Steve McDowell.

Kings Mills between, but much nearer Lebanon. It furnished badly needed commuter transportation to Peters workers during the war years. There is a telegram in Ordnance Department files at the National Archives from the IR&T agreeing to put on extra cars and bill the department for the added costs.

Passenger trains on both the Little Miami Division of the Pennsylvania Railroad (Cincinnati to Columbus) and the Cincinnati Lebanon and Northern which joined the Little Miami at Middletown Junction (a half-mile up river from the plant) were likely used to commute workers during this very busy period. It should be remembered that the Model T Ford was an increasingly used means of transportation. Still, the personal automobile had not attained nearly the popular status that it held by WWII.

Negotiations were under way to increase the production capacity of Peters Cartridge Company through purchase of the old property vacated by the R. K. LeBlond machine tool company in the Fulton District of Cincinnati, along the Ohio River on the east side of town. The end of the war halted the negotiations. The site is now LeBlond Park. There were also negotiations for the use of the old Ford Plant in Cincinnati for similar purposes. These negotiations also were stopped by the cessation of hostilities. This building was later used as the Sears and Roebuck Farm Store.

During WWI there was widespread paranoia concerning sabotage. This was caused by–or certainly exacerbated by–the large Germanic population of the area. Indeed, many workers at the plant were of German extraction, and it is likely that some of these workers still had ties in Europe. For more insight on this issue, see the chapter on explosions at the powder mills.

So intense was this concern that a good deal of anti-German sentiment was expressed. This sentiment found its way into actions both subtle and obvious. It is interesting to speculate what might have happened had the U.S. government been as sensitive to violations of civil rights as it became later.

It is probable that fear of arson fueled the fever to replace the wooden buildings at Peters with ones of more substantial construction.

It *is* certain that fear manifested itself in the stationing of soldiers around both the powder and the cartridge plants in order to protect them against subversive activity. This was done as early as mid-May, 1917, according to Felix Koch, who published a little booklet illustrating U.S. preparations for war in early 1917.

Soldiers of the Third Ohio Regiment were sent to the Peters and King Powder plants to supplement the plant guards. Joseph Warren King II told me in a 1985 interview that the soldiers were billeted at the lower end of town where the "tin whistle" building had been.

This influx certainly put more strain on the local infrastructure, although the military is usually thought to have the means of sustaining itself in the field. Still, these men were likely raw recruits and did not yet display the resourcefulness that soldiers are reputed to develop after campaigning for some time. One of the soldiers, Lavin Ingram, of Middletown, drowned while swimming in the Little Miami River shortly after arrival.

Soldiers of the Third Ohio Regiment guard the Peters and King operations during WWI, starting in mid-May 1917. A soldier, Lavin Ingram, of Middletown, Ohio drowned while swimming in the Little Miami River on May 20, 1917. He was said to be the first victim of the Great War to lose his life around Cincinnati.
Cline post card photo; information from Koch collection, Cincinnati Historical Society.

The Third Ohio Regiment was sent to guard "against incendiary and other attacks." The soldier here is no doubt taking the job seriously. Perhaps the girl on the left with the camera is a German spy*!*
Cincinnati Historical Society, Koch collection. Photo: Felix Koch.

Sack time for two members of the Third Ohio Regiment. Note the rifle leaning against the window at the left. *Cincinnati Historical Society, Koch collection. Photo: Felix Koch.*

Two of the usual watchmen of the Peters Cartridge Company. Here they are seated on the Cincinnati side of the Kings Mills Depot. Note the berm leading to the river bridge to the left. The watchman had to "hit" a key at each station along his route. The time he did so was recorded on a tape locked inside the clock he wore suspended by the strap. *Cincinnati Historical Society, Koch collection. Photo: Felix Koch.*

45-caliber shot cartridge for the Thompson submachine gun. The Thompson gun took a larger magazine to accommodate this longer than usual cartridge. Peters had a connection with Auto Ordnance, producers of the Thompson, through Philip Quayle, who did work for both Peters and Auto Ordnance. Quayle did work for Auto Ordnance to slow down the cyclic rate of that gun to make it more practical/saleable.

The period after World War I was one of readjustment. No doubt there were orders suddenly canceled and, hard on the heels of a worker shortage, there came layoffs. While there were certainly terrific adjustments to be made, the problems at some competitor's plants - like Winchester - were not evident at Peters.

Winchester also supplied vast amounts of ammunition to the war effort; however, unlike Peters, Winchester was also a large firearms manufacturer. Williamson noted that Winchester had invested heavily in replacing worn-out buildings, as Peters had done. In addition, it expanded its facilities very considerably to accommodate the wartime business, so much so that Winchester's debt burden after the war caused the company great concern.

As a consequence, Winchester expanded into the manufacture of items other than firearms and ammunition. The company produced roller skates, tools, hardware, flashlights, fishing tackle etc. – an endeavor that eventually moved the company into the hardware business. These unfamiliar activities ultimately created financial problems and arguably caused Winchester to declare bankruptcy.

Peters, after a period of adjustment, returned to the routine of a domestic ammunition supplier. This entailed storage of the wartime machinery and tooling and dusting off and setting up the equipment required to produce its peacetime line.

Peters at about this time (Frank Barnes, in *Cartridges of the World*, states 1920) introduced the .45 Auto-Rim cartridge. This was in response to the large numbers of .45-caliber revolvers produced during the war for the rimless .45 ACP cartridge. These cartridges were designed for use in the Model 1911 autoloading pistol and required a special "half moon" clip, which held three cartridges, to allow them to be extracted from a swing-cylinder revolver. Two of these clips were required to fully load a revolver. Both Smith & Wesson and Colt made these sidearms for the military and thousands of these revolvers were released to the civilian population when the war was over. To meet this special need, Peters simply produced cartridges with an extra-thick rim to function in these revolvers in a conventional manner, precluding need for the special clips.

Peters also produced some specialty ammunition. One was the .45 Thompson shot cartridge. It was perhaps easy to assume that this would be a great seller. After all, a Thompson submachine gun would have emptied a box of fifty cartridges in about eight seconds. Considering there were only 15,000 Thompson guns actually made in this period, and that it took many years to sell them, very likely this cartridge was not a moneymaker.

It is probably because of the association of Philip E. Quayle with both the Thompson gun and Peters Cartridge Company that production of the .45 Thompson shot cartridge came about. Information about the association of Quayle with Thompson came courtesy of John Appleton of Fairfax, Virginia. Phil Sharpe, in his book *The Rifle in America*, reports that: "[the Thompson could be used] with a special 18-shot magazine designed for use with a special .45 Thompson riot cartridge containing bird shot manufactured only by the Peters Cartridge Co."

Tom Nelson in his book *The World's Submachine Guns*, said the 18-shot magazine was similar to the 20-shot magazine except its front-to-rear dimension was longer. It was probably also used in the Model 1923 gun that took the special elongated .45 *Remington THOMPSON ball cartridge*. I do not know if Peters also produced some of these latter cartridges. The Model 1923 guns are extremely rare and it is presumed that Peters did not make these cartridges.

In 1927, Peters hired Philip Quayle from the U.S. Bureau of Standards to be their chief physicist. Quayle had concerned himself with physical phenomenon relating to firearms for some time, and had developed a method of photography that he termed "Sparkography".

In sparkography, Quayle perfected an old idea originated by Englishman William Henry Fox-Talbot in the mid-1800s. The idea was to utilize an electrical discharge across a spark gap to produce a brilliant light source of extremely short duration–about a millionth of a second. The original idea had not been successful due to the defective photographic plates available at the time.

Quayle arranged a box with a spark gap on one side and a photographic plate on the other. Upon firing a bullet between the two, an electrical discharge burst across the spark gap at the instant the bullet broke a wire. The resulting flash recorded the bullet's shadow on the photographic plate.

An additional benefit was that the escaping propellant gasses, shock waves and turbulence created by the bullet's passage through the air, were recorded as well. This latter was due to the refraction of the light waves as they passed through the variable density of the air. Bullets create shock waves in air, not unlike a boat passing through water. The extremely localized compression of the air by the bullet's shock waves refracted the light before it reached the photographic plate. A similar phenomenon can be observed when sunlight strikes your floor after passing through the unevenly heated air above a hot radiator.

Peters lost no time using such sparkographs in their advertising. No other cartridge company was using this medium. Booklets were published on sparkography as well as the magazine advertisements. They claimed that Peters utilized his method of "seeing" what was happening with wad efficiency and its effect on shot stringing and other information related to the efficiency and accuracy of Peter's cartridges. It was eye-catching and convincing.

It is of interest that a subsequent result of Quayle's efforts was the development of the strobe light. Quayle has been honored for his contribution by historically-minded authors in the field of photography.

The big news in the 1920s was the advent in the U.S. of non-corrosive priming. Corrosive priming had been with us from the beginning of the percussion era. The "trigger" ingredient was fulminate of mercury; the corrosive ingredient was potassium chlorate. Mixing mercury with nitric acid in the presence of alcohol made fulminate of mercury. The resulting compound is *very* sensitive to heat, friction, sparks and shock.

Those few allowed to make the priming mix at Peters were held somewhat in awe by the rest of the workers. Perhaps the 'dean' of these mixers was Steve Dragoo, who held this job for many years and was said to have been in three explosions. Mercury poisoning was an

Spark photographs taken by Philip Quayle.
Powder To Target *booklet, Peters Cartridge Co., by Philip Quayle.*

additional hazard; Steve suffered from that, too. In spite of the hazard attendant to fulminate mixing, Dragoo survived into his eighties. He was as well, or better, remembered for his initiative in being Santa at Christmas to all the kids in town.

The next most hazardous job at Peters was handling the priming mix after it was made. After it was placed in the priming cup, or spun into a rimfire case rim, it was relatively safe to handle. But handling it to that point was done with the priming compound wet, which made it much safer. By using exacting protocol, meticulous housekeeping and specially designed facilities in an area away from other personnel, handling the priming mix was done in relative safety, even after the compound dried.

According to Frank Barnes, there was a certain amount of free mercury in small globules in the resulting priming compound. This free mercury would amalgamate with the brass cartridge case when the cartridge was fired, rendering the case brittle and useless for reloading. This was not a big problem when loading with black powder, or–presumably–with Semi Smokeless powder.

When using these older powders, the mercury was diluted by the relatively large amount of residue left behind upon combustion. This, plus the relatively low pressures involved, mitigated in favor of the shooter–unless the reloaded cases were stored for a long period of time. The Europeans got away with using mercury priming compound by loading them in rimfire cases only. As we shall see, Peters did this too.

Later there was a general reformulation of priming compounds in favor of potassium chlorate. As noted above, this compound had been a lesser ingredient in the previous mercuric formulas, and had not been a problem because of the dilution by the considerable solids left by the combustion of black or Semi-Smokeless powder then in use. Anyone who reloads cartridge cases that have been fired with black powder has to clean them right away; which would likely remove any remaining mercury or chlorate salts.

During WWI, the U.S. government experienced primer problems in the ammunition made at its own Frankford Arsenal and with that of several contractors. This was later found to be due to defective primer drying associated with the general acceleration in manufacturing and worsened by damp storage in ships' holds on the way to war. As a result, the government required all contractors, as well as Frankford Arsenal, to use the formula then in use by Winchester. All of the cartridges involved were, by that date, loaded with smokeless powder. This Winchester priming compound consisted of 53% potassium chlorate.

This information is chronicled in *Hatcher's Notebook*. The Winchester compound cured the cartridge case embrittlement problem and produced an effective, *very* reliable primer with long shelf life–an important consideration for the military. This became the famous FA No. 70 primer, used by the military until about 1950. Winchester used it to produce some accuracy loads for 1000-yard shooting in the 1930s.

Williamson stated that Winchester provided Frankford Arsenal and Peters Cartridge with completed primers for government ammunition for the remainder of the war period.

The new compound proved to be quite corrosive to the bore of the firearm using smokeless powder. This was because of the formation of a salt upon combustion similar to table salt, potassium chloride.

On March 20, 1976, Harley Peck, who had been Peters' chief chemist, was nearly 91 at the

Harley Peck was chief chemist for the Peters Cartridge Company. Harley developed the famous FA 70 priming compound for Winchester, which was adopted by U.S. Ordnance for use in two world wars. After WWI, he came to work for Peters, developing non-corrosive primers for the company five years before any of the U.S. competition. He is shown here in retirement on his dahlia farm outside Lebanon, Ohio.

years before. The author has heard of no work stoppages or other labor difficulties associated with either Peters or Remington management. That is not to say that everyone was satisfied with events, as we shall see.

The production at Peters and the KMOP was the subject of praise as to both quantity and quality. As is shown in the chapter on KMOP, much of this was because of the skill, knowledge, dedication, and leadership of a relatively few of Peter's old time employees.

As the general war effort was seemingly hitting its stride, the War Department announced the success with which the Ordnance Department was meeting its production goals. This was bad news for the Axis powers and good news for Allied nations starved for good news. However, in a bitter irony, it was not good news for many workers of the KMOP and the old Peters facility. With the accolades of their country still ringing in their ears, even before D-Day, KMOP and other ammunition plants were shut down.

This terse story in the July 13, **1944** issue of *The Western Star* (Lebanon, Ohio, newspaper) says it all: *"All manufacturing operations of the Peters Cartridge Division Plant of the Remington Arms Co. at Kings Mills will cease Thursday or Friday of this week, as all components will be finished.*

"All machinery is to be dismantled and some of it will be shipped to the Bridgeport, Conn. Plant of the Company. Other machinery will either be sold or scrapped.

"The plant site is on the market according to the announcement made by the Company late in April."

Finis est!

Aerial photo of the Peters Cartridge Company taken by Leonard Michael from his open cockpit International biplane in 1935. It must have been a weekend or holiday; not a soul in sight. *Leonard Michael.*

Chapter 3

The Great Explosion and Fire of July 15, 1890

BY JULY OF 1890, the King Powder Company had become a mature manufacturing business. King was, however, still growing and still retained some of the freshness of a maturing company, then only twelve years old.

On the other hand, in 1890, the Peters Cartridge Company was only three years old and growing very rapidly. Peters had been organized to simply load paper shells bought from UMC and Winchester, who at first sold only the empty shells. These others suddenly saw profit in what Peters was doing, decided to load shells, too, and started pressuring Peters by raising the price of empty shells. To meet this threat, Peters, in late 1889, installed new machinery to manufacture their own paper shells.

There was a cluster of buildings, called by various names, around the Kings Mills Depot on the Little Miami Railroad (LMRR). In addition to the railroad depot, there was a warehouse that served both King Powder and Peters; magazines for the storage of powder for both King and Peters, about eight dwelling houses for employees, two three-story buildings, a boiler house, oil sheds, and a coal storage area for the cartridge factory. The Pittsburgh, Cincinnati and St. Louis Railroad leased the LMRR. By 1890 this trackage was operated by the Pennsylvania Railroad.

The events of July 15, 1890, became etched in the minds of all who lived or worked anywhere near Kings Mills on that day. *The Western Star*, a weekly newspaper in Lebanon, issue of July 17, 1890, tells what happened:

"At 3:50 o'clock, on Tuesday afternoon [July 15, 1890], *a terrific noise was heard all over Lebanon* [over six miles from King's Station] *as coming from the direction of the King's Powder Mills. Presently another report–then three more–were distinctly heard, but not so terrific as the first one. Crowds gathered on the streets to discuss the noise, and soon a huge volume of smoke was seen to rise far up towards the clouds in the same direction.*

"The telephone was used immediately to inquire the result, and wild rumors were circulated of all sorts, one of them being that twenty-five persons were killed and another that twelve poor souls were taken out of the burning debris. Then came a message from Mrs. A. [Ahimaaz] *King summoning all the physicians of Lebanon to repair as quickly as possible to the scene of destruction with necessary articles....*

"As soon as our reporter could get ready he went to the terrible scene, and witnessed a ghastly sight, and such a one as few ever witness in a life time.

"It was dark when we got there, and found the quiet little town on the hill [Kings Mills] *all full of intense excitement and grief at the sights enacted below and across the river.*

"The disaster occurred across the river [from Kings Mills], *at the south end of the county bridge which spans the Little Miami River. Here is what is known as King's Station. It is on the Little Miami Railroad.*

"It is here where the Peters Cartridge Company had their works, and some eight dwelling houses had been erected for employees. A new depot and a large warehouse, and Kings Powder Company office were also located here.

Scene before the explosion. Kings Mills town is located at the top of the hill on the left. This is, of course, an artist's rendering and shows the powder mill buildings on the far side of the river. The artist bunched the mills together to get as many in the picture as possible. Local freight train No.75 approached from the right *(headed toward Cincinnati)*. *Steve McDowell.*

"On the switch were two cars loaded with 800 kegs of powder from Kings Mills across the river and cartridges, and another one loaded with the same kind of goods.

"The local freight, No. 75, going west [toward Cincinnati], stopped at the station to discharge two cars loaded with nitrate of soda, and placed them on the switch [siding].

"Wm. Franey, a new brakeman, from Waynesville, about 27 years of age, who was making his first trip as a brakeman, undertook to ride the cars into the switch. Franey seems to have miscalculated the distance or the brakes refused to work, for the cars he rode struck the powder-laden cars with great force. Engineer Keck, who was some distance [away] on his engine, was looking out of the cab just as the cars came together.

"Poor Franey was standing on the running board of the foremost car, endeavoring to work the brake. Suddenly the cars seemed converted into a gigantic geyser of smoke and flame, which shot sky high, and then, spreading out like a fan, communicated immediately to the two three-story frame buildings used by the Peters Cartridge Company as a factory. These buildings were light in character, and burned like a tinderbox.

"There were about forty persons employed in these buildings, most of whom were young girls from the neighboring towns. The girls worked next to the windows facing the river, and although temporary fire escapes of ropes hung within their reach, the flames spread so rapidly that the escape of the girls was miraculous. Everything of an inflammable nature took fire and burnt like powder, not a piece of timber of any kind of all the buildings was left standing by six o'clock. A railroad pump was put to work to put out the fire alongside the tracks so that the workmen could repair the scattered rails in order to let by

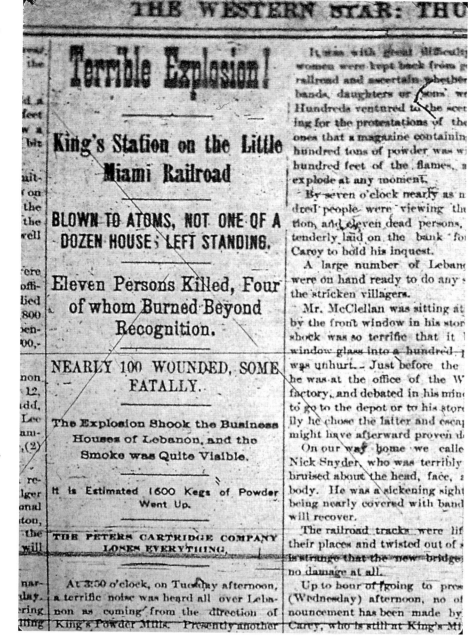

Headlines in the *Western Star*.
Warren County Historical Society.

the delayed trains at Morrow and Cincinnati.

"A steam fire engine was sent to the rescue from Loveland [about five miles south on the LMRR] and by eleven o'clock the track was in safe condition to let trains pass.

"The dead number eleven souls, viz: Wm Franey , brakeman; Henry Reynolds, teamster, Albert Williams, two other bodies who were unrecognizable, Moss family mother and two children, and three other children whose names we were unable to learn.

"The suffering of relatives and friends living on the surrounding hills was terrible and undescribable until they found out the fate of their loved ones.

"It was with great difficulty that the women were kept back from going to the railroad to ascertain whether their husbands, daughters or sons were killed....

"On our way home we called to see Nick Snyder, who was terribly cut and bruised about the head, face, arms and body. He is a

Beyond the wreckage of the Peters Cartridge Company and the railroad depot, the new bridge received no damage at all. The King Powder mills on the far side of the river were not harmed. The figure in the right foreground has been identified as A. King by Helen Bogart.

Joseph Warren King II.

sickening sight, his face being nearly covered with bandages. He will recover.

"The railroad tracks were lifted from their places and twisted out of shape. It is strange that the new bridge received no damage at all.

"AN EYEWITNESS" STORY

Mr. Jos. Proctor of Columbus...was an eyewitness. "The gentleman was still suffering from the effect of his terrible experience..." The Western Star went on: *"...and trembled visibly when talking. ...I turned around just as the freight train was making a running switch to the side track. I saw the brakeman on one of the cars as they shot onto the side track. And he was waving his hand to someone on the train.*

"As I looked, I saw the two detached cars bump against what I supposed was an empty car on the side track. An instant later there was a rumbling noise and, the very ground beneath seemed to open. I saw a puff of smoke

followed a second later by another and the cars disappeared. The station and a powder [power?] house and a dwelling seemed to follow, and the work of destruction had only just commenced....

'The dense volumes of smoke came pouring from the doors and windows of the cartridge factory, and I saw men, women and children tearing at each other in their frantic endeavors to escape.

'The explosion and the fire at the cartridge house seemed to be simultaneous. The building did not catch fire in an ordinary way, but the flame seemed to penetrate the doors and windows from all sides. I saw a number of the women come out, but some certainly perished in the flames [evidently none did]. A dwelling house below the cartridge house was blown from its foundation and dashed to the ground. In this building a mother and child lost their lives."

A week later, on July 24, *The Western Star* picked up a story from the *Times Star* [Cincinnati]

of the 17th. In it, J. H. McKibben, secretary to both King and Peters was quoted as saying:

"'We have not collected ourselves yet, and cannot state what our loss from the explosion will be. The estimates of $100,000...does [sic] not come from us....

"Mr. McKibben here pointed to a plan of the works and showed that the burned area was a very small part of the whole plant [although all of the Peters plant was destroyed]...'Up in the ravine we have a reservoir of water having a pressure equal to that in the city reservoir. But the fire at the shell and cartridge buildings seemed to burst out at all quarters at one time....'

"In order to get superintendent McKibben out safely, men had to play the hose on him. 'The shell houses were not death traps, as has been intimated, but were provided with plenty of means of escape. Indeed, outside of an accident of this sort, I cannot conceive how [an accident] of any proportions could happen...'

The steam engine which powered the cartridge plant is in the foreground, the boiler facing at the lower left. Beyond is a jumble of wrecked machinery. *Joseph Warren King II.*

Note the utter chaos. You are seeing what is left of the Peters Cartridge Company on July 16, 1890. That is the steam engine flywheel at the upper left. The boiler is beyond it. On the near side of the man standing near the middle, is a flat-bed planer of the wrecked machine shop. The barrels are for salvage. *Joseph Warren King II.*

This view looks toward the bridge, where the depot had been.

Joseph Warren King II.

"*Further inquiry developed the facts that this was the third powder plant in size of the country, and that the powder is chiefly used for blasting purposes in coal mines and elsewhere.*

"'*There is nothing left of the plant of the cartridge company, and outside of the powder lost in the cars* [and King Powder's office] *nothing of the powder plant was touched. The same men however are interested in both.*

"'*As soon as the debris about the railroad is cleared away, and some sort of landing* [loading dock] *constructed, the powder company will go on shipping its goods. The cartridge company will probably rebuild, but when and at what place can not yet be told.*'

"*With regard to the eighteen explosions which we referred to in yesterday's paper, Mr. McKibben said that only one had fatal results. That was about ten years ago and three men were killed in it.*"

The next issue of the *The Western Star* reported on Coroner George W. Carey's inquest. Carey conducted an "'*...inquest on the dead bodies of Samuel Stephenson, Henry J. Reynolds, Alfred Williams, William Franey, Mrs. Fred. Keller, Master Frank Keller, baby Fred Keller, Mrs. James L. Moss and her little daughter Goldie Moss...and found that... the explosion was caused by the too rapid run of the cut-off soda cars sent in on the spur switch at King's Station... from local freight train No.75, in charge of Engineer Charles Keck and Conductor James McDermott, in the Little Miami Division of the Pittsburgh, Cincinnati and St. Louis railway, on the afternoon of July 15, A.D. 1890... I further find, from the evidence that there was no negligence on the part of the Peters Cartridge Company nor on the part of the King Powder Company, but on the other hand, I do find that there was gross negligence on the part*

of the employees of the railroad company in charge of local freight No.75...'"

While little is said about the injured, it appears that none of the "young women" employed by the cartridge company were killed.

It took a decade for the subsequent litigation to wind its way through the legal system. The result was a settlement in favor of both the King Powder Company and the Peters Cartridge Company. There followed a payment by the railroad [probably their insurance company] of an undisclosed amount for damages. The writer finds nothing to reference the July 15, 1890, event in a comprehensive history of the Little Miami Railroad.

Marion Snyder in an April 20, 1981 article in the *Little Miami Express,* said that: "*Peters Cartridge sued the Pennsylvania Railroad for $125,000; King Powder for about $95,000 and won the cases. John Maag,* *driving a team hauling various materials on a wagon, was blown a considerable distance [and] was landed at the edge of the Little Miami River and was not found for over two hours. Scrapel [sic] had damaged him considerably.*

"He was an important witness on the court action when (J. A.) Runyan and (George) Stanley represented the explosives firms. After winning in the court, the Peters firm distributed monies to the victims or their families. Mr. Maag got $1,600 while 13-year old Lodie Behr who was a shell machine operator, lost an arm and was awarded $9,000.'"

Eighty years later, 87-year-old Timmy Dowdell, in a November 15, 1970, article in *The Cincinnati Enquirer*, remembered: "*I'll never forget it*", says Dowdell who was [in 1890] six years old when: "*It was July 15, 3 PM. I was playing under an apple tree with two other boys on the opposite side of the main office building when it happened. After the explosion, everything got dark and all the apples fell on top of us,*" he recalled.

He said he and his companions were as close [to the explosion] as anyone who lived. ...

Dowdell recalls, "*After the explosion, I ran as fast as I could into the woods and there I found my grandmother all bloody... but she wasn't hurt too bad even though her house burned down.*"

Long before the settlement, the company decided to rebuild the cartridge factory. They did so across the river from the depot, up on the hill. This was in the lower end of Kings Mills town. No photos of it as a shell factory are known to exist. The shell factory was converted to a department store. The King Powder Company, together with the Peters Company, in the same decade, built a new office half-way up that hill into Kings Mills.

Probably as a result of this explosion, all of the powder from the King Powder Company, or consigned to the Peters Cartridge Company, was subsequently loaded or unloaded

View from further up the hill reveals the scope of the destruction of the explosion and fire. Freight train No.75 approached *(and retreated)* from the right on the near *(spur)* track. Note the corn field *(middle left)* where much of the future plant would be built. *Joseph Warren King II.*

View from depot/bridge area looking at the devastated site of the works, the depot, warehouse and King's office. Note that cleanup is well under way. What appear to be sightseers can be seen above the head of the teamster. Much of the surviving machinery was sent to Cincinnati Screw and Tap Co. for rebuilding. The lonely chimney at left was a residence. *Bob and Betty Carter.*

from the railroad at Middletown Junction. This was the junction of the LMRR with the Cincinnati, Lebanon and Northern Railroad about a half-mile north of the Kings Mills depot. There was little in the way of habitation in the Middletown Junction area.

There were many explosions before this one, and many since.

Timmy Dowdell ran the Cliff [boarding] House *(background)* in King's Mills for over a quarter of a century. Shown here with his wife, he recalled 80 years after the event, that: "*... he and his companions were as close* [to the explosion] *as anyone who lived.*" *Fred Schweitert*

Many harmed no one. Some claimed as many as five victims. Most were at the King Powder Company but a few were at Peters. However many there were, the one on July 15, 1890, was always the *Big One*.

In subsequent years, Peters built a large cartridge works on the exact site of this explosion. The area was then full of the hustle and bustle, hum and hiss that was part and parcel of a large manufacturing concern: steam engines, dynamos, machinery in motion and the incessant rumbling of the comings and goings of locomotives, drays and trucks. Factory whistles and locomotive whistles saluted everything from morning reveille, the noon rest, to the quiet retreat that closed each workday.

For the past several years, the silence has returned. The cartridge factory has long since closed its doors. This railroad branch was abandoned by the Pennsylvania more than a quarter-century ago. There is now a quiet bicycle path, with only the shouts of children where screaming locomotives once warned everything from their path. There is, of course, auto traffic over old Grandin Road by people who have no idea of the drama that once unfolded here.

Perhaps it is fitting that peace has returned.

This bird's-eye view from the top of the shot tower in 1974 shows where the explosion occurred on July 15, 1890. Building R-21 stands *(center)* where the Dowdell boarding house was then. Note the "ghost trail" of the siding, long since removed, on which the fatal cars collided at a position some hundred feet or so beyond the white car. The original cartridge plant was located along the bottom edge of this photo.

Chapter 4

Peters, King, the Lindsleys and the "Grand" American Handicap

*T*HIS CHAPTER IS a look at the significance of trap shooting in general and of the Grand American Handicap on the fortunes of Peters, and to a lesser extent, King. We will also study the influence/involvement of Peters and King on the Grand itself. To accomplish this it is necessary to understand what was happening in the shooting world during the early days of both companies, and to see the Grand American was then, in many ways, very different from what it later became.

King was founded in 1878 and Peters in 1887, a time of significant changes in the shooting/hunting/military worlds. Muzzle-loading firearms had already lost ground to the encroachments of the breechloaders. Gunpowder was being called black powder to differentiate it from the recently introduced smokeless variety. The Smith and Wesson .44 Russian revolver was the darling of Anderton, the Bennet brothers, Paine and others

who had found the revolver was capable of accuracy that shooters had previously thought impossible. Some of these shooters were touring the world, exhibiting their shooting skills. The .22 Long Rifle cartridge, destined to become the most-produced cartridge in the world, was introduced in 1885. It was accurate out to 200 yards–more

Aerial view of Grand American Handicap of August, 1926. This was a splendid sight at that time, with twenty traps in view. There are now one hundred traps at Vandalia. *Courtesy of Dick Baldwin. Photo: Schiffer.*

accurate than most, if not all, center-fire cartridges. I have seen production estimates of between two-and-a-half and four billion produced annually!

The U.S. military was still embracing a single-shot .45/70 rifle and carbine, and although efficient as a fast-firing single-shot, there were a number of repeating rifles being adopted in Europe. While there were numerous breech-loading guns on the U.S. market, the Smith (L. C. Smith) and Parker double-barrel shotguns were elbowing each other in the press and each company was advertising its gun's superiority. At this time, "gun" was not a generic term for firearm, but specifically designated the shotgun. Since this discussion is about the Grand American, it is "the gun" that will be its focus.

The choke bore was a relatively new concept. Whether one considers Fred Kimbal or W. W. Greener–or yet another–the innovator, the choke bore was just consolidating

"Chamberlin Tournaments started the tremendous interest in the sport of target shooting, and a revival of them is a grand thing."

COL. J. T. ANTHONY, Charlotte, N. C.

AMERICAN WOOD POWDER CARTRIDGES

LOADED 12 GA BY THE

CHAMBERLIN CARTRIDGE & TARGET CO. CLEVELAND, OHIO U.S.A.

25 CHAMBERLIN CARTRIDGES 12 GA AMERICAN WOOD POWDER CARTRIDGES

LOADED IN SHELLS WITH SPECIAL PRIMERS 3 DRS WOOD POWDER 1 1/8 OZ NO 7 TRAP CHILLED SHOT COPY RIGHT HERE

SHOOT BLUE ROCKS

THEY ARE THE TARGET

"Chamberlin Cartridges have always been strictly first-class in every respect, and I have always found them most excellent for Blue Rock or Field Shooting."

D. M. PORTERFIELD, Vicksburg, Miss.

Chamberlin was an early presence in furnishing loaded shells to the trade. Note they were advertising Milton F. Lindsley's Wood Powder. Not all shotshells could withstand the pressures generated by early smokeless powders.
From undated shoot program ca. 1893, author's collection.

Glass balls used in early trap shooting *ca* 1880. Note Bogardus name on left-hand ball. *From Annie Oakley Foundation archives/Alex Kerr; courtesy of Bess Edwards, Annie Oakley's grandniece.*

itself in the shooter's domain. Confusion existed then, as now, regarding the relative merits of the various practitioners of the art of choke boring.

The well-known English gunmaker, W. W. Greener, published his famous book *The Gun and its Development* in 1881, and it greatly influenced shotgunning. In a subsequent (ninth) edition, Greener illustrates on page 363 the wonderful patterning of one of his guns, which won a trial at Leavenworth in 1886. *"A Greener 12-bore was shot at 40 yards with* **"King's Quick Shot"** *powder.*

...The gun beat all it's opponents easily."

Along with choke-bored, double-barreled, breech-loading shotguns came the relatively new paper shotshells that were manufactured by companies such as C. D. Leet of Springfield, Mass., and sold to the trade and individuals as unloaded shells. They were then loaded by local houses and sporting goods companies and offered to the trade under different brand names or loaded by the shooter. About 1873, Union Metallic Cartridge purchased paper shell-making equipment and started supplying empty paper shells to the trade. They were probably the first to offer widespread distribution of paper shells.

Around 1883, Chamberlin invented and introduced a manually operated, but self-indexing dial face cartridge loading machine. It was a great improvement over doing each step in batches. Prior to this, the operations were done on primitive loading machines that only performed one task at a time. Many local sporting goods houses soon adopted the Chamberlin automatic machine for producing loaded cartridges.

The first listing of Winchester **factory** *loaded* shotshells I have seen was in the July 17, 1890 issue of *Shooting and Fishing*. The first listing of *loaded* shotshells for UMC is August 14, 1890. I do not know for sure that this is their first, but in *Shooting and Fishing*, these are the first offerings I saw. Up to this time, they offered empty paper shells only. This illustrates the danger of using data gathered from published catalogs. If you look in the Winchester catalog offerings, the first listing *is* 1894. I prefer the information in *Shooting and Fishing*.

Before and during the early 1880s, there was a great interest in shooting at live birds, although artificial birds were extant in several forms and more would be introduced in subsequent years. There were glass balls; glass balls filled with feathers, clay "pigeons" in various. shapes and sizes; others were being invented. Along with them were means for launching the targets into the air to simulate the flight of birds. These alternative devices were received by the shooters with varying degrees of enthusiasm. Like near beer, they were just not the real thing to the live bird shooters. The terminology of the new devices, however, sprang from that of live bird shooting. The launchers were called traps, and the targets themselves, birds, names that persist to this day in trap, skeet and sporting clays shooting. Even today, soon after the sound of the shot, the scorer of inanimate targets will often announce his or her judgment of a shooter's efforts with the cry, "live" (miss), or "dead" (broken bird).

After the Civil War, there were a number of shooters who attempted to make a living at the shooting game, and some of them did so very successfully. In the days before game laws were in force, many shooters were cashing in on the taking of wild game for human consumption. Fred Kimball, Phoebe Ann Mosey (later known as Annie Oakley), "Buffalo Bill" Cody and many others did this on a small or large scale. The game was sold to hotels, distributors to the general public, or in support of some activity such as feeding railroad construction crews.

Some of the commercial hunters attempted to make their living as exhibition shooters who traveled from town to town individually, or with some performing troupe such as a circus. Of course, the great Wild West Show was, and is, the best known. Annie Oakley and Buffalo Bill are probably the best-known stars of the nineteenth century wild west shows.

The first manufactured moving target was the glass ball; they and a crude trap were first imported from England in 1866. Captain A. H. Bogardus. went on tour in 1872, shooting glass balls using a trap of his own devising, and popularized the sport. *Arms and the Man*'s December 4, 1918, issue stated that the Ligowsky trap and a saucer-shaped spinning clay bird were introduced by Bogardus and William "Doc" Carver on tour in 1881. The article stated that it was a tough bird to "kill."

George Ligowsky was from Cincinnati, Ohio. He appears elsewhere in this book relative to Peters' cartridge loading machinery patents. Prior to any affiliation with Peters, George invented the saucer-shaped clay bird that remains in use today, albeit in a somewhat different design. However, the principle remains the same. This was about 1880. Ligowsky also invented a means for throwing the bird to use it as a target simulating the flight of a flushed bird. The first targets truly were made from clay and were baked in a kiln like bricks.

George Morris in his book, *The Grand*, tells us that Ligowsky organized the first clay bird National Championship in New Orleans in February of 1885. It was at this shoot that Dr. Carver defeated Captain Bogardus.

George Ligowsky of Cincinnati invented the trap and clay bird, as we know it today. He sold loading machine patents, which were embroiled in litigation, to Peters.
Courtesy of Dick Baldwin. Photo: Schiffer.

Annie Oakley stated in a booklet she authored for Du Pont in 1914, titled *Powders I Have Used*, that some clay "birds" were over-baked (too hard) and the shot glanced off. She wrote that she used soft shot, which she felt would better break the birds since hardened shot would sometimes glance off a solid hit. For that reason, Ligowsky subsequently

Early Ligowsky clay pigeons are nested snugly in Ted Bacyk's collection.
Courtesy of Ted Bacyk. Photo: Schiffer.

adopted a mixture of limestone and pitch to form his "birds."

Doc Carver and Captain Bogardus were excellent trap shots who might travel with a show-or on their own. They shot for high stakes wherever they could generate sufficient interest, that is, money in the form of cash prizes. There were local shooters as well who could be counted upon to have sufficient support to assure a good betting pool for the traveling experts. High stakes wagering was common, and local pride was little different then from what it is now.

Still other shooters were employed or subsidized by ammunition companies to such an extent that the shooter then represented the company. Adolph Topperwein was perhaps the best-known shooter for Winchester. Capt. A. H. Hardy and Gus Peret were shooters for Peters. A factory representation relationship might be seen in either their own personal shooting activities, as with T. K. Lee for Peters – or going on the road in the name of the company itself (Hardy and Peret). Some of the shooters moved from one to the other of these activities as opportunity and their skill allowed. Some moved from one company to another.

Throughout the last part of the century, tabloid periodicals were published weekly in support of sporting interests. Nearly all had a large number of pages devoted to the shooting sports. *Shooting and Fishing, Forest and Stream* and *Sportsman's Review* are examples. They were much more intimate and personal in their presentations back then.

While these were still very much horse and buggy days, events were fast-paced compared to a generation or so before. The railroad could carry shooters unheard-of distances in a day or so. Railroads begat the telegraph, which was sometimes used to prevent the trains from running into each other. The telegraph, in turn, was used by the tabloids to gather information and–full circle–the railroads distributed the printed sporting papers throughout the country.

These newspaper-type publications generally maintained a knowledgeable editor to keep things on an even keel. Aside from editorials, one could say that these papers were, in fair part, written by their subscribers. There always seemed to be very knowledgeable amateur shooters who kept up a stream of erudite correspondence. They often used pseudonyms like "IRON RAMROD," "SMALL SHOT" and "DEAD BIRD" instead of their own names. The newspapers were published and distributed such that the shooting activities of one weekend would be in the hands of national readers by the following Thursday! And this well over one hundred years ago!

Judging from the dialogue found in the old issues, there was an active and far-reaching interest in the shooting activities. A hunter might never take part in a formal shoot, but the interest in it as a sport, and the relevance of spin-off technology to his own sport, was real. In the papers you find debate, challenge and support of shooting activities, methods and equipment. All shooting activities, including hunting were covered, but those under the heading of "The Gun" are of interest here.

Correspondents could be more or less depended upon to relate the local activities of gun clubs each week. These local reporters often used *noms de plume,* such as "Hottentot" from Cincinnati. Sometimes the contestants themselves wrote to the editor, sometimes it was their proponents; and there was no dearth of information about top shooters from opponents–some of it a bit inflammatory!

There is much to interest the reader who might be fortunate enough to review the originals of these old sporting publications. Some can be seen at the Trapshooter's Hall of Fame and Museum at Vandalia, Ohio – home of the Grand American. Many of the old magazines were found at Broadfoot Publishing Co. and Tom Rowe Books' reprints of *Shooting and Fishing*. These are extremely valuable and I certainly am indebted to Warren Greatbatch who supplied the originals from which these reprints were made. The survival rate of the old tabloid papers is not good. They suffered the same fate as most newspapers and were simply thrown out, used to wrap the garbage or when cleaning fish.

In the early days of smokeless powder, the loads were not as powerful as good black powder charges. Cartridges & shells had to be "loaded down" because of the varying pressures of very early smokeless powders. Bulged barrels and blown-up guns were

Doc W. F. Carver, shown here, and Bogardus traveled around the country as exhibition shooters. At first they used glass balls and then the new Ligowsky clay pigeon, no doubt because of the complicated logistics of using live birds. A spin-off was the promotion of in-animate flying targets as a shooting sport.
From Shooting and Fishing, *January 3, 1889.*

not all that rare among those who tried to duplicate black powder ballistics with smokeless. However, smokeless powder had a real advantage for the live bird shooters: no smoke!

The lack of smoke from a first shot allowed the shooter a clear view of the bird to determine if the second barrel was needed–and for aiming that second barrel. The second barrel load could then be a good stout one of black powder, giving the power to reach out to the bird that, by then, was some distance from the shooter. Since the smokeless loads produced less recoil than black powder loads, it was easier to get back "on" the bird for the second shot. Early live pigeon guns were invariably side-by-side doubles.

Early users of smokeless powder put a few grains of black powder next to the primer as a priming charge. This was because smokeless did, and still does, need a stronger primer than black powder did. Black powder primers generally did not have enough brisance *(oomph!)* to ignite the smokeless. Good, reliable smokeless primers were not then generally available.

The live pigeon shooter must not only drop the bird, but must do so within a circular fence surrounding the traps. The ability of a gun and load to do this was of great interest to the public. Both gun and load were well publicized in the press, along with the match results.

For this reason, the gun companies wanted their products used in competition. While game shooters were, by far, using more cartridges than the trap shooters, the successful game shooter was not likely to be written up in a national periodical. The game shooters often read the trap shoot results and the influence was as obvious then as today.

The main character in this chapter is Milton Fletcher Lindsley. In order to understand his involvement, some history of the explosives industry is appropriate. From the *History of*

the Explosives Industry in America, by Van Gelder and Schlatter, we know that Carl Dittmar was an important man in the development of smokeless powder. An officer in the Prussian Army, he later worked with Alfred Nobel. Dittmar later, briefly, became associated with Captain Johann F. E. Schultze. He came to the U.S. and, perhaps as a sideline to the manufacture of engineering explosives, produced Dittmar's Sporting Powder. This was commercialized in the U.S. as early as 1878.

Plagued by fire, explosions, lawsuits and ill health, Dittmar sold the powder part of his business in 1882 to a group of investors organized by sporting goods dealers Von Lengerke and Detmold. The investors were largely members of the Westminster Kennel Club. The investors employed the well-known sporting goods firm of Von Lengerke and Detmold as selling agents. Several of the Von Lengerkes were actively involved in trap shooting. Schultze was commercializing a similar product in England.

The newly formed company, which was split off from Dittmar,

Milton Fletcher Lindsley, active shooter and promoter, was super-intendent of American Wood Powder Company.
From unknown trap match bulletin, author's collection.

employed Milton F. Lindsley as superintendent. Milton had been associated with Dittmar as early as 1878. Lindsley called the new organization American Wood Powder Company. Undoubtedly

American Wood Powder Company claimed to be *(through Dittmar)* the first manufacturer of smokeless powder in the United States. After Wood ceased business in the panic of 1893, Milton F. Lindsley became superintendent of the King Powder Company in Kings Mills, Ohio.
Undated clipping from Lindsley scrapbook, courtesy of Edna Bowyer.

taking their origin as that of the Dittmar powder, American Wood claimed to be the first maker of smokeless powder in America.

As a split off of Schultze smokeless powder manufacturing in England, Captain Albert William Money came to the U.S. and started making and promoting Schultze and EC (Explosives Company) Powder here. Competitors in business, and shooters at the traps, Lindsley counted Money as a friend. American Wood and Schultze powders were very similar chemically, and in use. As mentioned above, Dittmar and Schultze had collaborated earlier but separated due to lack of capital.

Lindsley, who possessed an outgoing, affable personality, was an ideal promoter, not the least of which was his ability to charm the press. He coupled these attributes with a boundless energy and enthusiasm for his product. Other assets included his wife, Etta Butts Lindsley, who helped in the powder factory to the extent that she knew as much about the process as Milt, and more than any other man in the country. Etta often acted as superintendent of the powder factory when Milt was off handling promotions. He was an excellent shot and an enthusiastic competitor at the traps. Trap shooting was an ideal venue for getting his product before the public and in the press.

The following is one of Milt's promotions as seen through the eyes of "H. B. D." in *Shooting and Fishing*, January 31, 1889:

"Albany, N. Y., Jan.28.
The first tournament of the year was opened by the Elm Grove Gun Club, on Monday morning last, under unfavorable conditions, the weather being stormy...Two other strangers were present throughout the day and took part in the shooting; these were Archie Paul of Cohoes, and Milton F. Lindsley of New York. The first named is more famed as a kicker than a marksman, and

gave the manager of the tournament a fine taste of his quality at the close of the day, when he proved the justice of the transposition of his name by his acquaintances who call him Archie 'Bawl.' The New Yorker posed in delightful contrast to the spindle city bully, being quiet, well bred, obliging and courteous, as well as a splendid shot.

"Mr. Lindsley is the Superintendent of the American Wood Powder Company of New York, and during his two days' stay here made many converts to the use of that admirable powder for trap-shooting, the "special twelve bore trap." A large gripsack was filled with shells loaded with this explosive, which Lindsley handed out in prodigal profusion to all who wished to make a trial of "them firecrackers." No sportsman who ever visited this city, made a more pleasing impression–both as a marksman and as a man–than M. F. Lindsley, and this genial gentleman may be assured of a warm welcome whenever he visits our old Dutch city."

Al Bandle set a new record of one hundred straight live birds on December 25, 1888 with Wood powder in the first barrel and black powder in the second barrel. This match was a "friendly" one with Bogardus *(score 91)*. This record was never equaled, to my knowledge. *From* Shooting and Fishing, *January 10, 1889.*

In the 1880s, there were trap ranges scattered all over the U.S. Every major population center had several. The rural areas also had special places where people could shoot. Since many of them wired the weekly results to the nationally distributed sporting tabloids and the local newspapers, these were ideal places to promote the new smokeless powder.

As seen above, Milton F. Lindsley was a welcome addition at any shoot. Surviving newspaper reports of the shoots will often mention industry representatives at the event. Those that refer to Milton are often salted with adjectives like affable, jolly, jovial, genial, earnest, etc. He sometimes flapped his arms like a rooster when *mounting the score* (stepping to the line to shoot) and calling for his bird!

Far from being a buffoon, Lindsley was an excellent shot, in addition to being a keen organizer and promoter of the sport in general. He occasionally put together teams which traveled through the country in season, shooting against clubs east of the Mississippi River and sometimes west.

The *History of the Explosives Industry* states: *"American Wood Powder enjoyed considerable favor at the time and was used by a majority of the best shots in the country and held many of the shotgun records of the time. Lindsley himself was an excellent shot and did much to introduce smokeless powder among live bird shooters."* Perusal of the old records will often show Milton at a different shoot each weekend, for weeks on end.

On December 30, 1888 the great shotgunner Captain A. H. Bogardus met Al Bandle of Cincinnati in a friendly match at 100 live birds on the grounds of the Cincinnati Independent Gun Club. Bandle set a new record of 100 straight kills against Bogardus' 95, thirty yards rise. Al Bandle was the owner of the Bandle Arms Co. of Cincinnati and a relatively unknown shooter

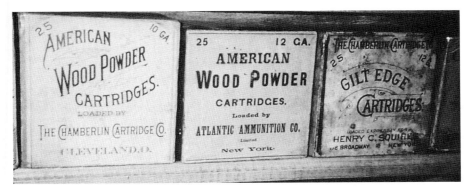

Cartridges loaded on Chamberlin's patent loading machine at their own house, at Atlantic Ammunition Co. and others, were not "machine loaded" in the sense that the machines were not externally powered and were much slower than Peters' loading machines. *Ted Bacyk collection. Photo: Schiffer.*

compared to the veteran Bogardus. The significance in this instance was the use of Wood Powder for the first barrel by both shooters.

The January 3, 1889 issue of *Shooting and Fishing* had this report on the match:

"Bandle had fifteen extra strong birds allotted him, and Bogardus sixteen. That number were extra strong birds, and the scores made will go on record as the most remarkable in the history of trap shooting, either in this country or in Europe. The score has heretofore never been equaled, nor is it likely to be within the next few years. The weather conditions were bad for the use of the second barrel... Bogardus used a 12-gauge 7 lb 14 oz hammerless loaded first barrel, 4 drs Wood Powder, 1 1/4 oz No.8 shot; second, 3 3/4 drs of Laflin and Rand's Orange Lightning [black powder], 1 1/4 oz of No.7 shot.

"Bandle used a 10-gauge hammerless, loaded first barrel, 4 drs of Wood Powder, 1 1/4 oz No.8 shot; second, 4 drs Laflin and Rand extra strong black powder, 1 1/4 oz No.7 shot."

Much was made of the merits of the various. gauges. Bandle, a big man at 246 pounds, liked the ten-gauge as the above indicates. It was popularly supposed that a 12-gauge was the minimum bore usable in pigeon shooting. Annie Oakley liked a 20-gauge. Annie wrote Bandle the following playful letter, which was published in *Shooting and Fishing* January 3, 1889:

"Bridgeton, N. J. Dec 26 (1888)
Mr. Al Bandle:
Dear Sir - I have been reading your scores of late and as we are both from the state of Ohio, I feel a little jealous of your fame, as I feel as if I should be the representative shot of that glorious state. Now I will make you an offer to see if we cannot decide who shall represent Ohio. I will shoot you 50 live or artificial birds, for as much money as you wish to shoot for; you to name rules, time, and place and referee. The only thing I shall ask in making the match is that we shall each weigh the same on the day the match takes place; or, in other words, neither shooter shall weigh more than 115 pounds. Hoping you will answer my very fair offer promptly, I am yours truly, Annie Oakley."

The above letter either resulted from, or was the cause of, two private matches between Annie and Al in Cincinnati in 1888 or 1889. The information concerning this is from two undated clippings in Annie's scrapbook. One match was held at the "Old Forest City grounds" near the zoo, and the second at the Cincinnati Zoological Garden itself. Both matches were for ten live birds each at 25 yards rise. In both matches, Al was the winner, ten to nine. Annie missed her eighth bird each time.

The significance of these matches is that both shooters used the same gun; Annie's little 20-gauge Lancaster double

Annie Oakley shot friendly matches with Al Bandle of Cincinnati. At least one was held at the Cincinnati Zoo. *From Annie Oakley Foundation archives, courtesy of Bess Edwards, Annie's grandniece.*

Annie Oakley in Scotland, note Scotch plaid outfit.
*From Annie Oakley Foundation archives,
courtesy of Bess Edwards, Annie's grandniece.*

2 drams of black powder and 7/8 ounce of No.7 shot in the left barrel. Annie used the same Schultze load in both barrels.

Al Bandle would have undoubtedly made a splash in the Grand; however, he died in 1892. The first Grand American Handicap was not held until 1893. This was at live birds. The first Grand American Handicap at clay birds was not held until 1900. Rolla (Pop) Heikes won that 1900 Grand. But, on New Year's day, 1889, Bandle beat Heikes 90 to 81 at live birds!

News of Al's death drew the following response from Annie (from Annie's scrapbook, undated clipping from *American Field*):

"I have just read with the greatest sorrow, of the death of

weighing five pounds, two ounces. Bandle used 2 drams of Schultze powder and 3/4 ounce of shot in the first (right) barrel and

Mr. Al Bandle. Only a year ago he wrote me a letter congratulating me on the false report of my own death. Poor Al: We have shot many a friendly contest, in which I generally came out second best, but that made no difference in our friendship, for I admired him, not alone because he was a good shot and a true sportsman, but for his many other manly qualities. May he rest in peace is my earnest wish.

Glasgow, Scotland. Annie Oakley."

The story illustrates that popular notions regarding shot loads were as far off in those days as they can be today. It also illustrates the regard some shooters had for their peers. If this is the same Lancaster 20 made for Annie by Lancaster himself in 1887, it is choked in both barrels.

As a side note to the above, I have photographed Annie Oakley's 16-gauge hammer Parker gun that is still in her family. It is believed to be "the first gun of quality" Annie ever owned, given to her by her family. It appears to be about a "G" grade gun. I found it to have a pull of 13 inches. It was lightning fast to handle even though it had 29-inch barrels.

There was no intention on my part to portray Annie as second best, but such things did happen. It is my opinion that *nobody* consistently equaled, let alone beat, Annie at *all* the types of shooting that she did. In the above vignette you can get a glimpse of the warmth and humanity of the little lady.

Meanwhile, Etta Lindsley was learning to shoot, and she became quite good at it. She soon reached the point where she not only held her own, but also claimed a share of the prizes. Remember that these were not women's matches; there weren't any at the time! Well aware of the novelty of a woman successfully competing at a man's sport, Milton actively promoted Etta's shooting. She adopted the shooting *nom de*

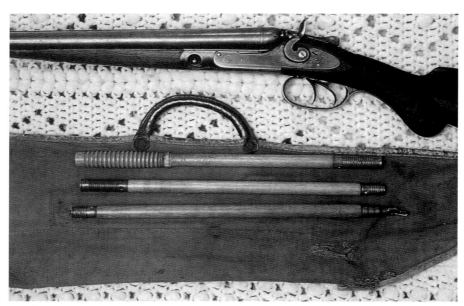

Annie Oakley gave this 16-gauge Parker shotgun to her brother John after she "wore it out." Nearly all checking is worn away; the barrels *(#17,486)* look like a flue pipe inside and do not match the receiver *(#30,203).* It rattles a bit when broken open for loading, but still snaps shut like a bank vault. It handles like greased lightning!

Courtesy of Bess Edwards, Annie's grandniece; photo: Schiffer.

view. The year 1894 saw Milton Lindsley a participant in the Grand American Handicap.

In 1896, both Lindsleys were entered in the Grand American and Annie Oakley was shooting in her first Grand. Neither Wanda nor Annie won anything in that event, but Wanda always remembered that she outscored Annie Oakley by one bird. Both women survived longer in the Grand American than many of the big-money shooters of that day and had reason to be proud. This fact drew praise from the press that has been preserved as newspaper clippings in both Annie's and Wanda's respective scrapbooks.

The rules of the International Association stipulated that information regarding the gun and load used by all competitors in the Grand American, not just the winner, be preserved. However, this stipulation was evidently soon ignored, as I could find nothing among the records of the ATA, successors of the International Association. The early Grands printed a hardbound book with photos of the year's contestants and officials, along with general information about the match.

Since live birds were the targets and two shots were allowed at each bird, special shooting loads evolved. As smokeless powder gained acceptance, black powder dropped off, even for the second shot. However, since the second shot was at extended yardage, a different loading might be employed to advantage. Perhaps No. 7 shot in the first barrel and No. 6 in the second barrel. Remember the competitor had not only to drop the bird, but also drop it within a circular fence. The bird was otherwise considered "lost" or "dead out of bounds" and was as good as a complete miss.

The early Grands were more intimate affairs than they are today where so many competitors gather. There were only 21 entries in that first 1893 Grand,

Women shooters in the 1896 Grand American captured the public eye. Here is Wanda on the left, Mrs. W. P. Shattuck, Mrs. Cornelia Crosby and Annie Oakley. *"These four women as a team would make the best four men in the country shoot carefully"* is part of the accompanying write-up.
From undated clipping in Lindsley scrapbook, courtesy of Edna Bowyer.

54 in 1894. Back then most competitors knew everyone else personally, or by reputation. While there was good will among most of them, all was not 'sweetness and light.'

There were disputes as to who was the better shot and these opinions were often backed by hard coin. There were differences of opinion not only as to the relative merits of powders and loads, but in how any such differences might be meaningfully measured.

Lindsley once got into such a verbal row (in the press) with Von Lengerke over Von Lengerke's previous remarks (in the press) about American Wood Powder. I never learned how—or if—it was resolved since it probably occurred during the time of Wood Powder's bankruptcy. The information came from undated newspaper clippings in Lindsley's scrapbook.

As might be supposed, the various interested

manufacturing companies lost no opportunity to publicize the fact that some product of theirs did well in the Grand. Ammunition and gun companies led the pack. Even when the Grand had only 21 shooters, it was a high-profile shoot and nice purses attracted many of the best shooters in the country.

It was true that some good shooters stayed away because of the handicap system. In theory– if the system works–all competitors have the same chance of winning. "Who will be right at the right time" was, and is a repeated slogan. To me, it seems that a hundred straight-run at long yardage says more for the equipment and ammunition than winning the Grand itself with, say, a 97 at 19 yards. But, winning the Grand was, and still is, winning the Grand!

The earliest use I've found of "Peters" shells in competition was at Walnut Hill (Boston area) on December 13, 1888. The shooter, G. H. Wheeler of Marlboro, did not do well in the challenge match but shot well in other matches that day. The following is from *Shooting and Fishing* of December 20, 1888, to give you an idea of the match reporting from those days. The name Peters is in quotations just as the reporter wrote it. Presumably this was because the brand was relatively unknown at the time, since Peters was not yet two years old.

"Walnut Hill Dec 13 (1888)

A special trap tournament was held at Walnut Hill to-day. The attendance was good, though many were undoubtedly kept away by the wretched weather conditions. The event of the day was the challenge match between Messers. Dickey and Wheeler, which was won easily by the former who put up a score of 93, a performance which, under the circumstances was remarkable. Mr. Wheeler failed to shoot up to his usual form, but pluckily fought the match through. Mr. Dickey used a 10-gauge Scott gun weighing 9 pounds 14 ounces, and the Climax shell loaded 4 drachms of Hazzard FF [black powder] and 1 1/4 grains [sic] of Taddams' "Trap 7" shot. Mr. Wheeler used a 10-gauge Smith [L. C. Smith] gun weighing ten pounds, and the "Peters" cartridges. Among the

guests of the club were Dr. Gerrish of Exeter, N. H. who at one time held the "Climax" badge and Mr. M. F. Lindsley, superintendent of the American (Wood) Powder Company.

The result of the shooting in the various events is as follows:

Six Standards- Wheeler first with six; Nichols and Perry second with five; Hartford, Swift and Wilbur third with four.

Six Standards, 21 yards straight away-Perry first with six; Stanton and Wheeler second with five; Lindsley third with four; Nichols fourth with three.

Ten clays- Dickey and Swift first with ten; Bowker and Stanton second with nine; Perry Wheeler and Wilbur third with eight.

Ten Standards- Dickey and Swift first with ten, Wheeler Stanton and Swift (?) Second with nine; Bowker and Perry third with eight; Chase and Nichols fourth with seven.

Ten clays- Stanton first with ten; Dickey Swift and Wheeler second with nine; Chase and Nichols third with seven; Bowker fourth with five.

Twenty-five clays, five traps-Perry and Wheeler first with twenty-four; Dicky and Nichols second with twenty-one; Chase, Lindsley and Stanton third with twenty.

Challenge match at 100 clay birds between O. R. Dickey of Boston and G. H. Wheeler of Marlboro:-

Dickey missed 3rd, 14th, 18th, 35th, 60th, 76th, 96th, birds; score 93.

Wheeler missed 1st, 7th, 10th, 18th, 22nd, 25th, 28th, 32nd, 38th, 41st, 58th, 64th 65th, 69th, 77th, 86th, 88th, 91st, 99th, birds; score 78.

Ten blackbirds- Dickey and Perry first with ten; Swift second with nine; Nichols and Webster third with eight; Bowker and Lindsley fourth with seven.

Ten clays- Perry first with ten; Dickey and Wheeler second with nine; Swift and Webster third with seven; Nichols and Stanton fourth with six.

Ten Standards- Stanton and wheeler first with ten; Lindsley second with nine; Chase Dickey and Perry third with eight.

Ten Clays- Perry and Stanton first with ten; Swift and Wheeler second with eight; Bowker Dickey and Webster third with seven.

Ten clays- Stanton first with ten; Bowker and Wheeler second with nine; Perry Swift and Webster third with eight"...

Note the presence and participation of Milton F. Lindsley, both as a factory representative and as a shooter.

Milton F. Lindsley was one of an elite group of shooters honored in a montage created by the U.S. Cartridge Company in 1890. Milt held the respect, affection and the attention of his competitors, his shooting peers and the press. *From Dick Baldwin.*

This montage is displayed in the Trap Shooting Hall of Fame and Museum, Vandalia, Ohio. *From Dick Baldwin.*

He did not do well with his shooting that day. (I also edited out a few matches in which neither Wheeler nor Lindsley participated.) It is interesting to note that Wheeler's opponent in the challenge match went on to win the Grand in 1896 and Wheeler himself did well in the 1902 Grand.

At this time, Peters was still putting up their loads in shells head-stamped UMC Star or WRA (Winchester Repeating Arms) Co. Star. As mentioned previously, before 1890 few if any of the large cartridge companies were loading their own shells. They were making the paper shells and selling them to those who then loaded them.

While it was a few years before the first Grand, it is interesting to note which loads were used in a local two-man team shoot at the Parkway Gun Club in Newark, N. J., on November 18, 1889:

"The guns and loads used were as follows:

Frank Class, 12-bore Lefever choked both barrels; weight 7 lb. 7 ozs.; Climax (U.S. Cartridge) shells, 3 drams **American Wood** *powder in first barrel, 3 drams Curtis and Harvey (black powder) in second; 1 1/4 oz. No.8 shot in first and 1 1/8 oz. No.7 in second barrel. Phil Daley, Jr. 10-bore L.C. Smith choked both barrels, weight 9 lbs., Kynoch shells; 4 1/4 drams* **American Wood powder** *and 1 1/4 ozs. No.7 shot in either barrel. J. Frank Kleinz, 12-bore Greener choked both barrels; weight 7 lbs. 14 ozs.; Ely shells, 3 1/4 drams Schultz powder and 1 1/4 ozs. shot in either barrel. Richard E. Irwin, 12-bore Parker choked both barrels; weight 7 lbs. 13 ozs.; Ely shells, 3 1/4 drams Schultze powder and 1 1/4 ozs. No.7 shot in either barrel. All contestant used chilled shot."*

While the above was selected more-or-less at random, notice that Frank Class and Phil. Daley won the team shoot with 41x50 live birds for $200 a side. Phil. Daley shot in the first and subsequent Grands. He also shot against Annie Oakley (Annie won: 50x70 vs. 45x70). Frank Class was a well-known shot as well, shooting above 90% at 100 birds.

Since the early results are seldom reported today, I will list the early winners of the Grand as taken from the official program of the *"eighth annual Grand American Handicap - April 2-6, 1900:*

"In 1893 the First Annual Grand American Handicap, held at Dexter Park, Long Island, had 21 entries. Robert A. Welch the winner.

"In 1894 there were 54 entries, the shoot being held at Dexter Park. Thomas W. Morfey the winner.

"In 1895 a move was made to Willard Park, Patterson, N.J.. But the number of entries was only 61. John G. Messner the winner.

"In 1896 Elkwood Park, N.J., was chosen as the scene of the great event. The big Casino had not then been built, and the shoot was held under the most adverse conditions, particularly as to weather. In that year there were 109 entries, with 104 competitors. O. R. Dickey the winner [probably used Peters shells].

"With the erection of the big Casino at Elkwood Park, with its three sets of traps, late in the fall of 1896, the success of the Grand American Handicap was secured. From that date the number of entries rose by leaps and bounds. Witness the following figures:

"1897, 146 entries, 135 shooters, Tom A. Marshall the winner.

"1898, 207 entries, 197 shooters, E. D. Fulford the winner.

"1899, 278 entries, 262 shooters, Tom A. Marshall the winner."

Peters and King were slow starters in the early Grand American Handicaps and had to be satisfied with the peripheral winnings. Not until 1902 did they start to generate the kinds of press they might have wanted.

G. H. Wheeler, long a user of Peters shells (remember his match with Dickey back in '89?) did quite well in the 1902 shoot. T. Keller, by now Peters' east coast representative, was well pleased with the results. Although he did not use Peters' shells, Peters subsequently hired the winner of the 1902 Grand, H. C. Hirschy, as an exhibition shooter.

According to A. H. Hardy in a letter to *The Sportman's Review* of December 9, 1944, the 1902 Grand, at Kansas City, was the greatest before or since at live birds. It hosted almost 500 entries. As noted, Hirschy won in a shoot off with 57 straight. However, C. G. Spencer, who tied Hirschy for first place and who used Peters Shells, stayed with Hirschy in the shoot off for 56 birds.

The Sportsman's Review of April 12, 1902 stated that during the 1902 Grand, Spencer ran 82 straight, going four days without a miss. Peters shells accounted for six straights in the Kansas City Sweepstakes, 13 in the Nitro Powder Handicap, two straights in the Grand American, and quite a few 24s in the Grand American Handicap. In all, 54 shooters used the Ideal shell in the big event. Spencer used Peters Ideal shells with 3 1/4 drams of King's Smokeless powder.

All told, 1902 was Peters and King's first big splash at the Grand American.

In 1905, Peters won the consolation match at the Grand. In 1907, H. E. Poston, using Peters shells, tied for third place. In 1908, Woolfolk Henderson tied for first using Peters shells. In 1909 Peters shells tied for second. All this was leading up to 1911 when Peters pretty well swept the boards, winning the Grand and many other matches in the event. Harvey Dixon won the Grand that year.

Woolfolk Henderson of Lexington, Kentucky, not only won the Grand in 1914 using Peters shells, he did something no shooter had done before, or has done since. Woolfolk,

Peters' fortunes in the 1905 Grand were not so grand, so they focused on positive events elsewhere.

From Shooting and Fishing, *courtesy of Dick Baldwin.*

shooting from 22 yards, also won all the other major shoots at the Grand! In addition to the Grand itself, these events included the Clay Target, the Doubles Championship and the Champion of Champions title. It is at least arguable that there is a certain amount of luck in winning the Grand. Woolfolk, shooting Peters shells, absolutely smoked that argument! At least he did for the year 1914.

The next year, J. J. Randall tied for first using Peters shells. After the war (WWI), in 1920 Woolfolk Henderson shot a 97 from 23 yards in the Grand, but it was not good enough to win against A. L. Ivin's 99 from 19 yards.

In 1921, E. F. Haak won the Grand with Peters shells with a 97 from 21 yards.

In 1927, Otto Newlin, using Peters shells, took the Grand. Peters had both a first and second in the Grand that year. It was not until 1939 that Peters

scored again with their "Peters New Crimp."

In 1942, a war year, shells were as scarce as the means to get to the Grand itself (gas rationing, priorities for rail travel, etc.). At this shoot, Peters shells dominated, but, as we shall see, did not win the Grand itself.

Naturally, when the big event itself was won, Peters trumpeted the fact with advertising. Full-page ads stated "**PETERS SHELLS WIN THE GRAND AMERICAN HANDICAP**" as they did in 1921 when E. F. Haak broke 97 x 100 from 21 yards. Or a double page ad they took out in the 1928 *Sportsman's Review:* *"PETERS WINS!"*

In years when Peters did not take the Grand, but the wins with Peters shells were arguably more impressive than taking the Grand itself, they might state, as they did in *The Primer,* a company newspaper:

"Kings Mills Shells Lead Field!

Dominating the field, Remington-Peters ammunition in all but two events was used by all the newly crowned Champions in the recently held Grand American. One of the two positions lost by Remington Ammunition was that of runner-up in the Sportswriter's event.

"Among the events in which Remington-Peters swept the field were the Champion of Champions event in which all State Champions competed, the Women's National Grand American Handicap, the High Over All Championship, the National 16-yard Championship, and the Preliminary Grand American Handicap.

"More contestants than ever before recorded, this year, were entered in the Grand American. It is a tribute to the fine workmanship incorporated in Remington-Peters Ammunition that more than 75% of all ammunition used in all events bore the Remington-Peters trademarks."

You may have to read the above very closely to see that Peters ammunition did not win the Grand itself!

In other years, 1924 for instance, Peters ran an ad simply offering: "Congratulations to the winners at the GAH. It was a wonderful meet." The ad goes on to chronicle the splendid doings of T. K. Lee along with Monroe, Hootman, Jenks, Nutt and Hutchinson in other events at the same meet.

In 1919, when the pickings were likely slim indeed for Peters in the Grand, Peters took a half page in *Arms and the Man* to extol the merits of amateurs using Peters shells in various other matches around the country.

In 1920, an ad in *The Sportsman's Review* headlined: "They smashed 'em with PETERS shells at the Grand American Handicap:" The ad goes on to list the several events at the Grand won with Peters shells. Among them: "The Grand American Handicap, Woolfolk Henderson, shooting from 23 yards made the remarkable score of 97 x 100." A casual reading might lead one to believe that Woolfolk had won the Grand. As mentioned above, A. L. Ivins did!

The Sportsman's Review stated the following about the 1929 Grand:

"A few minutes after the deciding shot had been fired and it was known that Newman was the winner, Johnny Wallace of the Peters Cartridge Co., who had been flying over the grounds in a big airplane, dropped thousands of yellow slips, "Congratulations to the Winner," in the form of a telegram from that company. This was something unique in the history of the G. A. H., and as there was no commercialization attached to it, it made a big hit with the shooters." Johnny Wallace was a grandson of G. M. Peters. This stunt was in keeping with his colorful character.

All told, Peters had an enviable record at the traps. Judging by Grand results I could find, Western, Winchester, Peters, UMC, and U.S. Cartridge had the largest number of wins in the Grand, in that order. Winchester dominated in the early years, Peters in the middle years, and Western, in the 1930s. There are several years for which I found no information regarding the shells used. Remember this book only covers the period up through 1944 for Peters (1958 for King).

When Peters was made a division of Remington Arms Company, it added a lot more wins at the Grand for the new "family" to crow about. With the UMC and the Peters wins, taken together, Remington had much to talk about.

It is hard to say just how much all this publicity meant. The amount of sales resulting from advertising and promotion can be highly subjective. This is particularly true where a lot of different efforts are going on at the same time. That is to say it is pretty much up to those who pay for the advertising to decide. As far as the customer is concerned, I go back to my original statement that there may well be more meaningful measures of

Peters was not bashful when they won big. Here is an example.

From Sportsman's Review, *1920, courtesy of Dick Baldwin.*

LAST PICTURE OF "WANDA."

Mrs. Etta Lindsley, who was known the country over as "Wanda," and had won several medals in most notable gun club tournaments of the United States in the last decade, was a descendant of one of New York's pioneer daily newspaper editors. The final resting place for the remains of the famous markswoman, whose death, as was mentioned in THE ENQUIRER, occurred at her Clifton home on Saturday, has been fittingly chosen within the city that was saved by "Wanda's" bravery from a fearful fate. She was buried yesterday in Forest Cemetery, at Binghamton, the city that was her forefathers' birthplace. The fearless spirit she possessed on the shooting field was manifest even in her girlhood. Once when all employes of a powder mill fled in terror from a fire that threatened an explosion which would have meant destruction to the entire city of Binghamton, Mrs. Lindsley, then Etta Butts, shoveled dirt fast and furiously upon the flames, and with the aid of one woman held the fire in check from a powder magazine until aid arrived.

Among the many handsome floral tributes at the funeral yesterday was a rifle made of roses from the King Powder Company. Those present from Cincinnati were Mrs. B. H. Hay, a sister of Mrs. Lindsley, and Harry King, of the King Powder Company.

This photo was taken in 1897 at the studios of W. N. Brenner in Cincinnati and was featured in Wanda's obituary in 1902. She died of chronic interstitial nephritis. Milton remarried and Rose Lindsley was the mother of Minton Fletcher Lindsley Jr. Rose was not a shooter, but Milt Jr. was. The text of the obituary is interesting.
From Lindsley scrapbook, undated clipping (probably) from a Binghamton, NY, newspaper, courtesy of Edna Bowyer.

shotshell excellence than who won the Grand.

The Grand contains the variable of possible handicapping errors and the chance of any given shooter being right at the right time with a given shotshell. Of course, this chance is part of the appeal of the Grand. But the statistics, in my opinion, lose more than a bit of their meaning because of this element of chance.

As evidence of how seriously Peters' management took the Grand American, I refer the reader to the chapter in this book on *Working At Peters*. In it, we see that when it came time to make shotshells for the Grand, machines and personnel were tuned up for the occasion. Himes worked there in the late 1920s. He tells how this was done and how any misfire at the Grand was watched carefully to see what color of shell came out of the gun when it was cleared. Shame to the maker!

Shotgunning excellence is a combination of shooter, gun and ammunition. Only by chance is the chain ever stronger than the weakest link–and never for very long. Shotgunning being what it is, a target that is merely

chipped, fragmented or completely smoked, are all scored as hits. On the other hand, the target drifting gently unscathed to the turf is obviously scored as "live." Even though it might have scuffmarks where the shot glanced off, it is still scored as "live," or lost–a miss. The instant of shot arrival is not frozen in time such that it might be subject to careful scrutiny. These situations do not lend themselves to careful analysis by the shooter as he fires.

This uncertainty of the real reason for a hit or miss causes the shooter to be more receptive to hard-content advertising claims of concrete results. It is perhaps those of us who buy a few boxes of shells a year who make up the vast majority of the shotshell market. Not many of us have really patterned a shotgun scientifically. We read of the feats of big-name shooters and, by substitution or extension, hope we might experience something similar.

Peters maintained a presence at the Grand American Handicap, as did all the others having a big stake in the results. In the early days, the Lindsleys erected a giant "teepee" on the

grounds and made the competitors welcome. It was a place to relax, meet new and old friends and absorb and spread the current gossip in the trade among the shooters and among those who make and keep the rules.

As mentioned, the first Grand American Handicap was held in 1893 at live birds. The live bird shooting stopped with the Grand held in 1902 at Kansas City. The nomadic existence of the Grand ended with its getting a "permanent" home in Vandalia, Ohio, in 1923. The Lindsleys, the Kings and the Peters are all gone. Their influence on the Grand is undeniable. The Peters brand shotshell, as made in Kings Mills, totally ended in 1944. Peters has, by now, all but disappeared from the Remington line.

The Grand hosted 8000 competitors in 1999. This is the largest sporting event in number of participants in the world, except for the Boston Marathon. But despite this, and all of the changes in the Grand and in the people who subscribe to its magic, the Grand has ever been the same.

The Grand is still ***The Grand!***

Chapter 5

Peters, King and the Shooting Sports

*I*T TOOK NO sage to realize the shooting sport that utilized the most gunpowder and cartridges was sport hunting. Market hunting was, at that time, all but dead. Early powder can labels, cartridge box labels, posters and cartoons put out by King and Peters reflect this interest in hunting. "Far Killing Duck" was an early powder brand of the King's Great Western Powder Company. The

earliest catalog of the Peters Cartridge Company featured a hunter and dog on the cover as did their most sought-after early Christmas Box–as well as other items.

As noted in the last chapter, the widely scattered nature of sport hunting prevented close monitoring of ammunition performance, and bag limits pretty well eliminated bragging about that aspect of the sport.

But the shooting sports created a venue where spirited competition took place; the expectation was that the sport hunter would read about shooting contests in the sporting papers and the outcome would influence purchases in the hunting market.

To be sure, trap, smallbore and bull's-eye pistol shooters consumed lots of powder and cartridges. There was more than a little interest from the military

The "Busted Duck" represented early art work used on labels and posters. It was an obvious appeal to hunters interested in far-reaching shotshells. *George King estate.*

This shooter is famous for his appearance on the coveted and rare Christmas box. He appears here on a trade card. *Eckler collection.*

and police in the competitions and, indeed, these were sizable markets themselves since both engaged in shooting exercises as training methods. The military issued contracts for cartridges and the police agencies, although much wider spread, bought lots of cartridges for their training.

The King Powder Company and the Peters Cartridge Company effectively used the shooting sports to promote their powders and cartridges. During the early years, both used the many promotional venues in common. Literature involved in the shooting sports, trade shows, match attendance and advertising were, more or less, shared between the two companies.

In the early days, King promoted on it's own. Promotional literature with the King's Great Western Powder Company name on it is relatively rare. But it is out there. One of the classics is a poster of a boatload of women shooting seagulls. Others feature cartoon characters in humorous situations.

When Peters came on the scene in 1887, their promotional literature consisted mostly of testimonials from users of the new machine-loaded shotshells, their only product at the time. The earliest catalog examined is dated 1889, owned by Ted Bacyk. Perusal of the text therein indicates there was no previous general catalog. Up to this point, Peters literature focused only on Peters products. As we move into the 1890s we see joint efforts, for instance: the *Handy Book for Sportsmen*, published in updated versions for a number of years. The booklets featured general information for shooters, including game laws as well as product information.

The chapter in this book regarding Peters, King and the Grand American Handicap pretty well sums up promotions regarding sporting events and shotshell production. There were efforts to reach the hunter directly. A perusal of the color section will graphically illustrate the artwork involved. The well-known Peters calendar art was primarily geared to the hunter's use of both shotshells and big game cartridges.

During the first years of production, Peters was hampered by lawsuits, explosions and the myriad other stumbling blocks involved in getting a new venture up and keeping it running. By the time King Powder got Milton Lindsley on board (1895), Peters was branching out into the metallic cartridge business (1896).

It is absolutely remarkable how quickly Peters got its act together regarding metallic cartridge production. Less than two years after their .22 Short cartridge hit the streets, Peters saw it begin to win in big matches. The introduction of Semi-Smokeless powder in .22 Short cartridges was soon reflected in winning the Indoor Championship of the United States, the first held, in 1898. Peters .22 cartridges loaded with

Early on, Peters formed a local gun club which, no doubt, included some King employees. Here you see dogs, trap boys, shooters, double-barreled shotguns and barrels of clay birds. This is how they appeared in 1890. *Bob and Betty Carter.*

CHAMPIONSHIP TOURNAMENT OF THE INDOOR .22 CALIBER RIFLE LEAGUE.
Impressions of the Pittsburg Press Cartoonist.

This cartoon celebrates the shooting of the Championship Tournament of the Indoor .22 Caliber Rifle League. The winner, Louis P. Ittel, won the title in 1902, 1903, 1905 and 1907.

Undated clipping from Shooting and Fishing. *George Kass collection.*

Semi-Smokeless powder won this match for twelve consecutive years and a record was set along the way (more about this later).

This was something for both King and Peters to crow about;

October 10, 1911.

Gentlemen:
You inquire if I am willing to give you a written endorsement of Peters Semi-smokeless Ammunition, and in reply beg leave to state that I am not only willing, but very glad to do so as I sincerely believe your goods to be the best on the market, and I know to a certainty that they have assisted me very materially in winning the .22 Cal. Indoor Championship as well as many other hotly contested matches during the past 10 years. I find your Semi-smokeless Cartridges wonderfully accurate and uniform and they will positively not injure the finest barrel—in fact have often marveled at their extreme cleanliness, and heartily commend "Peters" to all in search of thoroughly reliable and satisfactory ammunition. Again assuring you that I shall be pleased to have you use this endorsement as you see fit.

I remain,
Sincerely yours,
L. P. ITTEL.

Louis P. Ittel was well known at the Peters Cartridge Company. The employees there took great pride in his record with the fruits of their labor. Here's the Proof, *Peters Cartridge Company ca 1912. Author's collection.*

Peters was the exclusive user of Semi-Smokeless powder in their cartridges. King did sell Semi-Smokeless in canisters to individuals, but not to loading companies. Peters bragged that no bullet was loaded ahead of black powder in their entire line. That is to say they soon discontinued loading black powder into metallic cartridges. Peters could factually say that their metallic cartridges had no competition in kind until Du Pont introduced Lesmok powder in 1911.

This is all the more remarkable in light of the prominence in, and domination of, the metallic cartridge business by UMC—a mature firm making millions of cartridges *per day!* That company had already originated such fine new cartridges as the .22 Long Rifle. Not only that, but UMC had been supplying accurate cartridges to those who were busy making history in revolver accuracy.

A specialized group of competitive shooters had evolved in the United States, especially since the Civil War. Mostly of Germanic extraction, the schuetzen shooters were

devotees of offhand rifle shooting at 200 yards. These shooters were organized into groups all over the U.S. Towns big enough to have a ballpark usually had one or more schuetzen parks. Around 1900, there were seven in the Greater Cincinnati area alone.

The burghers were not to be ignored. There was gallery shooting available in many of the larger cities. Taking a page from the 200-yard schuetzen matches, shooting galleries offered indoor sport at 75 feet on a reduced schuetzen type target. The Zettler Brothers ran such an emporium on West 23rd Street in New York. In such places, the schuetzen shooter could indulge in good sport the year around. Zettler offered this testimonial about Peters .22 Short cartridges:

"Headquarters Zettler Rifle Club
150 West 23rd Street
New York, June 17, 1911
The Peters Cartridge Co
Cincinnati, Ohio

MR. L. P. ITTEL,
In a characteristic pose. Mr. Ittel is the winner of the recent indoor 100-shot match at New York. His score of 2468 was made with Peters .22 short cartridges.

Here is Louis P. Ittel as he appeared in the *Sportsman's Review* in 1905.

April 8, 1905 edition of the Sportsman's Review. Courtesy of Trapshooter's Hall of Fame and Museum.

Gentlemen:

For over fifty years we have been in the gunsmithing business. During that period we have conducted a shooting gallery for the accommodation of the general public and numerous clubs who make our place their headquarters.

We wish to state that for the last fifteen years we have used Peters .22 Short cartridges loaded with King's Semi-Smokeless powder almost exclusively in our gallery and have found them superior in accuracy and cleanliness and that it requires but little labor to keep our rifles in A-1 condition after using your ammunition.

Yours very truly
B. Zettler"

Local rifle clubs, like this one in Montana, were also vocal in their praise of Peters .22s.

"Butte, Montana, May 29, 1911
The Peters Cartridge Company
Cincinnati, Ohio
Dear Sirs:

I have been informed that it is the intention of your Company to issue a booklet setting forth the

Zettler's Gallery in New York was a popular venue for the success of Peters' .22 rimfire cartridges. American Rifleman's Encyclopedia, *Peters Cartridge Co. Courtesy of George McCluney*

merits of your Semi-Smokeless ammunition, and while the Rocky Mountain Rifle Club has at all times given due credit to your product, yet I feel that we have but poorly expressed our appreciation for **your unbeatable ammunition,** without a direct testimonial from us appearing in such booklet.

During the competition in the Small Bore Inter-Club Matches held during the years 1910 and 1911, our rifle team fired not less than fifty thousand of your .22 cal. Long Rifle Cartridges, and in this number of shots I can count the imperfect cartridges on the fingers of one hand and have fingers to spare: we look upon it

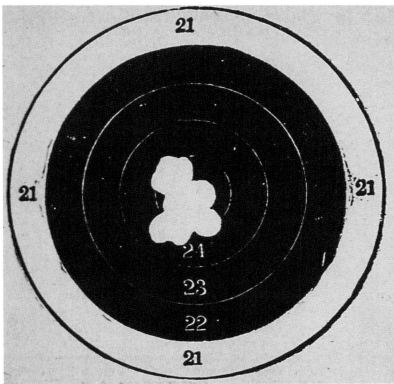

Perfect Scores Made With Perfect Ammunition

Score of 250 out of a possible 250, shot by M. DORRLER, at the Zettler Rifle Club Gallery. The ammunition used was

PETERS .22 SHORT

CARTRIDGES

Target Full Size

Dorrler was a well-known shooter at Zettler's Gallery and elsewhere, among schuetzen shooters.
Rifleman's Record and Score Book, *Peters Cartridge Company. Author's collection.*

as a record of almost marvelous perfection and it engendered a feeling of absolute confidence in our ammunition, which was the greatest possible factor in the success of our team in both of these championship series; in fact, we feel the medals and trophies awarded us could, with perfect propriety, be inscribed "Won by Peters Semi-Smokeless Cartridges."

Yours very Truly
T. E. Booth
Secretary Rocky Mountain Rifle Club of Butte Montana"

Perhaps the most impressive evidence is that of the aforementioned Indoor Championship. The individual winners were a Who's Who of schuetzen shooting in that day.

1898-H. M. Spencer 2424
1899-F. C. Ross 2425
1900-F. C. Ross 2429
1901-F. C. Ross 2451
1902-L. P. Ittel 2458
1903-L. P. Ittel 2457
1904-L. C. Buss. 2456
1905-L. P. Ittel 2459
1906-W.A. Tewes —
World Record 2481
1907-L. P. Ittel 2465
1908-Arthur Hubalek. 2464
1909-W. A. Tewes 2470

W. A. Tewes became an employee of Peters in later years. It was he that Elmer Keith erroneously thought was the plant manager at Peters in the 1930s. Elmer, without doubt, knew him from the matches– likely Camp Perry. I have seen his signature as technical manager under Peters letterheads dated as early as 1931. Some of the matches listed above were shot in **Madison Square Garden**, in Grand Rapids in 1906, the rest at Zettler's gallery.

The following quote illustrates the fact that many of the advertisements in the industry needed careful reading. Even then, the reader might not always be able to tell just who did what. When Mr. Louis P. Ittel shot a record score of 2468 at the Zettler Rifle Club Open

At Armbruster's Greenville rifle range, an interesting 100-shot match took place on Jan. 2, between two of New Jersey's leading riflemen. This contest was originally arranged for Dec. 26, but owing to Mr. Tewes' rifle having become disabled on that date, after he had secured a score of 232, the match was postponed until the present occasion. The weather conditions were favorable, excepting for the mist which hung over the range, obliging Mr. Tewes to use a pinhead instead of his favorite aperture front sight.

Both contestants were in good form, and the match progressed smoothly from start to finish. Mr. Tewes obtained a lead of one point on the first string, which he steadily increased, finishing with a lead of 53 points, all of his shots being in the 12-inch black. His rifle is a .33-220 Stevens-Pope-Ballard, barrel 29½ inches, using 4 grains of Du Pont No. 1 Rifle Smokeless, and balance of shell filled with King's Semi-Smokeless, FG, felt wad, Peters shells and Peters nitro primers. As usual he used no palm rest, shooting from the hip-rest position with the rifle rested on the finger tips.

Mr. Dorrler shot his Stevens-Pope-Ballard .32-40-200, 32-inch barrel, 4 grains of Du Pont No. 1 Rifle Smokeless, balance of load, King's Semi-Smokeless, FG, U. M. C. shells and 7½ primers, cardboard wad, palm rest. This outfit is a recent acquisition of Mr. Dorrler's, who is an expert mechanic and has made the stock and lever after his own ideas. He remarked after the match was over that he was perfectly satisfied with the shooting qualities of the weapon.

Owen Smith completed a 100-shot score of 1958, as runner-up. Among the other riflemen in attendance were Thomas Anderton, formerly of Boston, Major Brinkerhoff, W. H. French, of Colorado, Ed. Taylor, of the Laflin & Rand Co., W. J. Coons, H. F. Barning, J. Kaufmann, V. R. Olmstead, and Major R. W. Evans.

W. A. Tewes . . . . 220 223 219 219=218
                                  224 220 221 225 215=2204
M. Dorrler 219 215 213 213 221
                                  219 206 211 217 217=2151

(vertical text in margin: SHOOTING AND FISHING 3-16-01)

This clipping from *Shooting and Fishing* tells of a match between Dorrler and Bill Tewes with centerfire schuetzen rifles and their loads, both using King's Semi-Smokeless Powder.
March 16, 1901 issue of Shooting and Fishing.
ASSRA Archives, courtesy of Rudi Prusok.

WM. A. TEWES
Winner of .22 Cal. Indoor Championship of the U. S. in 1906, by a World's Record Score, 2481 out of a possible 2500. Also champion in 1909.

156 Glenwood Ave.,
Jersey City, N. J., October 19, 1911.

THE PETERS CARTRIDGE CO.,
Cincinnati, Ohio.

Gentlemen:

I cannot let the Season of 1911 go by without complimenting you on the accuracy of your .30 caliber ammunition. The long list of matches won with it speaks for itself. The .22 caliber cartridges, too, of your latest output, are better than ever, being fast, clean, and beautifully accurate and should prove winners in this winter's matches.

Very truly yours,

W. A. TEWES,
Lieutenant Colonel,
Ass't Ins. Gen'l of Rifle Prac., N. J.

This testimonial letter from Bill Tewes is typical of many. What is not typical is that Bill later went to work for Peters. Here's the Proof, *Peters Cartridge Co. ca 1912.*
Author's collection.

FOR GALLERY SHOOTING

The Uniform Accuracy of PETERS CARTRIDGES
Make Them The Chosen Ammunition of Experts

This illustration shows fifty consecutive shots at 75 feet, by W. A. Tewes, shot with Peters .22 Calibre Cartridges.

Target Full Size

An example of Bill Tewes' shooting and Peters performance.
Rifleman's Record and Score Book, *Peters Cartridge Co.* ca *1902. Author's collection.*

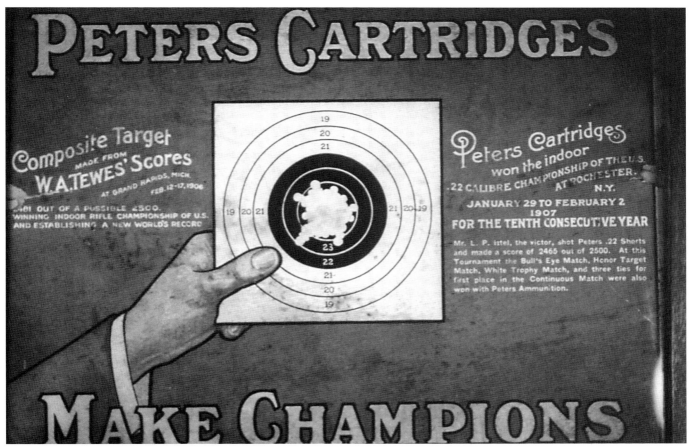

Bill Tewes established a world record of 2481, which stood for many years, shot at Grand Rapids in 1906. Peters also heralded the performance of Louis Ittel at Rochester, N. Y., on this counter felt advertising.
Peters' counter felt. Courtesy of Bob and Betty Carter.

Bill Tewes as he must have looked leaving the line after he won the Wimbledon Cup in 1905. He did it with a Krag rifle during the days of the 1903 Springfield. Bill must have used service ammunition to win this event or Peters would have crowed about it.

Clipping from unidentified source. George Kass collection.

Tournament in 1905, Winchester advertised: *"three of the four first prizes [at the shoot] were won by shooters who used Winchester Cartridges."* They failed to specify that *"the match record for that class of shooting"* was won with Peters cartridges in that shoot!

Not only did Peters crow about Winchester's convoluted reporting, they advertised the telegram and letter that Mr. Ittel fired off to Winchester asking for the record to be set straight. I have not found that Winchester ever responded. It should be said that Peters, too, was known to accentuate the positive and ignore any negative aspects of their own product's performance, although not to the degree illustrated above.

The Marlin Fire Arms Catalog of June 1897 is extensive and informative. It stated the following about King's powders:

*"**We can recommend the following brands** of black powder for reloading these cartridges (32/40): **King's "Special FFG"** (Among seven other powders)*

The catalog also mentions King's Semi-Smokeless and Smokeless as follows:

*"**King's Semi-Smokeless FG** bulk for bulk with black powder..."* and *"**King's Smokeless** Rifle Powder No.4 bulk for bulk with black powder."*

The only other smokeless powder listed is the imported powder Walsrode. Of course there is no alternative powder listed under the Semi-Smokeless category, as there was no competition to Semi-Smokeless for more than a decade.

The catalog goes on to list the loadings, with appropriate changes in load, for most of the cartridges in the catalog.

Will Hayes was a well-known schuetzen rifleman and rest shooter. He was a particular

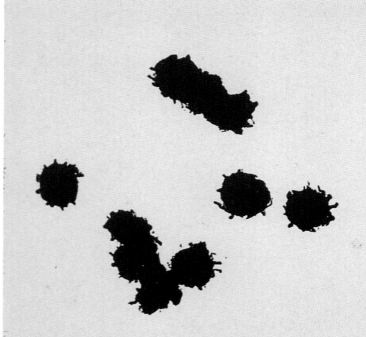

Tested at 200 Yards

The accompanying group of shoots, ten consecutive, were shot by WILLIAM HAYES, at 200 yards, at Armbuster's Shooting Park, Greenville, N. J., with

C. G. BRAND OF

KING'S SEMI-SMOKELESS

POWDER

A group shot at 200 yards by Will Hayes, a famous schuetzen rifleman, using King's Semi-Smokeless powder.
Rifleman's Record and Score Book, Peters Cartridge Co. ca 1902. Author's collection.

friend of the well-known barrel maker H. M. Pope. On April 23, 1898, Will Hayes tested the various brands of King's Semi-Smokeless Powder at Armbruster's Greenville Schuetzen Park in Greenville, N. J. Mr. Hayes shot his .32-40 rifle from a machine rest. His first ten-shot group with FG brand measured one minute-of-angle at 200 yards. His second ten-shot group measured about 1-7/8 inches; nine of them in 1-1/4 inches. There is shown a twenty-shot group in less than a minute-of-angle at 200 yards. Try that with anything available a century later! This information is from *Hints on King's Semi-Smokeless Powder and Peters Cartridges*.

Harry Pope stated, as quoted in a Peters booklet *Here's the Proof*:

"H. M. Pope,
Rifle Barrels and Tools,
18 Morris Street,
Jersey City N. J., July 17, 1911
Peters Cartridge Co.,
98 Chambers St. New York.
Gentlemen,
I am happy to tell you that I have used **Peters cartridges** *in*

Testing King's Semi-Smokeless powder at Schuetzen Park, Greenville, N. J.
American Rifleman's Encyclopedia, *Peters Cartridge Co.*
Courtesy of George McCluney.

testing my rifle barrels for the last fifteen years or more, wherever I have had occasion to use fixed ammunition, and that during that time I have found these to run more uniformly than those of any other make, so that they **have become My Standard**.
Yours sincerely,
H. M. Pope"

Ray M. Smith's book *The Story of Pope's Barrels*, shows illustrations (from *Shooting and Fishing*) a composite group of fifty shots on the Standard American Target shot by **Harry Pope** at 200 yards offhand. *Shooting and Fishing* called it a record score for 50 shots, scoring 467 x 500 points. On one of the

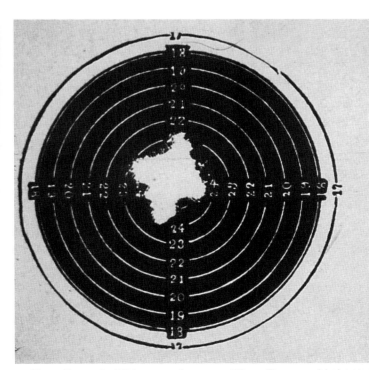

H. M. Pope

the well-known rifle maker and expert shot uses

PETERS CARTRIDGES

to test his fine rifle barrels. He has many fine scores to his credit. The one presented herewith was made in a match at a range of 75 feet, off-hand. Shot with Peters .22 Calibre Cartridges.

Harry Pope shot this group in competition. Pope could shoot, as well as make barrels of legendary accuracy.
Rifleman's Record and Score Book, *Peters Cartridge Co.* ca *1902. Author's collection.*

ten-shot targets, Harry dropped but three points. The 13-pound rifle was a Stevens with a Stevens Pope .32-40 barrel. The powder used was King's FFG Semi-Smokeless.

Also shown are groups that Pope shot with a Stevens Pope .22, with Peters .22 Short ammunition (loaded with Semi-Smokeless Powder). The ten-shot group is one ragged hole. The 50-shot and 100-shot composites with it show remarkable uniformity of point of impact as well as tight grouping without cleaning the barrel. These were shot in February of 1903.

The *Hints* publication quoted earlier also mentioned another well-known schuetzen rifleman of a century ago, **E. A. Leopold**. Leopold is perhaps best known today for the excellent bullet lubricant he developed and sold under his name. At 200 yards, Leopold tested a *"32 caliber Pope system* (muzzle-breech loading system developed by Harry Pope); *no cleaning; 40 grains* **King's Semi-Smokeless** *FG powder, 202 grain bullet. Diameter of group 2-3/32" from*

center to center of outlaying shots." This is a ten-shot group from machine rest.

Hints also relates that King's Semi-Smokeless was used to win the rifle championship of Greater New York and vicinity, representing 100 consecutive shots at 200 yards offhand. *"This being one of the great annual rifle shooting events and participated in by many of the leading rifle shots of this country.* ***King's Semi-Smokeless Powder won this championship in 1899, 1900, 1901, 1902 and 1903."***

The well-known shooter and experimenter ***"Iron Ramrod"*** (Ruben Harwood) tested King's Semi-Smokeless in a .25-21 for small game shooting. He found accuracy the best yet with that cartridge and the killing power on small game excellent. Dr. Baker, with the same cartridge produced a ten-shot group at fifty yards that could be easily circumscribed by a dime, the edges of the holes not coming as near the circle as 1/32", anywhere. This was also shot with **King's Semi-Smokeless.** This, and the following

information, came from the *Hints* booklet.

In September 1900, **Wm. De V. Foulke won the Wimbledon Cup** at the Sea Girt range in New Jersey using **King's Semi-Smokeless Powder**. The distance then, as the Wimbledon remains today, was 1000 yards (5/8 of a mile); the number of shots, 30. *"The same powder, loaded in Peters .45 caliber cartridges for the U. S. Springfield rifle, scored victory after victory at this same meeting."*

While we are dropping names, how about **Dr. Hudson**, the "human machine rest?" The good doctor undoubtedly used his famous Remington Walker rifle when he shot a 'possible' of 125 x 125 in one of the legs of the Indoor Rifle Championship of the U.S. in 1905. The Doctor used Peters Cartridge .22 Shorts.

Major Ned H. Roberts wrote in the 1930s about the old schuetzen rifles. Gerald Kelver, long-time secretary of the ASSRA, collected some of Ned's writings from the 1930s and published them in 1951. In the

King's Semi-Smokeless powder was used by Wm. deV. Foulke to win the Wimbledon Cup match in 1900.
American Rifleman's Encyclopedia, *Peters Cartridge Co. Courtesy of George McCluney.*

down roots at the latter place in 1940, where shoots have been held ever since.

Friend and NMLRA past president Merrill Deer provided an old NMLRA shoot bulletin dated 1939 showing a King Powder advertisement, since found in shoot bulletins dating back to 1935. King also advertised in the NMLRA's house organ, *Muzzle Blasts*. Interestingly, all of these ads are for King's Semi-Smokeless Powder. Quick Shot, their then current brand of black powder, was not mentioned.

The popularity of the NMLRA shoots was no doubt due in part to the fact the old rifles could be had quite cheaply. The ammunition, too, was the cheapest available. In the depths of the Great Depression those were big factors.

Soon after the NMLRA got started, Walter Cline became involved, first as a competitor and author of articles about muzzle loading, which were

This fellow is obviously a smallbore rifle shooter of the 1920s. Here he is with his Model 52 Winchester with sling, scope and shooting jacket. While he was known in smallbore circles, he became much better known as one of the fathers of the National Muzzle Loading Rifle Association. E. M. (Red) Farris was Secretary to the NMLRA for many years. In later years, he ran a gun shop on Gallia Street in Portsmouth, Ohio.

May 1927 issue of the American Rifleman. ASSRA Archives, courtesy of Rudi Prusok.

published in *The American Rifleman* in the early 30s. Walter Cline later became President of the NMLRA. The big 500+ acre range at Friendship, Indiana, is named in his honor. When the NMLRA bought the first 52 acres to found this range in 1942, The King Powder Company donated $25 toward the purchase. Only four, including Powell Crosley Jr. and the Cline family, donated more. That amount of money

KING'S SEMI-SMOKELESS
POWDER

The Best of All Powder for
MUZZLE LOADING FIREARMS

It shoots clean, is reliable, and will make an improvement in your score

Write us for prices and booklet fully describing the use of King's Semi-Smokeless Powder

The King Powder Company, Inc.

CINCINNATI, OHIO

PROGRAM

Combined
W. L. W.-Crosley *and*
National Muzzle Loading
Rifle Association
Matches

Laughery Park
Rising Sun, Indiana

October 23rd, 24th and 25th

1936

The National Muzzle Loading Rifle Association was founded in 1933 in Portsmouth, Ohio. The King Powder Company was an early supporter of the NMLRA, recognizing that they represented a resurgence of demand for their sporting powders. Here is an advertisement for the King Powder Company in an early NMLRA match bulletin. *1936 NMLRA Match Bulletin. Courtesy of Merrill P. Deer.*

Adolph Niedner was one of the Grand Old Men of schuetzen shooting, custom rifle building and collaboration with Franklin Mann (author of *The Bullet's Flight From Powder To Target*). *Pop*, as he was called, was an active competitor in the National Muzzle Loading Rifle matches in the early days at the Walter Cline Range.

Courtesy of Muzzle Blasts.

represented over two week's salary in that post-Depression era.

It soon was demonstrated that in the matches requiring pinpoint accuracy, Kings Semi-Smokeless Powder developed a devoted following. Edna Bowyer, long-time secretary of King Powder remembers that Red Farris, perennial NMLRA Secretary and editor of their magazine *Muzzle Blasts*, would stop by Kings Mills on the way to a shoot and buy a stock of powder to sell at that shoot.

Walter Cline had an especially fine rifle made by Whitmore. It came cased with all accessories

and a full-length telescope. This rifle shot a picket bullet. A picket bullet has a flat base (usually) and a spire-shaped point, but no cylindrical section. The Whitmore displayed great accuracy in his hands and in the hands of several of Cline's friends. In 1934 it took 1st, 3rd, 4th and 5th places in a 220-yard NMLRA match. Walter fed it King's Semi-Smokeless Powder.

In the early '30s, Walter Cline took the Whitmore to Kings Mills where it was tested at the request of Peters' Chief Physicist, Phillip Quayle. Walter Cline tells the story as he wrote it and as was published in *The American Rifleman* issue of May 1931:

The rifle tested...was made by N. J. Whitmore of Pottsdam, NY. The grooves were cut on a gaining twist...ending in one turn in 3 feet 4 inches; bore diameter .432; depth of grooves .008; weight of

1935. . . .Rising Sun (Ind.) Range. Left to right: Powel Crosley, Walter Cline, E. M. Farris. The huddle is in the interest of getting more information to Mr. Crosley about that rifle held like it is about to pop a Jap plane It is a Whitworth hex bored match rifle. . . .and became the property of Mr. Crosley as a result of this alfalfa patch confab.

Confab in a cornfield. And, yes, that is a Whitmore in the text and a Whitworth in this cut. These three notables were active in promoting the early National Muzzle Loading Rifle Association. Powell Crosley was a well-known industrialist (radios, automobiles, appliances, radio broadcasting etc.). Cline and Farris were founders of the NMLRA.

Courtesy of Muzzle Blasts.

This is an early shoot on the Walter Cline range with sway-backed benches, no covered firing line and few other amenities. The range now features over a quarter-mile of covered firing line and shooting in about any discipline you might desire or imagine for muzzle-loading rifles, pistols and shotguns. There is a large primitive range, too, on part of the over 500 acres of NMLRA land.

Courtesy of Muzzle Blasts.

rifle 16 pounds. The bullets are flat pointed picket type, with slightly rounded base measuring .440 at the base, .740 in length and weighing 225 grains. The bullets were formed of pure lead. ...Experiments were conducted in the laboratory with various powder charges in which velocity was carefully measured and **a charge of 64.7 grains of King's Semi-Smokeless, FFG granulation** *was selected, giving a mean muzzle velocity of 1,638 feet per second. ...This rifle has a full length telescope of about 12 power. ...*

"The bullet was ...centered on a circular patch wet with saliva ...and the bullet starter forced the bullet into the bore... five shots were fired for group, the bore being carefully cleaned after each shot; distance 186 yards. This group measured: extreme horizontal 1 1/8 inches; extreme vertical 7/8 inch. **Every shot would have touched a five-cent piece."**

The above shooting is the more remarkable in that it does not consist of a selected group from many shot. This is excellent work as anyone with experience in lead bullet shooting can attest. Cline wrote a book, *The Muzzle Loading Rifle–Then and Now* (Standard Publishing Co., Huntington, WV, 1942). Cline tested many conventional round-ball rifles of both flint and percussion ignition and had this to say:

"With the various calibers (of rifles), that we were using, **we found that FFG Kings Semi-Smokeless gave the best results."**

Alas, King's Semi-Smokeless Powder is no longer available, nor is anything like it made today. Noryl Hamilton, King's chief chemist during the 1930s told me that, as far as he knew, he made the last batch of Semi-Smokeless in the early '30s. It was made in batches and sold until stocks were exhausted.

Indications are that stocks of Semi-Smokeless lasted up into the 1950s. By the 1930s, King only made a single grade of black sporting powder, Quick Shot. It had a following, too. Gunmaker Jack Haugh said he preferred King's blasting powder for quarry work in his younger days and that he found King's sporting powder was excellent, too. While they both were called Quick Shot, there was a difference in the formulation–and considerable difference in the granulation of powder for blasting and sporting purposes.

The NMLRA is alive and well and has a current membership in the neighborhood of 20,000. They have their own journal, *Muzzle Blasts.*

The NMLRA was father to another shooting group active today, the American Single Shot Rifle Association (ASSRA). The ASSRA was founded by John Amber, late editor of the *Gun Digest,* prolific writer

Gerald Kelver and others, on the NMLRA grounds in the late 1940s. The firearms to which the ASSRA is dedicated had their heyday during that of both King and Peters. Although Peters had long since moved to Bridgeport before the ASSRA was founded, lots of the records celebrated by the ASSRA were made using their respective products. Early writings of the ASSRA show the use of King's Semi-Smokeless Powder in their schuetzen loadings. King did not close for about a decade after the ASSRA was founded. Today, the ASSRA has about 2,000 active members and, like NMLRA, publishes its own *Single Shot Rifle Journal*.

Col. Townsend Whelen was 'Dean' of rifle shooters for the first half of the twentieth century. A half-century after his death, the colonel is still often quoted as saying: *"Only accurate rifles are interesting."* There is a corollary to that. The corollary is the dead certainty that **the finest rifle ever made can be no more accurate than the ammunition available.**

Occasional cans of King's powders will surface, while shootable Peters ammunition, made at Kings Mills, is long since history. Like the men and women who made them, the powder and the ammunition are becoming increasingly rare.

ily, 1942   MUZZLE BLASTS   Page 7

SCHUETZEN STYLE

HERB 1941
SHERLOCK

This cartoon will be of interest to members of both the American Single Shot Rifle Association and the National Muzzle Loading Rifle Association. Both have full-blown schuetzen programs of their own. But, no, I'm afraid you will not find the beer keg on the line with either association.
Courtesy of Muzzle Blasts.

Chapter 6

Kings Mills Ordnance Plant (KMOP)

THE STORY OF the Kings Mills Ordnance Plant (KMOP) is perhaps the most remarkable of those in this book. The full impact of the Peters Cartridge contribution to the Allies' World War II effort went far beyond Warren County, and far beyond the cartridges manufactured at KMOP and Peters. The story of the KMOP within Warren County is remarkable in itself; however, the plant was a relatively small WWII ordnance operation. Peters provided the seed that took root

in the huge new Denver Arsenal and others. Some background information at this point will be of use in understanding this story.

World War I had been a very busy time for Peters. The large contracts from the British Government alone assured more business than Peters could handle. After the U.S. entered the war, government contracts took the place of others and, it is to be supposed, pushed aside domestic sporting production. The cash flow from these

contracts went a long way toward financing the new plant that Peters built and equipped to replace the old wooden works constructed after the 1890 explosion.

The U.S. government found that the method of procuring ammunition during 1917-1918 produced widely varying quality in cartridges furnished to the troops in Europe. Experienced commercial cartridge companies like Peters gave little trouble in this regard. However, many government contractors produced

This is a photo of the KMOP site, looking south. You see the "old" plant with the shot tower and chimney at the middle left. The "new" (1942) KMOP is the complex beyond, on top of the hill, with its two water towers. The river is winding its way down to Foster, Loveland, and the Ohio River not far from Cincinnati. Trees *(right foreground)* obscure the little town of Kings Mills. The Pennsylvania Railroad follows the river quite closely on the far side. The "bright spot" among the trees well above the plant smokestack is the fire-fighting water reservoir. *Warren County Historical Society.*

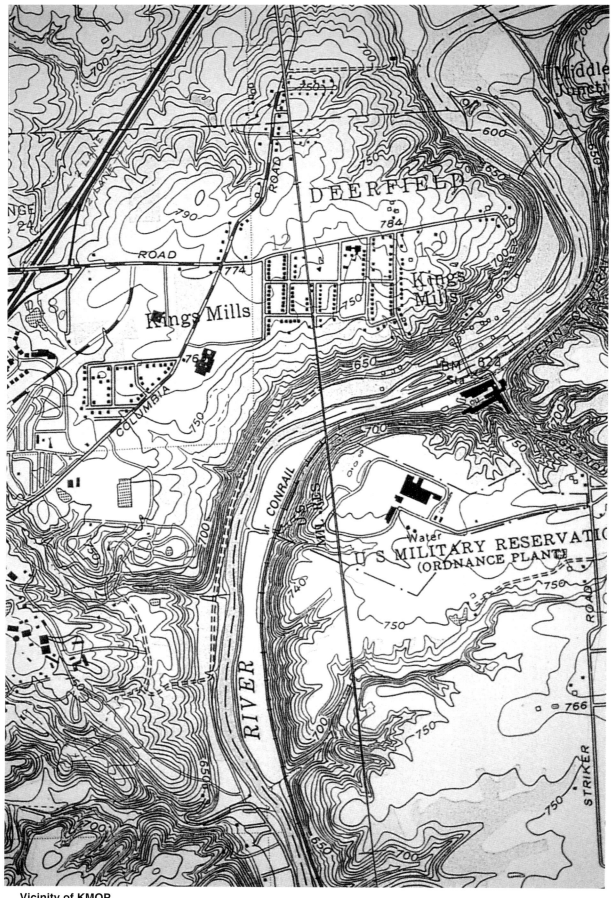

Vicinity of KMOP.

ammunition that was worse than useless. It was said almost anyone could contract with the U.S. government for small arms ammunition.

I suppose that cupping, drawing, and annealing cartridge cases and the manufacture of primers were the biggest headaches to would-be ammunition producers. When I was growing up, there was still a fair amount of surplus WWI ammunition available. I can remember blown-out cartridge cases and inaccuracy in much of it (none of it was of Peters manufacture). Admittedly all of it was, by the early 1950s, about 35 years old. But well-made ammunition should age more gracefully.

As a reaction to their WWI experience, the U.S. Army Ordnance Department developed a plan. For the full text of the information the author found in ordnance records on file with the Cincinnati Historical Society, see the appendix. It obviously believed that a close relationship with privately owned industrial capacity was of the greatest importance in time of war. Therefore, the Ordnance Department set about establishing and maintaining an ongoing relationship with industry in time of peace.

The U.S. was divided into ordnance districts. The one of interest here, Cincinnati Ordnance District, took in all of Kentucky and Tennessee plus parts of Ohio and Indiana. The district was headed by an Ordnance officer and supplemented by reserve officers, plus industrial leaders known as dollar-a-year men. Obviously, the expense to the government was small in peacetime.

It was the job of Ordnance personnel to identify potential contractors from industry who were able to manufacture military materiel. These firms were further matched to specific items needed. This was all on paper. There was some actual procurement under peacetime conditions. The quantity was minuscule compared to wartime needs. Congress was by no means willing to fund a large standing army, let alone enough hardware to sustain one.

It is obvious, however, that preparations were being made to enable the government to gather vast amounts of war materiel very quickly. The thought was undoubtedly to maximize the preparedness without making large appropriations for hardware. The disadvantage of this system was that on *Day One* of a war, there was not enough hardware available for immediate issue. On the other hand, there was a distinct economic advantage to doing it this way. There was no squandering of tax money on equipment that might become obsolete awaiting a need that many citizens of that day thought—or at least hoped—would never come.

This plan should be considered in light of events and feelings of those times: World War I was, by the late 1930s, still popularly supposed to be the "War To End All Wars." If true, there was no need for a large armed force or for stockpiled materiel.

Furthermore, there was a very strong isolationist movement in the United States that held that what went on in Europe—or elsewhere in the world—was not any business of the United States. Further, in the late 1930s, the U.S. was still in the grip of a *very* severe economic depression.

There had been depressions, economic downturns, and financial panics aplenty in the history of the country. However, this one had lasted for nearly a decade. Hence the attempt by Congress to set things up on a shoestring.

Let's take a look at how well the Ordnance Plan actually worked with respect to the manufacture of small arms ammunition.

Events in the rest of the world in the late 1930s gave many isolationists pause. The Lightning War *(Blitzkrieg)* that Hitler loosed on selected countries in Europe issued a grim warning to the rest of the world. President Roosevelt made the United States' official neutrality a mockery by helping foes of Germany and Japan in one way or another. This was done long before the U.S.

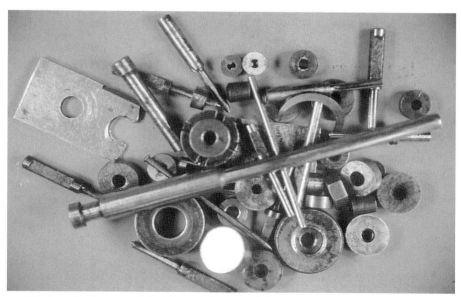

This is a double handful of the original precision tooling used to produce .30 Carbine ammunition at KMOP. There are punches and dies for case- and jacket-forming, as well as tiny primer anvils. This tooling was mostly, if not entirely, produced in the machine shop in the old plant. It came from Jim Rodgers, the engineer who set the machinery up to produce .45 ACP, and soon after changed it over to make .30 Carbine.

officially entered the war. The Neutrality Act of 1936 became increasingly meaningless as sales of munitions, and programs like Lend Lease, increased.

The beneficiaries of all of these U.S. efforts were clearly those nations opposed to the expansionist activities of what became known as the Axis Powers. Such events would have furnished more than ample provocation to both Germany and Japan to open hostilities with the U.S. had they, themselves, been ready for such an event at the time.

Harold Himes, local author and historian and one-time employee of Peters, reported that in 1939, Remington requested Peters to bring their military cartridge-loading machines out of storage. This in a plant devoted 100 percent to shotshell production for some years (after the sale of Peters, *metallic* ammunition production had been shifted to Bridgeport, Conn.). The Battle of Britain (the *Blitz*), which was totally an air war, used huge quantities of small-arms ammunition. The Nazi aircraft involved in the *Blitz* were bombers, with fighter escort. The defenders were nearly all fighter aircraft, hence the need for small-arms ammunition.

Phil Sharpe, in the June 1954 issue of *The American Rifleman*, reported the British government purchasing commission had a contract with Remington in 1941. It was for .30-'06 ammunition. The headstamp was "RA 1941, 300 Z". Sharpe noted this ammunition was marked in the British way, 300 denoting .30 caliber, and the letter "Z" indicating nitrocellulose powder to distinguish it from the British cordite. It is not known if any of this was made at Kings Mills.

Major General Julian S. Hatcher was the 'Dean' of Ordnance personnel from WWI through WWII. The writings of the good general introduce the author of the next remarks: "...*Captain* [Phil B.] *Sharpe had*

the enviable and valuable experience of serving as an officer in the Ordnance Department for three years during the recent war [WWII], and as an Ordnance Intelligence Officer in Europe he had an unprecedented opportunity to get firsthand information on continental arms and ammunition factories and their products."

Captain Sharpe, in his book *The Rifle In America,* had this to say about the situation in general, and the Kings Mills Ordnance Plant in particular:

"*When it came to ammunition consumption, World War I was a weekend practice shoot compared to World War II. In the United States alone, the production of small arms ammunition reached a point where* **more cartridges were made every eight days than were produced in the entire wartime period 1917-1918!** [emphasis the writer's]

"*The United States made many mistakes, but it did profit from World War I experience. In 1917, contracts were given to practically anyone who asked for them. Ammunition was produced at a number of fly-by-night plants that were unable to make a single acceptable cartridge. Small arms ammunition production actually fell to the big commercial firms including the United States Cartridge Company, Peters Cartridge Company, Winchester Repeating Arms Company, Western Cartridge Company and Remington Arms-Union Metallic Arms Company. The sole Government ammunition plant was Frankford Arsenal.*

"*Due to the demands from overseas, commercial makers of arms and ammunition had been expanded even before Pearl Harbor Day, but war plans for the protection of the United States had been formulated in the early 1930s—at least on paper. New plants would be built when required. That they were not ready earlier was due to public apathy against military spending. Had this country been fully ready, Hitler might have*

thought twice before he embarked upon his program of world conquest. One does not slap a big fellow with a club in his hand...

"*The 'On-Paper' program was known as the 'Unit Plan.' It involved the use of the major arms and ammunition plants, kept alive in this country because of the demands of American Sportsmen for hunting and target weapons and ammunition. In the ammunition field commercial plants were to expand to capacity production. Frankford Arsenal was to be a key planning point, and each manufacturer would work with Ordnance technicians and planners in developing, constructing, equipping, training personnel, and operating a series of new plants. These new plants were to be known as GOCO plants-'Government Owned, Contractor Operated.'*

"*In June 1940, following the Dunkirk debacle, Remington received British ammunition orders which required them to increase their .30 caliber military ammunition production 600 % [this would include Peters], and their .50 caliber production 2000%. With the United States entrance into the war* **anticipated** [author's emphasis], *the Ordnance "Unit Plan" was called into action. Late in the summer of 1940, Remington was asked to recommend sites for new ammunition plants. A study was made covering 50 sites in eleven cities. In the 'first wave' stage, Remington was asked to build two plants.*

"*Remember these were to be new plants, designed and built from the ground up for but one purpose–to build small arms military ammunition in quantity. These two new plants were built, equipped, manned, and were in production on ammunition before that fateful Sunday, December 7, 1941 now known as Pearl Harbor Day.*

"*The first of the new plants was the Lake City Ordnance Plant.... constructed on 3,800 acres...26 miles from Kansas City.... actual daily capacity 8,900,000 rounds of all types [.30 (1906), .50 and .30 carbine].... Some 20,000 people were employed here...*

"The second...was the Denver Ordnance Plant–also Remington designed, constructed, equipped and operated. This plant is believed to be the world's largest small arms ammunition plant. It far tops the big Polti plants at Magdeberg, Germany, or the Rheinische Wesfalische Sprengstoff, A.G. [RWS], plants at Nurnberg and Stadln, Bavaria–which have been visited many times by the author.

"The Denver Ordnance Plant was located on a 2,080 acre tract in the suburbs of Denver... It had at its peak 20,000 employees daily. ...

"Construction was started March 3, 1941. Seven months later and five months before the estimated completion date, the plant was in production...eventually 10 million rounds per day! In 1942 and 1943, this one plant produced 4,156,377,343 rounds of accepted Caliber .30 ammunition.

"[another] GOCO Plant [was the] Kings Mills Ordnance Plant at Kings Mills, Ohio, near Cincinnati.

"This Kings Mills plant was a revision of the old Peters Cartridge Company plant, previously purchased and operated by the Remington-DuPont combine. In the fall of 1941, the government decided to take over the Peters works and construct a large additional plant, the combination to be known as the Kings Mills Ordnance Plant. Construction began that December. Only 90 days later the buildings were substantially completed, and plans were well under way to produce 2,500,000 caliber .45 pistol cartridges daily. In June 1942, some .45 production was started.

[These cartridges are relatively rare; should be head-stamped "PC 42"; WWI (and earlier and later) .45 caliber cartridges manufactured by Peters were marked "P.C.CO 18" etc.; Sharpe reported the WWII code for Kings Mills Ordnance Plant as "PC." In actual KMOP carbine production, the "P" and "C" stamps were widely separated as at ten and two o'clock; the last two digits of the date (only two used) are located at six o'clock. Cartridge collector Otto Witt reports that of the major collections today, only Steve Fuller's has a specimen.]

"At this time Ordnance changed its plans. The entire project was revised. The active production of the U. S. M1 carbine and consequent drop in pistol cartridge requirements, made it necessary to convert the plant to the manufacture of carbine ammunition, caliber .30, then acutely needed. Such a change was not simple. Buildings had to be altered and many new ones constructed. A million dollar's worth of .45 machinery had to be moved. Of 548 pieces of .45 equipment, 493 had to be replaced or converted.

"Carbine ammunition went into production on November 10, 1942. By the following summer, the monthly output was up to sixty million. But as ammunition demands were being met, the plant was stabilized at this figure although its monthly capacity was 90,000,000 rounds.

"Kings Mills used most of the original Peters layout in the

This is some rare ammunition produced at KMOP. Bridgeport sent engineer Jim Rodgers 50,000 steel blanks to process, as an experiment, into steel-cased .45 ACP. It was to be run on their new equipment in KMOP but head-stamped "RA". Jim said there were about 50% casualties. The one on top is a primed empty; bottom is a loaded round. The dark coating on the case is the special lubricant used.

manufacture of over 125,000,000 shotgun cartridges, chiefly for Air Corps training.

"On March 3, 1944, the Kings Mills plant suspended operations. At the close of the war [August 1945], Remington was faced with the problem of disposing of the Peters plant-should they continue to operate it in the post-war production of Peters ammunition? The decision was made to abandon it. The expansion of Remington's

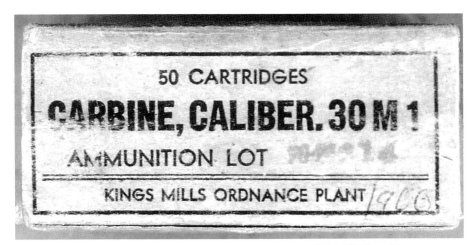

This .30 Carbine ammunition was the main product of KMOP after the very short run of .45 ACP.

ammunition facilities at Bridgeport left them with a large plant, and the surplus facilities could be used for the production of the Peters line for commercial markets. Accordingly, Peters equipment privately owned by Remington was transferred to Bridgeport, and the plant went out of existence. The new section, government owned, was converted to other needed military and naval equipment."

Dick [Richard F.] Dietz, then Public Relations Director of Remington Arms Co., wrote to me on January 31, 1974, sending what he could find in the Remington archives at that time. He appended a photocopy of an "old book that summarizes the military production of various Remington plants during World War II." This old book read:

"Kings Mills"

"Beginning late in 1940, the facilities of the company's Kings Mills Works come under consideration by the U. S. Ordnance Department, British Purchasing Commission, and other agencies. Various plans for military production were discussed and several engineering studies made. Finally, in the fall of 1941, the Ordnance Department decided to proceed with a proposal, previously suggested by Remington for caliber .45 manufacture....

"One of the plant's significant contributions was adoption of the "Record of Performance" plan (ROP) to military production. This plan, which originated at Kings Mills in 1938, is designed to measure productivity and achieve a more effective use of personnel in each operation. The Ordnance Department was much interested and full information was sent to other facilities."

The balance of this article reads almost identically to the quotation from Sharpe above. It may be from *In Abundance And On Time*, a Remington booklet.

Dietz also sent me a photocopy of a page from *Remington Arms*

in American History, by Alden Hatch. It offers the following:

"...The next step in rounding out Remington production was the purchase of the Peters Cartridge Company in May, 1934. Peters had been an honorable rival of Remington ever since G. M. Peters founded it in 1887. ...

"When Remington had bought the company it had fallen on evil days like so many of its competitors, but the plant was up-to-date and the operation was efficient. More important still, as later events proved, was the acquisition of Peters' skilled workers, many of whom lived in the model village of Kings Mills, and the well-trained executive personnel, many of whom became invaluable to Remington.

"Among valuable men who came to Remington from Peters were Bernard E. Stroder who became Vice President and Director of Sales; Dewey Godfrey who became Assistant Director of Sales and was later elevated to Vice President and Director of Sales, and top production men such as Charley Green, Roy Holden and Harvey Hackman."

The reason for bringing this out is that Harold Himes reported in *A History of Miami Land*, that back at the beginning of the war, *"Charles M. Green, the former Manager of the Peters Plant, was promoted to Director of Production, responsible for the operation of* [Remington operated] *Ordnance Plants, which at their peak, employed over 50.000. He was a good manager of people, material and processes."*

Himes further states that "...Remington Arms Company rented one floor of the Brown Palace Hotel in Denver [still there in 1997 and still *the* place to stay] to be used by transfers, and the many specialists visiting the plant to assist in the start-up [of the Denver Ordnance Plant]. This is a partial list of Peters employees who worked day and night to put the production lines in motion:

"Pargal La Mar - a specialist on the bullet assembly machine, perhaps one of the most complex on the production line.

"Ernest Moon - a specialist in the manufacture of tools and dies.

"Frank Wilson - a self-made mechanical engineering genius, who was noted for repairing any mechanical device and devising ways to keep machinery running efficiently.

"Percy Bolmer - a specialist with a talent for putting the right people in the right job.

"Bill Bowyer - prepared a training manual on the manufacture of small arms ammunition. It became the textbook for thousands of supervisors who had never been in a cartridge plant prior to this time. His manual helped to train over 50,000 employees to manufacture millions [billions!] of rounds of small arms ammunition. The backgrounds of these (new plant) employees were quite varied. There were cowboys, and cowgirls, store clerks, auto mechanics, waitresses, and wives of service men, who wanted to help in the war effort."

The Paso Del Norte Gun Collectors Inc., El Paso, Texas published a brochure on the .30 Carbine. The brochure had the following to offer on the cartridge and carbine:

"Federal Stock Number - RA Pd 10666

Overall length - 1.68 in

Weight of Ball Cartridge - 193 grains

Weight of Bullet - 111 grains

Muzzle Velocity - 2000 ft per second

Pressure in Chamber per square inch maximum - 40,000 lbs

Cost to U. S. Government - 2.1 cents each

"The M1 carbine was first used in battle during the invasion of North Africa in November of 1942." They list Sicily, Tarawa, New Britain, Burma, D-Day, Battle of the Bulge and Okinawa as some of the campaigns in which the carbine was used.

Sharpe's history of the development of the .30 carbine is the most interesting narration of that story I have seen. The interested reader is referred the story as told in his book *The Rifle in America*. It is not in his first edition; it is in the third; I don't know about the second edition.

All of this is to show that Peters had an impact far beyond the limits of Warren County. But what about the situation at KMOP itself? As we have seen, KMOP was the combination of the old Peters works and a new building–or, more accurately, building complex.

A plot of ground was purchased by the government at the top of the hill thirteen hundred feet south of the main works and 136 feet higher.

As far as utilities were concerned, it was decided to use steam from the old Peters power plant. This was a coal-fired (stoker) facility with a battery of Babcock and Wilcox boilers that had produced the steam-generated electricity at the old plant. The boilers fed two high-speed Buckeye reciprocating steam engines and one Rice and Sargent Corliss-style engine. There was excess steam capacity available. Therefore, 125-psi steam was piped above ground to the new site through a 6-inch line. The steam sent to the Ordnance plant was used there for process heat such as primer drying, comfort heat, producing hot water for showers, etc.

Evidently there was not enough electrical capacity from the old plant to serve the new ordnance plant. Electricity was obtained from the local utility. An emergency gasoline-powered generator was part of the ordnance plant.

Potable water, supplied to the new plant through an 8-inch line, was obtained from wells and chlorinated onsite. Water for firefighting was supplied from a storage pond between the new and the old plant. The fire water pump was steam turbine-driven from a branch of the steam line

This is .30 Carbine ammunition. The top right and bottom left cases are of steel. The others are brass. Note the old "PCCO" head stamp of WWI has given way to a simple "PC". There are no periods after the initials.

supplying the new plant. There were two above-ground water storage tanks at the ordnance plant: one for potable water and one for fire-fighting water.

Sewage treatment was provided for both domestic waste and Polnol waste. The Polnol was from the tracer mix, or the tracer igniter. As revised, this plant supplied tracer ammunition for the carbine as well as ball ammunition.

The new facility had its own employee examination room, clock house, change (shower) rooms (2), main manufacturing building, primer manufacturing house, tracer mixing house, tracer igniter house, ballistic range house, ammunition storage house, office building, and cafeteria. All were separated from each other. The main manufacturing building alone covered about 100,000 square feet [equal to a building 30 feet wide and well over a half mile long, although it was not configured that way].

The facility had a large system of bunkers with barricades to safely store priming mixture and chemicals as well as tracer materials, plus miscellaneous storage sheds. All of this was in a rectangular plot of ground 1,300 ft. by 1,450 ft.–slightly over 43 acres. The buildings were connected by covered outside

walkways and service roads. The perimeter fence featured what look like guard towers at the corners.

Anyone familiar with World War II construction would know there were a lot of relatively non-strategic materials used in the ordnance plant construction; wood, concrete and brick chief among them. Still, a staggering amount of steel for piping, nails, tanks and fencing - and copper for wiring - was necessary.

The design and specifications on all drawings were reviewed. Three or four signatures were required for 'official' drawings. *All* prints–not the original tracing, but the individual prints themselves–had to be signed off by the proper official. This was an extraordinary and time-consuming control step. It looks like the U.S. Corps of Engineers did the construction work, or supervised it. Some of the signatories on surviving prints in my possession were C. L. Holden, G. Mackey, Q. V. du Pont and others. On most of them, W. V. Luck, AIO, signed for the Ordnance Department.

It may be of interest that Captain Luck, the first resident

CAPT. W. V. LUCK

Captain Luck was the Ordnance Department's official representative. Peters Primer, *a Peters publication.*

These are extremely rare official Army Signal Corps photos of the KMOP operation. Under normal circumstances, no cameras were allowed in the plant due to wartime security concerns. None of the workers are identified.

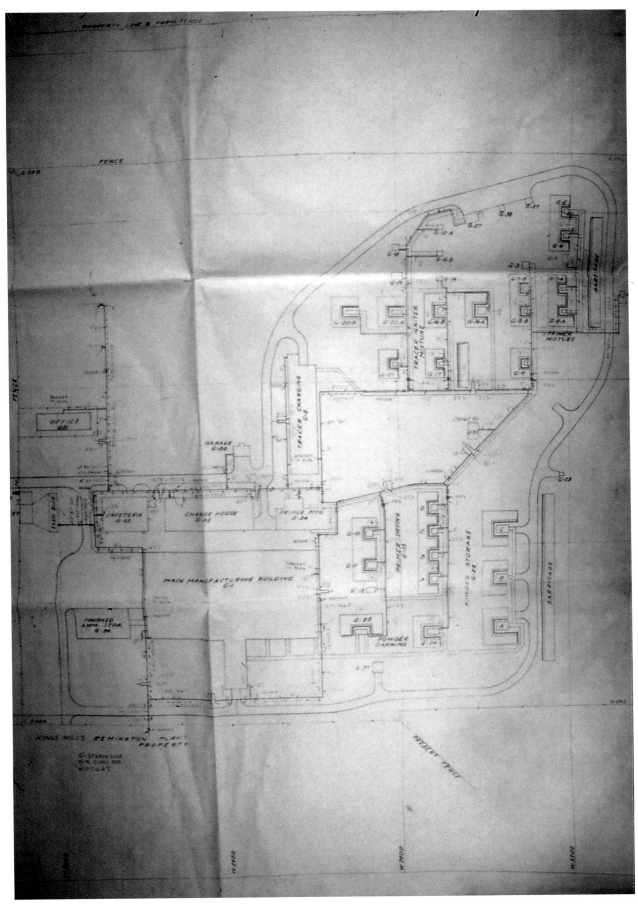

KMOP plant layout.

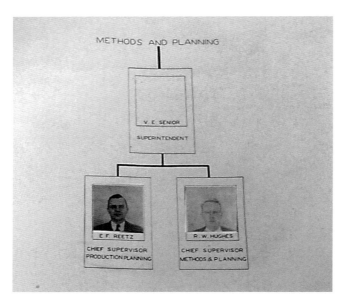

Ordnance officer, was a relative of Ahimaaz King's wife; Holden had been plant manager at Peters. There were two Holdens associated with Peters; this one was the father.

J. Maag signed the print showing a revision of the layout of the loading presses at the ordnance plant on January 16, 1943.

J. Q. du Pont was a Du Pont engineer sent to do "punch list" items as the ordnance plant construction finished up. He was later reassigned to Tennessee and became part of the development of the well-known Manhattan Project that developed the atomic bomb.

There were said to be 5,000 people employed in Kings Mills during the war. Maybe 1,000 worked for King Powder, and another 1,000 at the old works. This would leave about 3,000 working at the new ordnance plant.

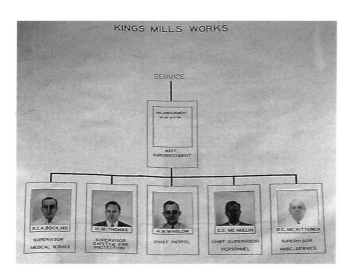

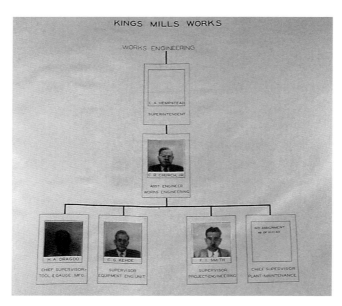

These are original organization charts of KMOP. Jim Rodgers does not appear since he had long since joined the Navy. This was dated 11-1-43.

George Kass collection.

Where did they all come from?

As in the past, the local towns: Mason, Morrow, Lebanon, South Lebanon, Foster, Brecon and many crossroads places we never heard of supplied many workers. Long before WWII, the traction line had ceased to exist (1903-1922) and passenger service on the railroad was not what it had been. Therefore, busses came in from Hamilton and Cincinnati, picking up from points in between. There had to be mass transit and car-pooling because there simply was not room to park the automobiles.

For the convenience of the employees, the company provided a bus, which ran every fifteen minutes over the mile or so from the old plant to the new. Shotgun shells, used for training machine gunners, were produced in the old plant on preexisting machinery. The old plant also did supplemental work for the new ordnance plant. Blueprints dated 1942 and 1943 in my possession indicate that machine shop floor space and bullet-making were among the support resources provided by the old plant to KMOP.

There are photos of the guard force lined up in front of the flagpole to receive an award. There must have been fifty guards in the photo! John Murphy, a friend, was one of them. John reported that FBI personnel would occasionally test their security. It was with no little amusement that John reported that an agent once got in all right, but couldn't get back out!

As you would expect, both plants ran around the clock during this period. There is no lack of testimonial for the quality of their product. The Army-Navy "E" was awarded them for quality and quantity of production.

With the accolades of a grateful and much-relieved nation still ringing in their ears, the ordnance plant was shut down on March 3, 1944! It is hard to imagine both plants were

closed at this time; the war still had nearly a year and a half to run its course. It can be supposed that the ability, know-how and dedication of the Peters management and workers allowed this to be so.

In eloquent testimony to this thought, Admiral Yamamoto, the Japanese Navy architect of the Pearl Harbor attack, is said to have remarked after that infamous attack: *"We have awakened a sleeping giant and*

filled him with a terrible resolve."

After examining the evidence, I believe Remington's boast of *In Abundance And On Time* was appropriate. I also believe that a disproportionate share of the credit was due the Peters plant and the quality, dedication and hard work of Peters personnel. Plenty of Americans were filled with resolve, but not many were in a position to do as much about it as were many of the Peters

ARMY MEN HIGHLY PRAISE KINGS MILLS AMMUNITION

Lt. Hollis B. Hale, former employee of the Kings Mills Ordnance Plant, now is in charge of the Rifle Range at Jefferson barracks, Missouri.

As part of his responsibility, he makes regular report to the War department on the efficiency of the ammunition used on the range. He is, therefore, an accepted authority in determining the value of the work which has been done by the employees of the Kings Mills Ordnance Plant.

In a recent letter to Robert F. Rothrock, Jr., assistant editor of the PRIMER, Lt. Hale said:

Dear Bob,—

Have just received another copy of the PRIMER. I enjoy reading every edition and want to thank Remington Arms Co., Inc., for sending me the publication. Although I was with the Company only a short time I know many employees and receipt of your publication makes me feel I still am part of the organization.

I am in charge of the Rifle range here. We are using .30 carbine ammunition. It is necessary that I make detailed report on the efficiency of every lot of ammunition used on the range. I'm always glad when we receive a lot made by the Kings Mills Ordnance Plant. The ammunition we get from Remington is tops. There are less misfires than any other we use.

Only on one occasion have I found a bad lot. Lately we have bene receiving quite a bit from another factory which uses the steel case instead of brass. You should see some of the reports that go in.

To give you an idea of the amount of ammunition we use every month, about 9000 men use the range in that time. You readily can see that a few hangfires and

misfires can slow us down. Then, too, faulty ammunition causes broken ejectors and extractors on the pieces.

So I wish all ammunition that we get would be marked "PC43" on the case and our troubles would be over.

Give my regards to all and Merry Christmas.

Lt. Hollis B. Hale.

Robert Cornett, son of Virgil Cornett of maintenance, now in training at Keesler field, reports that his outfit has been cited for proficiency in the use of the carbine.

The citation reads:

"(1) It has come to my attention that the men of squadron 584, Class 119, have qualified 100% with the U. S. Carbine Cal. .30M1 at Firing Center No. 2, Basic Training No. 2.

"(2) Class 119 is the first class to qualify 100% of its men. Therefore it is desired that they be highly commended for this.

"(3) With the spirit, team-work and ability to receive instructions that this class has shown, these men will be an asset to any command in which they may serve.

(Signed) William J. Hanlon,
Col., Air Corps,
Commanding."

There can be no doubt of the importance attached to efficient use of the Carbine Caliber .30M1 in U. S. Military operations. The success of the weapon lies not with the men who are using it but with the men and women who are making the ammunition which it fires. That seems to leave the proposition strictly up to us.

Testimonials about KMOP production.   The Primer, *a Peters publication.*

personnel. These key people were in a position to channel much of the resolve of many ordinary citizens into the production of countless rounds of small arms ammunition...*and they did just that!*

Epilogue

After March of 1944, the new ordnance plant building was taken over by Delco Remy, contractors to the Navy for landing boat parts. This information came from Steve McDowell who worked in Stores/Receiving for KMOP down in the old plant during the war and later went "Up the Hill" to work for Delco after the ordnance plant was closed. According to Lillian Sackett, who still lives at the top of Magazine Hill, the company made starting motors for landing boat engines. In later years, this same facility was used for storage of government materiel and a Military Reserve facility.

Today, nearly half of the main manufacturing building has been razed—and it still has lots of unused space. Sergeant Foster kindly allowed me to wander through it. The old cafeteria has been abandoned and the roof has fallen in. A newer administration building for military personnel has been erected near the plant entrance. The access road now is host to a new potable water treatment facility for that general area. A new generation of military "weekend warriors" (Army Reserve personnel) now use it, little suspecting the drama that took place a half century gone.

Recently, it was reported that beaver had taken up residence in a creek bed near the old ordnance plant. Building a dam, the beaver(s) had made a nice pond for themselves in a short time. What with guards and the FBI running around, this would have been unheard of in this busy place fifty years ago. On the other hand, the goings-on in the Kings Mills Ordnance Plant some half-century ago, are about as strange-sounding to the area residents of today!

Chapter 7

Explosions at The King Powder Company

BOTH KING POWDER and Peters Cartridge handled flammable and explosive materials on a daily basis. However, it was at King Powder that the bulk of the explosions and injuries took place. At Peters, the most hazardous material was priming compound but the quantity was quite small–measured in pounds–and only one person was exposed to the most hazardous operations. Other hazardous materials at Peters were confined to small lots and treated, stored and handled carefully. But across the river at King there were literally hundreds of pounds of powder, sometimes tons. Any explosion there was likely to be of some magnitude. Powder manufacture involves using lots of mechanical energy and heat. In spite of strict safety rules, no foolproof methods for preventing these accidents have been found.

In most such accidents the evidence was destroyed, or too widely scattered to interpret. In addition, the workman on duty was often no longer able to bear witness to what happened. There must have been some temptation, after a fruitless investigation, to assume the worker violated some safety stricture and to then go on with business, more or less as usual.

In general, the wheel mills and structures were separated far enough to assure that one mill's explosion would not communicate to another. This evidently did not always work out as intended. Perhaps burning embers rained down on another area where they "found" powder. However, separating mills was effective to the point that there does not seem to have been any explosion that involved

the destruction of more than four of King's powder mills or structures (1890 explosion excepted).

Beyond the above precaution, King constructed and used its own narrow-gauge railroad within the powder plant. Powder was moved from one operation to another using four-wheeled cars, which ran on rails. A horse or mule supplied the motive power. These animals were shod with bronze, using copper nails. The rails themselves were iron. The wheels that ran on the rails were of brass. These materials, with the exception of the iron, were considered non-sparking.

Edna Bowyer says that the company grazed sheep over the

powder property to keep the grass down. This allowed the vegetation to be controlled without resorting to the use of mowers and scythes, which might strike a spark. Revenue could also be realized from the sale of wool and sheep. This likely counterbalanced any expense for tending the sheep.

Powder workers were not allowed to wear shoes made with steel nails or shanks. Naturally, smoking and matches were strictly forbidden anywhere near the powder line. The possession of matches would result in the miscreant being fired on the spot. The buildings themselves were made of flimsy wood with metal roofs, and painted red.

While some foreshortening makes these mills appear closer than they really were, the separation of the mills and their flimsy construction is clear. The millrace is on the left and the river, parallel to it, out of sight on the right. Photo taken from the main bridge approach. *Cincinnati Historical Society.*

RULES AND REGULATIONS

FOR THE WORKS OF

THE KING POWDER CO.

1. THE MANAGER shall have the direct charge of the Plant, through the Superintendents and Foremen of the various departments.

2. A DAY'S WORK shall be nine hours, commencing at 6:30 A. M. and closing at 4:30 P. M., with an intermission of one hour at noon, with the exception that powder men will be permitted to leave their work after 3 P. M. provided they have cleaned up their mill and leave it in a condition satisfactory to their foreman, *as per article No. 8.*

3. ALL EMPLOYEES are required to be at their respective places of work promptly at the times fixed for beginning, and are to look to the Foreman for instructions connected with their work.

4. WHEEL-MILL MEN are not to be governed by Rule 2, but are to work twelve hours per day, commencing at midnight and working until noon, commencing at noon and working until midnight, each taking his turn as assigned by his Foreman.

5. EMPLOYEES WORKING IN POWDER are not allowed to wear boots or shoes with nails or metal pegs, nor are they permitted to carry matches or to smoke anywhere in the neighborhood of the Mills.

6. CAUTION AND DILIGENCE are required at all times of employees while on duty, and any one engaged in night-work, who shall lie down or sleep while on duty, shall be subject to immediate discharge.

7. EMPLOYEES HAVING CHARGE OF MACHINERY must keep strict watch and care of same, and particularly examine every part to see that the bearings are well oiled and in proper condition before starting.

8. BEFORE LEAVING WORK every mill-man must see to it that his respective mill is cleaned up and in good order, at the close of the day's work.

9. REPAIRS ON MILLS shall not be made by a powder man, nor shall he be permitted to take tools into a mill for that purpose.

10. ON CLOSING DOWN A MILL for repairs during the day or night, the man in charge must at once notify his Foreman.

11. TRANSPORTATION OF MATERIAL by teamster and truck men, will be handled on special orders from the team Foreman.

12. ABSENCE FROM DUTY shall not be allowed any employee without permission from his Foreman.

13. VISITORS are not allowed along the line of the Works unless accompanied by an officer of the Company, or by written permission from the President or Manager. Employees are not allowed to conduct their friends through the Works except by permission. All employees are especially requested to prevent all strangers from approaching the Mills or trespassing on the property, and are earnestly requested to assist the Management in the enforcement of this rule.

14. INTOXICATING LIQUORS of any kind are not permitted on the premises of the Company.

15. WHEN AN ACCIDENT OCCURS and an alarm is given, every employee having machinery in charge must immediately stop and secure same, and all employees except powder men must at once hasten to the scene of the accident, place themselves under the direction of some one in authority and render every possible assistance. Coolness and absolute subjection to authority are all important on such an occasion.

16. PAY DAYS will be on the 5th and 20th of each month, or on the day following, when either of those days falls on Sunday. All disbursements and adjustments of accounts will be made at the office of the Company.

17. ALL EMPLOYEES are POSITIVELY PROHIBITED from VISITING other operations or mills than those wherein they are assigned to DUTY. Truckmen transporting materials from one building to another, will handle same expeditiously and not visit at either end of the trip with the men in charge of the operating mills. This rule must be carefully observed, as we must depend upon the assistance and co-operation of all employees to make the work as safe as possible.

GEORGE G. KING, President
R. A. KING, Manager

Kings Mills, Ohio, July 1, 1922.

The Work Rules give more than a hint of the dangers involved in powder making.

Courtesy of Bob and Betty Carter.

The men were not allowed to wear shoes with steel nails or shanks in them and the horses and mules were shod with brass or bronze shoes held on with copper nails. These were from the King Powder stores department.

Photo: Schiffer.
Shoe courtesy of
Edna Bowyer.

The flimsy construction provided little resistance to an explosion. This allowed the blast to expend most of its energy on the atmosphere. A rigid structure might provide lethal missiles and cause the explosion to raise pressures within the building before the structure yielded. Flimsy construction tended to favor survival of any hapless employee within, or anywhere near, the structure. Further, it was easier, faster and cheaper to replace. The heavy wheel mills themselves were seldom damaged, beyond the wooden curbing around the bedplate or other easily-replaced items.

The wheel mills were not the only places where explosions took place but they had more than their share. Corning, glazing, packaging and other areas came in for their share of grief, too. Unlike wheel mills, the machinery in some of these structures seems to have suffered more from an explosion because of lighter construction.

The buildings were illuminated by electricity, in later years, by placing a light source *outside* the structure, and having the light shine in through a window. As mentioned, no small pains were taken to avoid any source of sparks. In addition, controls located outside the building allowed workers to shut

down a wheel mill *before* entering.

The worker then went to a designated safe place while the mills were running, or else serviced a different mill, which was shut down.

The wheel mills were charged with the powder-making components. While these materials were initially not very —if at all—explosive, intimate mixing, or *incorporation* as it was called (in the wheel mills), transformed it into an explosive. Generally, unincorporated powder in the mills would not explode; it would be more likely to fiercely burn and sputter like a firecracker fuze. As incorporation progressed, the powder became potentially more dangerous. This was because of loss of moisture in addition to being more intimately mixed.

When a wheel mill had incorporated powder for the allotted time (perhaps two hours for blasting powder; four for sporting powder) it was shut down from outside, and the operator entered and shoveled the incorporated powder from the mill with a wooden shovel. The semi-finished powder was loaded into a horse- or mule-drawn car

and pulled along the track to the next operation. The explosive force of the mix in a mill was in some proportion to the degree of incorporation, or intimate mixing.

When an electrical storm approached, the worker was to shut down the mill and go to a safe area. Lightning could initiate an explosion. In response to the specific question during an interview with Joseph Warren King (II) in 1985, he indicated that placing lightning rods around a given area seemed to reduce the number of explosions within the area.

Reports read that witnesses saw bodies hurled some distance into the air by the explosion. Others speculated this could not be, since the worker would not have been on top of the exploding powder, but beside it. The following explosion did not take place at King's, but is the best description I have seen of the type of explosion we are talking about.

In his *History of the Confederate Powder Works*, Col. (General) George W. Rains gave a vivid verbal description of the only fatal explosion at that works in the course of manufacturing the 2,750,000 pounds of the same kinds of powder that King was manufacturing. General Rains said:

"There was a temporary structure about one hundred yards from the permanent building, on the opposite side of the canal; this after a use of some months, exploded with about three tons of gunpowder.

"The explosion was heavy, shaking the earth for some distance, and throwing up a convolving column of white smoke five hundred feet in height. It was composed of a series of confused masses of smoke and heated air revolving in vertical planes with extraordinary velocity, through which the flames flashed outwards in all directions; this

was followed by the thundering sound of the explosion, which vibrated the air for a mile around, and was heard within the limits of the city.

*There were seven men in the structure, a sentinel outside and a boy with a mule in a shed adjoining. The bodies of the seven men and the boy, with the debris, were carried up with the ascending column, and by its revolving action, reduced to small fragments and dispersed; the sentinel was killed by the shock, but his body was not otherwise disturbed. A growth of small pines surrounded the place, which effectually intercepted the lateral flying fragments; in fact the force of the explosion **did not extend outside the diameter of 100 feet** [emphasis the writer's], but within that area the trees were destroyed and the space where the structure stood was ploughed up, and nothing remained. At the time there was no work being done, as the workmen were awaiting the arrival of the boat with the mill cake. The careful foreman, Gibson, had been called away, and probably the accident happened from matches falling on the floor, as it had been found impossible to prevent their use by the workmen, for smoking, when off duty."*

Explosions at the King Powder Company usually involved less than the three tons of powder talked of by General Raines. The stage of completion of the powder, as well as the quantity and degree of confinement, affected the force of the explosion.

Stephen McDowell, who worked at the Peters Cartridge Company, noted in the Enquirer article quoted earlier, that: *"Once in the early '30s I was walking to school when I saw a man flying through the air before I heard the explosion"* says McDowell. *"Blew him clear across the river. The explosion looked like the sun coming out of the hill side."*

Black powder is considered to be a low explosive. That is to say,

the velocity or rate of propagation of the explosion is much lower than that of a high explosive. The term used is *deflagration* in talking of the burning of black powder. A high explosive (nitroglycerine, ammonium nitrate, picric acid Dynamite, etc.) is said to *detonate*. The velocity at which detonation progresses is many times the deflagration rate of black powder

There is, however, some evidence that—under unique conditions—black powder might detonate. This may be related to the amount involved and the containment. Those who would say this is impossible have not likely been in the position of having to explain the unexplainable!

Where large quantities of black powder are concerned, sympathetic explosions at a site considered remote from the initial explosion, and other phenomena commonly associated with detonation, have been reported. Similar, but rare, events have been noted in the usage of smokeless powder in cartridge firearms. Theories abound. There are many questions the experts have not answered satisfactorily.

At the King Powder Company, explosions were not rare. An analysis of the situation might well show many explosions were associated with personnel not familiar with powder manufacture. It was common in wartime that demand would increase, the labor pool (particularly men) would decrease and there would be an influx of inexperienced workers in the trade.

The King family "always sought to do their duty" by those killed or maimed in an explosion. This took many forms. The funeral expenses were paid for, but other—perhaps more subtle—things were done. It was sometimes seen to that a surviving widow got the job as post master in Kings Mills. Or, perhaps, an injured worker no

longer able to perform ordinary work would be given a job, waiving the usual requirements for being able-bodied.

The U.S. government was called in, or came in, to investigate many of the explosions on the supposition they might have been caused by foreign agents. Aside from a single incident during the Spanish American War, I do not know of any such final determination. During that episode, a stranger (not identified) was found badly burned in a nearby barn after an explosion. He lived long enough to speak in a foreign tongue. As in most cases of an explosion, you are left with little besides your imagination to determine what really happened.

The following happened during WWI and is from the August 21, 1917, edition of the *Cincinnati Enquirer:*

*"**EXPLOSION***

Blast at Powder Plant Planned 'Tis Said.

Plotter at Kings Mills May Have Perished.

Employee Seen near to Burning Tramcar. Tons of Explosives Detonate, Causing Havoc For Miles

---Federal Investigation To Be Made.

Federal authorities will investigate circumstances leading to the explosion yesterday of four tons of blasting powder in grinding mills of the King Powder Company, Kings Mills, Ohio. Four men were killed instantly, their bodies blown to atoms and one man was injured seriously.

The shock of three separate explosions was felt in a radius of 20 miles. Windows in the village were shattered. Trees were blown to the ground and foliage stripped from them. At Fosters Crossing, five miles away, houses shook upon their foundations.

Conversation of employees of the powder company centers upon one man, an alien. He had been employed in the mills but three days. His residence is not known to residents of Kings Mills and he gave no name of relative to be notified in case of accident. If he was responsible for the explosion, he sacrificed his life in a plot which cost the lives of other men. Those killed were Alvie Joseph, 50 years old, 726 west Eighth Street, Cincinnati, Ohio; T. M. Mc Donald, 58 years old, New Albany, Indiana; Frank Howell, 30 years old, Gracy, Alabama; and Rudolph August, James H. Owens, 27 years old, Athens, Ala., was seriously injured. William Cornet, Kings Mills Ohio, escaped with minor injuries. ...

"August and William Cornet, Kings Mills, were employed in hauling a carload of powder, possibly one ton, from the press house to the granulating mill. Cornet was driving a mule hitched to a car along a small tramway. He heard a scratching sound and turned to see August sitting on the back of the car, which just was beginning to burn. Realizing the danger, he leaped from the car, rolling down the bank near the track just as the first explosion occurred. August made no attempt to escape, though he probably had more time than Cornet, for he was sitting directly behind the compartment where the fire started.

The tramway cars are approximately 12 feet long.

Flames from the first blast caused powder in a grinding mill to explode. Here Alvie Joseph and T. M. Mc Donald were killed and the small building was wrecked. Both men were working in the building where the powder and ingredients are ground beneath massive wheels. Neither man had a chance to escape.

The second explosion caused a similar effect in a press mill where the powder is subjected to a hydraulic pressure of [several thousand] pounds and molded into cakes. Frank Howell was killed and James Owens seriously injured in the blast.

Howell, according to R. A. King, was in the press mill visiting Owens. Howell's position with the company did not compel him to subject himself to danger. He had gone into the mill along the powder line without permission of officials.

Both Cornet and the mule which was drawing the powder car escaped injury. The animal was blown many yards down an embankment into a small stream which serves as a mill race along the line of buildings. The mills are built along the millrace for nearly three miles. The isolation is made to avoid large explosions and casualties.

The destructive force of an explosion can be roughly gauged by the hole in the ground. Too often, that was the evidence still recognizable. Upon seeing this photo, David Spencer, head of Detonite maintenance at KICO, said the deep hole seen here was made by Detonite.

Bob and Betty Carter.

Some explosions did not leave this much evidence. This is what remains of a powder buggy. Note the wheels still on the rails and the leaking steam line (*middle right*). A sharp eye will see a sheep grazing against the far fence just to the right of the left-hand post.

Bob and Betty Carter.

Employees of the powder company and the Peters Cartridge Company which adjoins the powder mills, ceased all work and hurried to the wrecked buildings. Large clouds of white smoke rose from the valley. Women and children from the town, whose husbands and brothers were employed in the powder mills, hurried to the place. Anxiously they awaited the announcement of the names of those men killed and injured.

Officials of the company declare none of the men killed had a family.

Bodies of the men killed were carried into the emergency hospital. Dr. Withman, Kings Mills was on the scene immediately. He directed his labor to saving the life of James Owens.

Owen's wife, who was living in the Homestead Hotel, became hysterical when told of the injury

to her husband. He was carried in the hotel. Physicians despair of saving his life.

Coroner ...of Lebanon, Ohio hurried to the place. He will cooperate with officials in investigating circumstances surrounding the explosion.

Windows were broken in the Peters Cartridge Company plant.

In the office of the King Powder Company, the glass was hurled across the room in tiny splinters. Transoms and window frames were blown inward. Farther within the village, the vacuum of the explosion caused the windows to be blown outward.

R. A. King declared the warm weather, which permitted windows to be open, saved many dwellings from loss of windowpanes. The windows in the public library were shattered.

For several months, a company of Third Regiment soldiers had been guarding the powder plant

and the Peters Cartridge Company. During their stay on the grounds there were no explosions and only trivial accidents.

When the Third Regiment was ordered away all guards were withdrawn from the plant. The explosion yesterday followed. It is believed the Government will be requested to place another detail of soldiers at the place.

Work in the unit of five mills will be stopped for five days, during which time the new buildings will be built and machinery placed in working order. The damage to the property is estimated by Mr. King at $5000.

The bodies of the four men were forwarded to Lebanon, Ohio."

The follow-up the next day:
"BLAST
Claims Another Victim.
Fifth Employee of Powder Factory Dies of Burns

Explosions which Monday rocked the country for miles around Kings Mills, Ohio and devastated a sector of the powder line of the King Powder Company, yesterday claimed a fifth victim in James Harry Owens, Athens Alabama

Owens died at Good Samaritan Hospital at 1:30 o'clock yesterday afternoon. He was burned from head to foot when enveloped in flame from detonated powder, which swept the hydraulic press room, where Owens was working. The press mill was shattered in the third and last of three explosions which originated in a tram car loaded with blasting powder. Owens was the only one of the five to die as a result of the Kings Mills explosion who was married. His widow has been living at the Homestead Hotel. Owens was taken to Good Samaritan Hospital Wednesday night, being brought from Kings Mills by train. At that time it was feared he would not recover. Relatives announced yesterday his body would be forwarded to Athens for burial. Whether accident or design of plotters was responsible for the Kings Mills explosion probably will never be known, it was conceded yesterday.

Searching investigation by officials of the King Powder Company, cooperating with Warren County officials failed to develop substantial conformation of "plot" theories advanced by officials of the company Wednesday. The force of the blast was sufficient to obliterate any circumstantial evidence, if such existed, it was said.

George G. King, president of the King Powder Company, said he was inclined to the belief that the explosion was accidental.

Mr. King and Prosecuter Stanley of Warren County, were in conference yesterday afternoon with Calvin S. Weakley Special Agent of the United States Department of Justice, and United States Attorney Stuart R. Bolin. Results of the investigation of Warren County and company

officials were laid before the Federal Agents.

As a consequence it was said investigation by Federal authorities probably would not be pushed further.

Activities of the King Powder Company in filling Government orders was uninterrupted yesterday. Little trace of the havoc wrought by the three explosions existed yesterday other than shattered window glass and debris from the two company shacks used as grinding and press houses.

Company officials said the explosion, affecting only one small unit of the three mile long chain of powder houses, [had little effect] on the shipment of powder.

It is understood that no request for guards for the powder company's property will be made of the Government. Company officials believe their private guards to be ample protection.

Following investigation yesterday by the County Coroner H. E. Dilatush released the bodies of the four men whose lives were snuffed out instantly.

The bodies [of three of them] were claimed by relatives. That of Rudolph August, address unknown to authorities, will be buried by the King Powder Company.

Witnesses examined by the

Coroner Dilatush yesterday said that August told fellow workers the morning of the day he was killed that he intended to quit his position that night.

Witnesses declared August said he was a German. [!]

These two articles are quoted nearly in their entirety because of the many facets of the explosion issue touched.

Fred Schwietert grew up in Kings Mills and states that his father worked on the King powder line in the 1930s. He was working in the corning mill with a coworker, who was sweeping up when his father left for the day. A subsequent explosion killed his father's friend. His father immediately quit the powder line. There are any number of

This is Fred Schwietert's father when he was working on the powder line in the 1930s. He is standing on the King Powder Company's bridge over the Little Miami River. You can see the rail of the tramway linking the mills to Middletown Junction, the shipping/receiving point on the railroad. The King Powder Company dam is not far above this bridge. *Fred Schwietert.*

similar anecdotes regarding near misses and concerning the gruesome task of locating the bodies and body parts.

During WWII, a similar event on July 30, 1942 claimed five lives. On December 11, 1942, in the *Cincinnati Times Star* of the following day, we note the following:

Kings Mills Blast Takes the Life of Second Brother.
Another victim planned to be married Saturday.

The brother of a man killed in a similar fashion last July and a prospective bridegroom were listed as dead Saturday following the latest explosion at the King Powder Company plant, Kings Mills, O. in which five other men were injured, one seriously.

The victims were Hugh Abner, 32, South Lebanon, O. and John Hacker, 26, Kings Mills, O.

Abner's brother, Sid Abner, 33, South Lebanon, was one of five men killed in a blast at the plant July 30, in which 11 men were injured. Hacker had planned to be married on Saturday, acquaintances said

An investigation into the second blast at the plant in three days was under way by the local FBI office and the Explosives Safety Branch of the Army Ordnance Department in Chicago. The injured were Turner Harrison, 50, Kings Mills, seriously burned; Amos Johnson, 35, South Lebanon, back injury; Frank Noe, 26, Kings Mills, perforated ear drum; Clarence Baker, 40, South Lebanon, leg injury; and Webb Pancake, leg injury. He is a powder line foreman.

All the injured were treated at Blair Hospital, Lebanon. All except Harrison were sent home. His condition was reported as somewhat improved.

The blast occurred late Friday when the corning mill and separator building exploded a few minutes after Harrison and Pancake had been in it.

When Harrison and Pancake heard the corning mill blow up, they started running. They had

not traveled more than a few feet when the separator building also exploded.

Harrison's clothing was set on fire but his life was saved when Pancake threw him in a tub of water extinguishing flames.

The two buildings where the blasts occurred were approximately 20 x 40 feet. They were surrounded by earthwork to cushion the effect of a blast and save other buildings in the vicinity.

A cause for the explosion of the extent of damage could not be immediately determined. It was reported that 5,000 pounds of powder went up, although no confirmation could be obtained.

On Wednesday, [three days previous] 600 pounds of powder blew up although no one was injured.

Three persons were killed in a explosion at the plant Aug. 7, 1940.

Lt. A. C. Smith, Ohio Highway Patrolman, reported that the force of the Friday explosion was felt at Sabina, O., 40 miles northeast of Kings Mills. At Clarksville, O., 20 miles northeast, the blast was reported to have been felt as severely as the one in July. Washington Court House also was aware of the explosion indicating that the full force traveled north.

An undated clipping found in the Warren County Historical Society files undoubtedly refers to an event that occurred in August 1944. The newspaper is unknown. The clipping says:

A series of four explosions at 12:30 am last Thursday killed Woodrow Cornett, 26, and destroyed four buildings of the King Powder co at Kings Mills. The explosions were felt as far away as Centerville and Cincinnati. Houses in Lebanon, Morrow, Mason, South Lebanon and other nearby communities were rocked violently.

Cornett was the only person at work at the scene of the explosions, other men having gone home at Midnight. Driving a horse and cart, he had been

going from mill to mill to check on grinding operations.

The first explosion was muffled. It was followed rapidly by three very loud jarring blasts, which persons 15 miles away said were accompanied by flashes rising high in the air.

Two grinding mills, a powder press and a stock house were destroyed.

The horse which Cornett had been driving, and which was standing outside the mill in which the first explosion took place was uninjured except for having its hair singed slightly.

A friction spark resulting from a foreign substance in the powder was believed to have caused the first explosion.

There were more accidents and more serious ones during wartime, without doubt because of the influx of inexperienced workers. Manpower was in short supply and recruiters went to remote areas to get workers for the mills.

It has been said that some of the recruited workers did not know what hazards awaited them. I find it hard to believe that even the most callous management would knowingly allow this. Even if the company had no regard for life, the loss of powder, production and profit would dictate otherwise. I can, however, believe that some workers would not believe the hazards were as serious as the foremen made out.

It has been said by a firm with a far larger database than my own, that 93 percent of all lost-time accidents are because of unsafe acts, such as failure to follow established procedures, leaving items to be tripped over, etc.

At a safety training session conducted by the DuPont Co. some years ago, I asked why that company (about 1972) divested themselves of the last black powder plant in the U.S. After all, black powder had brought them into the chemical business and was their pride for over a century. Their answer was simple

know why. Anyway they said he was Russian and you couldn't understand him when he talked...That is as much as I know about that.

"They sent different ones over here. Of course we down there in the shop wouldn't have any idea or notion of who they were because they were strangers to us. We didn't mingle with those people when we were working and they didn't mingle with us. Of course they would sometimes come through there and ask us questions about the work, but that is all. We would not know who they were and they wouldn't know who we were.

"At noon we spent our hour eating our dinner and dancing, some of us, not all of us. They had a big back room for storage for those [paper] tubes; they called those tubes that they made the shell out of. There we would go, lots of us, and just dance at noon. So we would go out there and dance or take a walk. You see we had a whole hour and then finally they cut us down to a half hour. Before I quit, they served dinners, fresh cooked dinners down in the basement. Of course, you had to pay for it, but it was a fresh cooked dinner.

"I can't begin to tell you how many people they employed or anything like that. Of course, this doesn't have anything to do with the powder line [King Powder Co. across the river] but that [King] is where the explosions were. One explosion I remember I was rocked. I had gotten so I could do other things besides run the wad winder. If they could spare me

from the wad winder or someone was off, sick or something I'd go there. Well, this day I was running the primer; I didn't ever like that very well, I was afraid of [it] but I was working there. I did as I was told to do. There was an explosion [across the river], a dreadful one. It must have socked me awful because when I came to, I was sitting in the middle of the factory...on my chair and my brother was coming in the back way hunting me.

"There was only one woman that I can remember of who ever died from any effects of an explosion; she inspected primers. They had a little house up on the hillside [fulminate hollow] and nobody was allowed in that. No other help was allowed to go in there, only the ones that worked in there and she worked there. There was an explosion and she got hurt so bad that she passed away-not then but later."

Elsie Black lived in Foster. She walked two miles up the river to the Peters plant to put in a ten-hour day and walked back home. She did this for

twenty-one years. And that is to say nothing of dancing or taking a walk at noon!

The following was taken from an interview, by Miriam Lukens and Alma Kintzel, of Viola Knapp of Mainville. Mrs. Knapp worked for Peters for eight years starting in 1907. The interview was held in 1976.

"...When I started, we just did simple things, maybe sort shells or something like that. I worked there for $5.00 a week, ten hours a day for five days and the sixth day was eight hours. I was there a little while and I was given a raise of [to?] $1.00 a day. Then I think, in maybe two months I was put on a gang of piecework. There were five in the gang–the plate filler [this must have been the metallics loading department], the greaser, the packer, the boxer and the lidder. I did the boxing.

"...There was a bad explosion near the river bridge [King Powder Company across the river]. We were changing gangs and the packer was up on the table when the [window] glass

This is a bird's-eye view of a .22 rimfire work station; probably final inspection and box packing, the plates being used to organize and orient the cartridges. *Cincinnati Historical Society.*

INSPECTION TABLE—One of the many inspections which Peters Cartridges must pass before being approved for shipment.

These women are inspectors. Women were used in many jobs because of their sharp eyes, nimble fingers and lower wages–not necessarily in that order.
Peters Catalog No.27 (1927).

came. I remember grabbing his legs thinking this was going to the last because the glass blew in and the doors were all bulged in. That was a scare.

"...I worked there in the 1913 flood and we had a lot of things to put on the second floor. There were five or six of us [who] stayed who could get [home by going up] magazine hill.

"...[Peters] employed a lot of women in [our area] and in other areas [of the plant]. Where they made the paper shell, they had a lot of women there...

"...we went [to work] on a hack...the man at the end of the road where I got on drove one of the hacks. We always stopped at the old spring in Foster to water the horses and to get a drink and then we went up the river road into Kings Mills...I always left home at six [am].

Constance Witt went to work for Peters in 1913 and worked at assembling or loading metallic

cartridges. This is her story as told to Miriam Lukens and Alma Kintzel in 1975 again selected and edited by the author.

"We loaded the .22s, .22 Shorts, .22 Longs, .22 Extra Longs, .22 Winchesters and .32s and .38s and .45s.

"...I worked in the loading department. There were four girls and one man working together. There were two first-class girls and two second-class girls and we called it a gang. When the shells [components] came to us they were separate and when they left us they were ready for the shooting gallery. They were ready to be packed and sent up to the packing department. They were ready to go out when we got through with them.

"...the [components] were in separate bins. There were two girls [who] worked in the bullet bin and one girl on the shells [primed cartridge cases] and the other girl around the crimper. We

changed jobs every two hours and 15 minutes-we changed jobs.

"[the crimper] put some kind of fancy mark around the shell [cartridge case] and it also helped to hold the bullet and the shell together.

"...often times these shells would go off. Of course you might get burned a little but nobody was ever seriously hurt.

"...there was one man [who] worked with us...we called him a loader. He was the man who put the things together–put them in the press and tripped the machine [loading press]. Each press held 832 shells. We would take them out and when they left us, they were all in boxes [bins] ready to go to the inspectors, then to the packing department.

"...every shell [cartridge] was inspected...[these inspectors] were different girls...that was their regular job.

"I started at ten cents per hour...after you were there a while

This was the Wilson's pleasure boat on the Little Miami River. It was pressed into service, whenever the bridge washed out, to ferry workers over to the cartridge works. The Wilsons made kegs for the King Powder Company.

Steve McDowell.

you got a small increase...Then I was put on piece work. That brought our wages up.

"I rode the streetcar [interurban, to work]...from Brecon...it took us about 28 minutes.

"...shortly after I went to work there, we had the big flood [1913]...and it took the bridge out. We were all off from work until they got the mud cleaned out of the place and the machinery back in operation. Then we had to cross the river in boats, morning and night. That was a job! We always got to go first because we had to catch the car [interurban]. [The interurban] wouldn't wait on us. People who drove their own cars had to wait until we crossed the river but in the mornings we had to take our turns...[the interurban car] was up there at twenty of five-[you] had to be up there or else you missed it.

"...We never had any serious accidents, not in the factory. Of course there were explosions on the powder line–things like that where some of the men were killed. But there was nothing serious, not in our place [metallic cartridge loading].

"...we started to work in the morning...about 7:30 when the bell rang. Then about twenty after nine the first girl would go on a break. There was no coffee break or anything like that–we just changed jobs. But you could go to the restroom and then come back, and, of course you knew which girl's place you were going to take...It was that way until all four girls got to go. Of course, we didn't have a lunchroom or anything like that or coffee breaks...We had to take our lunch.

"There were lots of times that we weren't real busy, especially when the shells went haywire. Something would happen–maybe

the fulminate [priming compound] wouldn't be right or something [else] would go wrong and [the finished cartridges] weren't firing like they should [in the testing department]. We were stopped and we had to wait until they found out what the trouble was. We were allowed to crochet or read. You just had to stay at your place though; you were not allowed to run around the factory and visit or bother anybody else.

In an article in the *Primer*, a Peters publication, in the 1940s Joe Weine had this to say:

"I came here [Peters] in the Fall of 1900, I don't remember the date. In those days there was no employment office. When a man wanted a job he went direct to the department in which he wanted work and made application for employment to the department foreman.

"When I came up I waited until the first whistle blew in the

morning and then asked the Metallic Loading Room Foreman, G. P. Deming, for a job. When the second whistle sounded I went to work. How is that for efficiency, neatness and dispatch compared with present methods[?] In those days we had no passes to show [or lose], no time clock to show us up, no watchman to inspect our lunch boxes or coffee bottles and no fence around the place.

"We came in wherever it was convenient. There was no plant hospital. The foreman gave first aid until a doctor could be summoned from the hill [Kings Mills]. There was no lunchroom although some of the higher priced help [those who were making $1.50 or $1.75 per day] had their dinner sent down from the hotel on the hill.

"We came to work at seven in the morning and quit at six in the evening, with an hour off at noon. We worked nine hours on Saturday. Perhaps I might correct that and say we were supposed to work until six, for in the winter some would hurry a bit and have a good start home when the whistle blew.

"The main office was located where the Cupping Department is now. [Building R6]. It was a room about 20 feet square and had three or four employees. Usually the timekeeper came around on Wednesdays to see if we had been there on Monday and Tuesday. And again on Saturday to see if we had been there Thursday and Friday. I might add that there seldom was anyone who had been absent.

"Where the Machine Shop now is located [the building is still there as this is written] there was a stable as those were horse and buggy days. A little further up there was a dwelling and a small orchard and across the road where the warehouse [warehouse end of Richmond's building] now stands there was a boarding house and another house with an old windless well in front.

"The drinking water was carried in buckets from a spring at the foot of Magazine Hill, and a dipper or tin cup was used by all although some of the more fastidious had cups of their own. What wasn't drunk was poured back in the bucket or thrown on the floor, whichever was easiest. There was a salt well where the carpenter shop now stands.

"The power came from across the river [King Powder Company] and every so often something would break and we would be sent home for a day or so until repairs could be made. The plant usually shut down for a week at Christmas for inventory. This always was a week of good cheer as some of the older employees will remember. We won't go into detail there. Those days are gone forever."

Joe Weine's story offers an ideal glimpse of life in the early days and by, inference, something of what it was like toward the end of the tenure of the Peters plant in the Kings Mills area. In more recent times Peters added watchmen, badges, a personnel department, cafeteria, company nurse, doctor, clinic, engineering/drafting department, machine shop and other support.

Parts of the plant itself were a veritable forest of belting descending from the line shafts that seemingly ran everywhere.

This is a group of Peters workers, probably photographed in the 1920s.

Steve McDowell.

Gesselshaft of Covington, Kentucky, at the time the Peters Arms and Sporting Goods Company was in business. There was definitely a demand for schuetzen rifles in the area, but there could not have been many rifles sold by Peters Arms like the one I saw at the gun show. Output of this quality is always small. The Peters Arms Company name on such fine hardware must have engendered prestige far out of proportion to the small number of rifles produced. I am surely not the only shooter who remembered these rifles—and the name Peters associated with them—many years after seeing one.

I believe that there are only about a half dozen or so of these rifles in existence. Others I have heard about may actually be these same rifles under a previous owner. There are several interesting things concerning rifles marked "Peters Arms Co. Cincinnati, O." that I have examined. They are:

- All Peters Arms Co. rifles that I have seen or heard of are fine double set-trigger schuetzen rifles.

- All of them are built on Sharps Model 78 actions.

- All of them generally look like Zischang's design.

- Serial numbers are not evident.

- Of the two rifles I have examined recently, the top of the breechblock on the "plain" Peters Arms Co. rifle is fitted with the same setscrew arrangement that Zischang used on his; the engraved one is not.

- The engraved rifle has "A. Lux" engraved on the trigger guard. There are three "A. Lux" listings in the Cincinnati City Directory of 1904. One was the superintendent of a tannery.

- Both Peters Arms Co. rifles that I have examined have

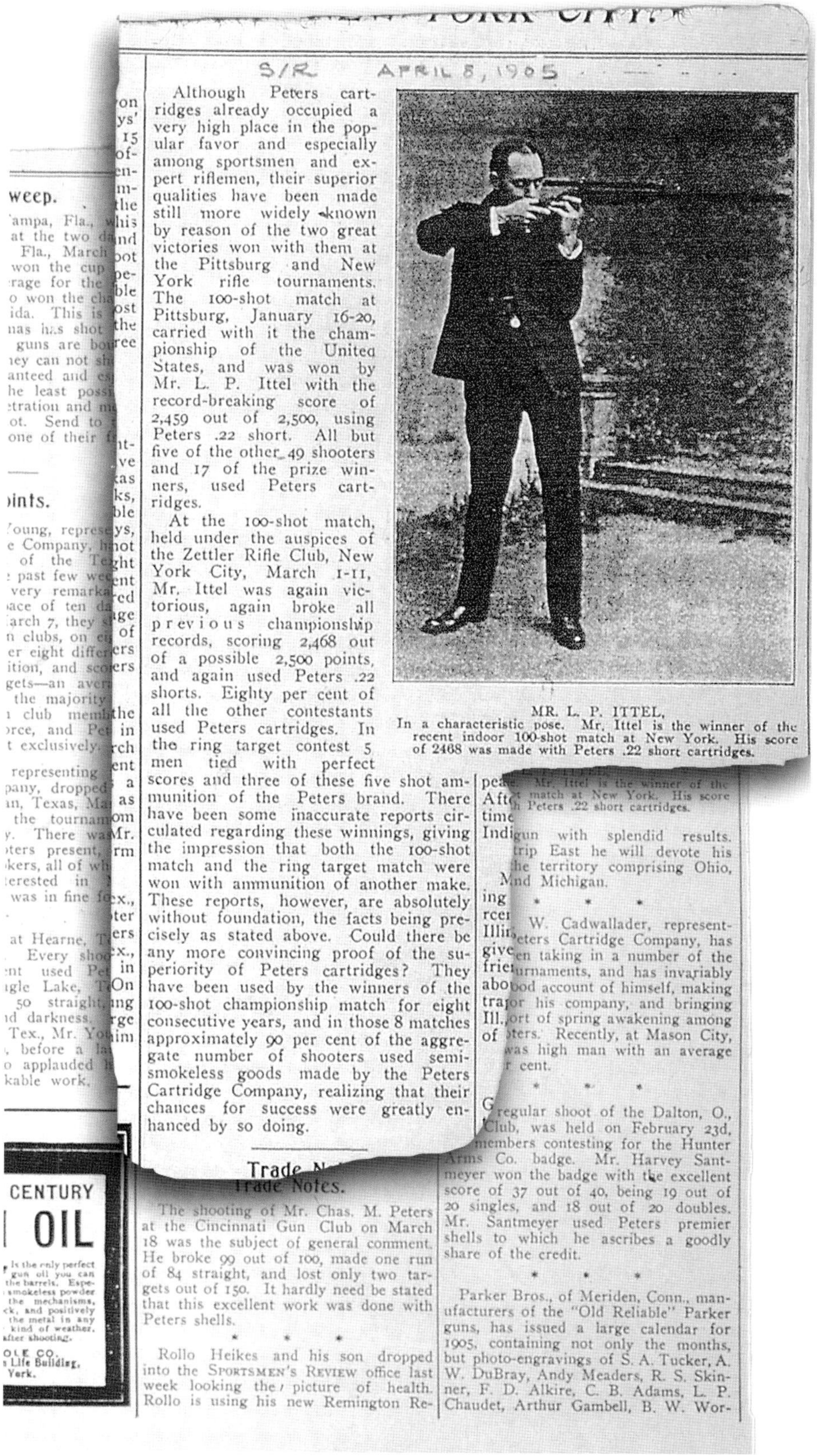

S/R   APRIL 8, 1905

Although Peters cartridges already occupied a very high place in the popular favor and especially among sportsmen and expert riflemen, their superior qualities have been made still more widely known by reason of the two great victories won with them at the Pittsburg and New York rifle tournaments. The 100-shot match at Pittsburg, January 16-20, carried with it the championship of the United States, and was won by Mr. L. P. Ittel with the record-breaking score of 2,459 out of 2,500, using Peters .22 short. All but five of the other 49 shooters and 17 of the prize winners, used Peters cartridges.

At the 100-shot match, held under the auspices of the Zettler Rifle Club, New York City, March 1-11, Mr. Ittel was again victorious, again broke all previous championship records, scoring 2,468 out of a possible 2,500 points, and again used Peters .22 shorts. Eighty per cent of all the other contestants used Peters cartridges. In the ring target contest 5 men tied with perfect scores and three of these five shot ammunition of the Peters brand. There have been some inaccurate reports circulated regarding these winnings, giving the impression that both the 100-shot match and the ring target match were won with ammunition of another make. These reports, however, are absolutely without foundation, the facts being precisely as stated above. Could there be any more convincing proof of the superiority of Peters cartridges? They have been used by the winners of the 100-shot championship match for eight consecutive years, and in those 8 matches approximately 90 per cent of the aggregate number of shooters used semi-smokeless goods made by the Peters Cartridge Company, realizing that their chances for success were greatly enhanced by so doing.

MR. L. P. ITTEL
In a characteristic pose. Mr. Ittel is the winner of the recent indoor 100-shot match at New York. His score of 2468 was made with Peters .22 short cartridges.

Trade Notes.

The shooting of Mr. Chas. M. Peters at the Cincinnati Gun Club on March 18 was the subject of general comment. He broke 99 out of 100, made one run of 84 straight, and lost only two targets out of 150. It hardly need be stated that this excellent work was done with Peters shells.

Rollo Heikes and his son dropped into the SPORTSMEN'S REVIEW office last week looking the picture of health. Rollo is using his new Remington Re-

[column fragments:]
...pea... Mr. Ittel is the winner of the... After... match at New York. His score time... Peters .22 short cartridges. Indigun with splendid results. ...trip East he will devote his ...the territory comprising Ohio, ...and Michigan.

...W. Cadwallader, represent...Peters Cartridge Company, has...been taking in a number of the...tournaments, and has invariably...good account of himself, making...for his company, and bringing...sort of spring awakening among...Peters. Recently, at Mason City, ...was high man with an average ...per cent.

...regular shoot of the Dalton, O., ...Club, was held on February 23d, ...members contesting for the Hunter ...Arms Co. badge. Mr. Harvey Santmeyer won the badge with the excellent score of 37 out of 40, being 19 out of 20 singles, and 18 out of 20 doubles. Mr. Santmeyer used Peters premier shells to which he ascribes a goodly share of the credit.

Parker Bros., of Meriden, Conn., manufacturers of the "Old Reliable" Parker guns, has issued a large calendar for 1905, containing not only the months, but photo-engravings of S. A. Tucker, A. W. DuBray, Andy Meaders, R. S. Skinner, F. D. Alkire, C. B. Adams, L. P. Chaudet, Arthur Gambell, B. W. Wor-

The Peters Cartridge Company was well known in schuetzen circles as revealed in this 1905 article in *The Sportsman's Review*. By extension, the Peters Arms and Sporting Goods Company was well aware of the needs of the schuetzen class of shooters.
April 5, 1905 issue of Sportsman's Review.
Courtesy of Trapshooter's Hall of Fame and Museum.

This Peters Arms Company rifle is engraved. It has a small finger lever similar to the Sharps factory lever. The name *A. Lux* is engraved on the trigger guard.
Photo: Schiffer. Courtesy of Tom Rowe.

- Both rifles examined are essentially original, although both show a bit of TLC by skillful hands at one time or another.

Some choices suggest themselves:

- The rifles were made in-house by the 'smiths of the Peters Arms and Sporting Goods Co.
- The rifles were made in-house, but with some items farmed out (barrels, buttplates, actions, engraving, etc.).
- The rifles were made by some other party, Zischang or ?? for Peters Arms and Sporting Goods Company.
- With the exception of the engraving–and the probable exception of the Pope-style rifling– the only person that we *know* did this kind of work is A. O. Zischang of Syracuse, N.Y. or his son William, both of whom were active 1900-1908.
- The "Peters Arms Co., Cincinnati, O." that made the rifles discussed in this chapter is not the same company as the Peters Arms and Sporting Goods Company of Cincinnati, Ohio. (*While I do not believe this idea has any merit whatsoever, I feel I must mention it as a possibility.*)

buttplates that look like they were made off the same distinctive pattern as those on the Zischang rifles I have examined, be they Ballards or Borchardts.

- The modeling, or reshaping of the action, is different on both Peters Arms Co. rifles, as it is on Zischang rifles.
- One of the Peters Arms Co. rifles has a barrel with a left hand twist that looks like Pope-style rifling, however it is not a gain twist barrel.

- Both rifles I have examined are in .32-40 caliber.
- The double set triggers on the Peters Arms Co. rifles are of generally the same configuration although not interchangeable. The Zischang triggers are a bit longer and larger.
- Both rifles examined were at one time fitted with a palm rest, which has been removed from the engraved one and the holes skillfully plugged.

The information for this chapter came from three published sources; an obituary in a 1940 issue of the *Peters Informer* for George W. Collins; *Cincinnati City Directory* in the years before and after 1900 and Jim Eckler's Peters Arms and Sporting Goods Catalog No.2. There were telephone conversations with Gary Quinlin, collector and dealer who has owned Peters Arms rifles, Marvin Huey, who has owned one of the rifles examined and Ron Long, then a Denver gunsmith who has made Borchardt actions. There

This is the roll stamp on the engraved rifle. While saying the same thing, it is different from that on the non-engraved rifle. Note that "Cincinnati" is spelled incorrectly.
Photo: Schiffer. Courtesy of Tom Rowe.

was the visit to Dan Schlegel to compare two of the rifles in question. And there was the personal letter from John Dutcher, and the information gleaned in a visit to Tom Rowe.

But all of the rhetoric and speculation aside, the most fascinating evidence of all are the rifles themselves!

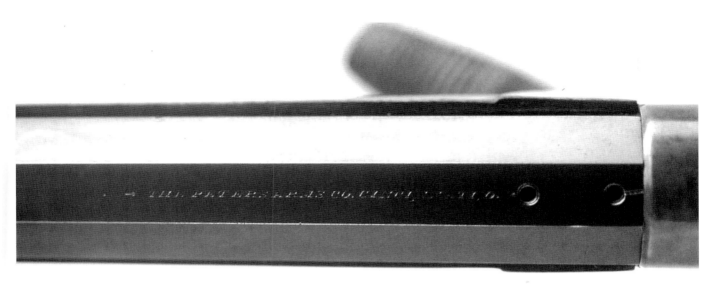

This is the roll stamp on the "plain" rifle of the Peters Arms Co. Both this and the roll stamp on the other rifle read front to rear. This one reads "THE PETERS ARMS CO. CINCINNATI, O."

Photo: Schiffer. Courtesy of Dan Schlegel.

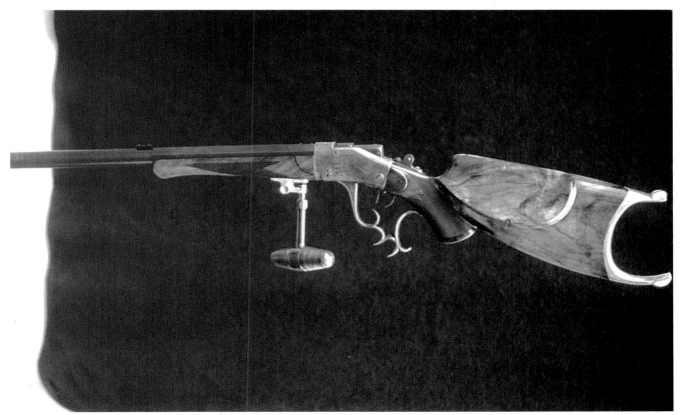

Note the classic schuetzen lines on this Peters Arms Co. rifle. The modeling of the stock, the checkering, palm rest and trigger guard blend to make an artistic statement beyond mere form follows function.

Photo: Schiffer. Courtesy of Dan Schlegel.

Chapter 10

Life as a Resident of Kings Mills

LIFE IN KINGS Mills village was said, by Peters management, to be idyllic. In 1927, they celebrated their fiftieth year in business. In their catalog they said:

"The Peters Company employs the highest type of workman, most of whom are residents of the model village of Kings Mills, Ohio. Their happy and contented disposition is the result of the very pleasant home life enjoyed by all, made possible by the systematic way the village is operated. Rents are cheap, with ample ground for home gardening. Inhabitants have unusual opportunities for recreation, including swimming

and fishing in the picturesque Little Miami River, theater, library, gun and rifle club, athletic sports, etc. In addition, the village maintains a fine church. The big majority of these employees are enthusiastic shooters either in the field, at the traps or on the range. Wherever producers are consumers, it follows that the more interest will be taken in the manufacture of that which is produced and that greater care will be exercised by each and every employee in the performance of his duties–for being entirely familiar with the consumer's requirements, he knows how very important it is

that every operation in the making of a shell or cartridge be exactly as it should be to produce the desired results.

"The education of young folks is taken care of at a fine school, both Elementary and High.

"Such are the surroundings of those who work in the great factory of the Peters Cartridge Company. The standard of home life enjoyed by each and every employee is bound to reflect itself in the work performed by these people. It is a well known axiom that a good workman makes a good citizen, and vice versa, and the fact that in the village there are no police of any kind

The home of Ahimaaz King was, perhaps, the very first home built in Kings Mills. *Joseph Warren King II.*

School District included the Peters Cartridge Company (across the Little Miami River and hence in a different township). Early on, it was insisted that the teachers be college graduates. The first school was founded in 1889. The high school was built in 1890. The first graduating class was in 1895. A gym was built in 1928 by the Kings and deeded to the school board in 1941.

As far as there being no police needed, this is a mixed blessing. During normal production, the workers were rather under the thumb of the management. Those who would make trouble were subject to losing their job *and* their home. A bigger stick, arguably, than police hold over most citizenry today.

On the other hand, John Murphy was a guard at the Peters Cartridge Company and quoted Mr. King as saying he would rather have the monetary value of the cartridges that found their way out the door in lunch boxes, etc., than the profit!

Fine rhetoric to the contrary, during the WWI years, a small building behind–and across the street from–the church was requisitioned to serve as a jail. A foreman of the plant labor gang, Squire Currans, was deputized to do whatever was necessary to isolate the occasional unruly revelers from the source of their inspiration.

The town was founded in 1886 when Ahimaaz King built his house atop King Avenue. The bricks were burned nearby and the site platted to serve as a company town for the King Powder Company workmen. The original town of Gainesboro (in this same general vicinity), founded in 1815 by Ralph W. Hunt, had been located hard by Isaak Stubbs' mill. It never had more than 150 inhabitants. It was Stubbs' long millrace and hydraulic potential that attracted the Kings in the first place; that and the fact the Little Miami Railroad was just across the river. Whereas Gainesboro

This building was used as an unofficial jail in Kings Mills. In later years, and perhaps before, it hosted the Kings Mills Band for their practice sessions. The band was in demand for many events throughout the area.   *Steve McDowell.*

was clustered on the riverbank, Gainesboro was deserted by the time King's Great Western Powder Company was founded. Periodic flooding had much to do with both the desertion of Gainesboro and the location of the new town of Kings Mills on the hill.

At first, there were only two long streets, King Ave., and College streets. The houses were of substantial but modest

construction. As mentioned, rents were modest, too.

By September of 1903, an electric interurban line was extended from Cincinnati, 25 miles away, through Kings Mills to Lebanon, some seven miles north. This line hauled light freight as well as passengers. There was a depot or station in the town. The interurban ceased operation in March of 1922. The cars were 47 feet long and would

The King mansion at the top of King Avenue. Note that it had its own water system with windmill to pump water from a deep well into the *(right)* water tower.   *Warren County Historical Society.*

King Avenue, not paved, about 1887. The church under construction at left was dedicated in 1887.

Joseph Warren King II

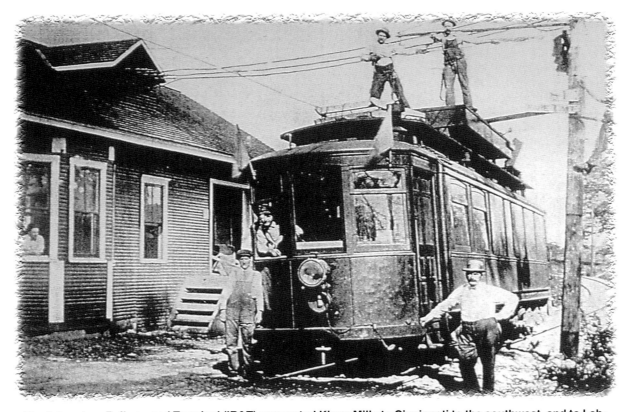

The Interurban Railway and Terminal (IR&T) connected Kings Mills to Cincinnati to the southwest, and to Lebanon to the north, via a single-track system. This station was on King Avenue across the street and just down the hill from the church. Streetcars were used for both freight and passenger service. There was a loading dock on the side of this depot.

Post Master Ruth Fisher.

The Cliff House was built to house and feed workers constructing the millrace, before powder was made. It had sixteen rooms and a large dining room. Timmy Dowdell was the manager for over 25 years.
Photo: Cline. Courtesy of Joseph Warren King II.

hold 52 passengers. Four 60 hp motors would have moved them along at a swift pace. The King Powder offices were relocated to the interurban depot after the King Powder Company office burned in 1950.

The Little Miami Railroad was located just across the Little Miami River from the town, providing passenger as well as freight service. This line was later taken over by the Pennsylvania Railroad but operated under a number of different names until then. In later years, the passenger service gave way to the influence of the Model T. Much later, after the cartridge factory and the powder mill had closed in the 1960s, the entire Division was abandoned, thanks to the inroads of the trucking industry. The plant closings were no doubt a factor in the decision to close the rail service.

The Cliff House Hotel was erected early in the town's history. It is shown on a map dated in the early 1890s. The Cliff House had 16 guest rooms, a kitchen and large dining room for the residents. It had a prominent position overlooking the valley, river and the Peters Works and was built for King Powder Company workers.

The Manse was located just up the hill from the shell factory (when it was briefly located in town) and one block over from King Avenue. Some of the King Powder supervisors lived here. This was in the "King" part of town. The Peters section was farther west.
The King Powder Company, Illustrated 1896.
Courtesy of Bob and Betty Carter.

Helen Dowdell Bogart, whose father ran the Cliff House for 26 or 27 years, remembered:

"The first level contained the dining room and the showers...When we first went there, if you turned one electric light on, you turned five different ones on in a series. It had the storage rooms and the boiler room. On the next floor were living quarters and the bedrooms, and upstairs, I think there were 16 rooms altogether. [There was a] huge dining room–there were at least two tables and usually they were more than filled with people."

Another location for collective habitation was "The Manse," also known as "the barracks." It was a Philadelphia- or row-style structure and housed a dozen or so families of powder company workers. This building was constructed after the 1890 explosion to support the cartridge factory as a warehouse when the factory was relocated to the lower end of town. It is a soccer field today.

THE MANSE.

"Transferring and Moving Carefully and Promptly Done". Feed was sold as well.

For the most part, work was located close enough to the residence section for everybody to walk to work. Later, when Peters Cartridge became a growing concern, the town was extended considerably to the west, but never actually expanded past the east side of Walnut Street, although platted past there. West of Walnut Street is where the post office and Kings Mills High School are located today.

For the most part, the commercial establishments were located in the lower part of town near the Cliff House Hotel and the livery stable. There were dry goods stores, meat and confectioners establishments as well as a post office. Simonton, Tufts, Hanes, McClelland,

Most homes had no stable for horse and buggy, but there was Zentmeyer's livery in town. Zentmeyer's daughter remembered he had about a dozen horses. There were *"Swift Horses, Fine Buggies, Carriages, Wagons &c for Hire"*...

The Park Department store was located in the lower end of Kings Mills. Originally I believe this was the shell factory, briefly located in town after the explosion of 1890.
Warren County Historical Society.

This was the Cline/Wilson store for many years. The post office was located in the library, on College Street, then in this building on King Avenue–before it moved to the present location on Walnut Street. In the very early years of the town, school was held upstairs and, later, a meeting room was there.

Steve McDowell.

Coates, McAdams and others ran these concerns.

Pauline McElwain Lauterwasser recalls her grandfather James T. McClelland's general store in this way: *"He had beautiful dishes for sale. He had a wooden cookie box at the back of the store. After school, boys came in and sampled the cookies with no questions asked [girls wouldn't do this?]. Benches surrounded the stove and a pickle barrel stood nearby. Men who gathered there in the evenings dipped into the pickle barrel. When customers paid their bills on pay day, they were given a sack of candy."*

The post office (which was located in at least four places over the years; in the library building; further up the street on King Avenue; and on Kings Mill Road on the powder mill side of the school, before being relocated where it is today at Walnut

Street and Kings Mill Road), expanded and contracted with the activities of the two companies nearby. In 1932, when business got slow, Peters moved its advertising department from nearby Cincinnati to the factory, which increased the post office traffic.

The town featured another hotel, the Homestead. According to Edna Bowyer, it was opened on July 4, 1905. A hotel of this size was unusual in a town the size of Kings Mills. Not only was the town fairly small but, more importantly for a hotel, Kings Mills was located in a place that was on the way to no place in particular.

The Homestead was originally built as a residence for the then-expanding cartridge company workers. Unmarried schoolteachers also took residence there. The Homestead was situated in the "Petersburg"

section of town and consisted of two floors, a basement and attic. In the basement was a rifle range in the north wing. The men's showers, furnace and kitchen and dining room were in the basement's south wing.

The first floor had a poolroom and the rest, plus the second floor, was divided into sleeping rooms. Some residents of Kings Mills claim there were 250 rooms in the hotel; others say 100. The latter appears to be more accurate. I can believe that 250 people lived in 100 rooms.

Swanson, Johnson, Kendall, Price, Hanna and Mc Kitterick were successive managers from 1905 to about 1938. When Remington (Du Pont) took over Peters, the Homestead was considered a firetrap, due to its wooden construction, and torn down.

We'll let Marjorie Mc Kitterick Stevenson (daughter of the last manager) give you an idea of what living there was like. She wrote the following in 1975:

"The chefs and helpers were all good... a feeling of nostalgia sweeps over me as I remember those huge pans with beef, or loin of pork, roasting in the ovens; macaroni and cheese, scalloped potatoes, and always a huge pot of mashed potatoes, also army-navy beans. Mrs. Charles Lane made Parker House rolls that surpassed any I have ever eaten. Mrs. Elizabeth Begley, who still lives at Morrow, was superb. I remember her butterscotch and chocolate meringue pies. Mr. and Mrs. Charles Callahan and Jerry Callahan and Mrs. Wilson and a man named Silas all cooked good food.

"There was a cafeteria in the Peters Cartridge factory (Bldg. No. 1 basement) so every working day noon, lunch was served from the hotel kitchen. At 10 am, the Model T truck was backed up to the (hotel) kitchen door. (It had to be cranked to start). Then came the mad rush. A carrying case with about a dozen compartments came out first. There were always two hot meat selections (usually more), potatoes, mashed or au gratin, beans, three or four more vegetables and gravy. Then came the pie carrying case - perhaps four meringue and six apple, peach, cherry, raisin, etc. – box of sliced bread and cut butter. Then salads and other side dishes, perhaps fruit desserts. The hot food was put on a steam counter until time to be served. A few people started coming in at 11:45, then at 12:30 it was all over!

"Ben Sparks ran the pool room (in the hotel) for as long as I can remember. He came on duty at 5:00 pm and went off about 5:30 am. The poolroom closed at 10 pm (after all it had been a long day!). From then on, Ben was the night watchman–every hour he walked the halls, punched his clock with the keys in the metal boxes at the ends of the corridors. We all said he wore wooden shoes–he didn't, but they were heavy laced high-top shoes with thick soles so that he clumped along, really a comforting sound if you had fears during the night. Then at 5:30 am he took the brass bell from the dining room, went along all halls ringing the bell to alert people it was time to get up. Breakfast would be served from 6:00 until 7:30 for people who went to work at 8:00 am...

"For entertainment there was the "parlor," a room with a large table and chairs and a Wurlitzer player piano. There were many rolls for it. One man who played the violin occasionally played for us there - music that was the forerunner of our contemporary country music.

"Dances were held occasionally on Saturday nights so one year

The Homestead Hotel. Company literature stated the hotel could accommodate 200 people. I believe there were 100 rooms, with the men's side physically separated from the women's side. Dances, etc., were held in the dining room and there was a rifle range *(smallbore)* in the basement. It was razed after Du Pont took over Peters.

Courtesy of Postmaster Ruth Fisher.

The King Mansion at the head of King Avenue. The fountain in the yard *(center)* probably gave the name 'Fountain Square' to the general area.

Courtesy of Bob and Betty Carter.

the company - Peters Cartridge Company - had a hardwood floor put in the dining room—what a difference it made for dancers."

The attic of the hotel was said by some to have been a dormitory for men during WWI. Cots placed there were said not to get cold since successive shifts of workers used the same beds in succession. In keeping with the Victorian traditions of the day, there were partitions in both the first and second floor halls segregating the men's and women's side! Each side had their own stairway. The women's side was to the right as you entered.

There was a "Fountain Square" section of town. It was an area that included a few houses and the King Powder Company stables, located just east of A. King's big house at the

This view of the King Mansion's side yard with the servants in sight gives some idea of the lifestyle the Kings enjoyed. *Courtesy of Bob and Betty Carter.*

Colonel George King was a prominent Republican and was on Ohio governor Nash's staff. Son of Ahimaaz King, he took over upon his father's death. Colonel King was the only president of both Peters and King. He was instrumental in founding Camp Perry in Ohio, where the National Matches have been held for so many years.

The King Powder Company, Illustrated 1896.
Courtesy of Bob and Betty Carter.

high ceilings, it featured fancy-grained imitation oak woodwork. It had its own stables, ice house and running water when these luxuries were a curiosity in the county. There was a deep well and tall windmill to pump the water into an equally tall elevated tank to supply the pressure.

Louis Romohr (born in 1911) grew up in the Fountain Square section. *"This was a little community of half a dozen houses and two huge barns. My dad was farm manager for over 500 acres of the King Powder Company land. (Louis Whitnack) was the manager of horses and mules used to pull the powder wagons. I've seen them bring those mules up from the powder line burned so badly that some would have to be destroyed and some were saved by packing them in linseed oil. I've seen, as a little boy, huge 2 x 4s ten feet long and 4 x 4s blown from the explosions into our field next to our house.* [Note: those boards would have to be blown some 200 feet, or more, in the air and several hundred feet horizontally to do this!]

"I was fortunate as a young lad who lived there to have access to many pets and did have. The King family (Col. George King) was very wonderful to me. They furnished me with goats to drive the wagon; they furnished me with bantam chickens to play with when I was a child and so I became very fond of the King family. They were sort of the du Ponts of the Warren County area. They had a huge operation... really a shame to see it leave that area. They owned the entire town of Kings Mills (and) most of the land around it."

Mrs. Sherwood remembered the young children were not allowed to skate on the frozen river until they were teenagers. Until then, they skated on the pond near the big barn at Fountain Square. They were not allowed to coast on the big hill, either, but used what they called Acorn Hill at the other end of town.

The Wilsons, recruited by the Kings early in the company history, lived on the extension of Kings Mill Road, which accessed the Fountain Square area. They were persuaded to relocate from Delaware to manufacture powder tins and kegs for King. They evidently did very well and were respected citizens of the town.

top of King Avenue. King's horse training track was also located in this general area. The fountain in King's front yard probably gave the name to this area.

The King mansion itself was (and is) a source of pride to the town. Of brick construction with

Ice skating on the Little Miami River just above the Foster Bridge, downstream from Kings Mills about two miles. Edna Bowyer is on the left, with a friend.
Edna Bowyer.

Left to right: William Wilson, J. C., Bertha, Frank, Annie Chandler Wilson and John

The closest house to the King mansion was the Wilson house, across the street. James Wilson invented the double-seam can and was recruited to make cans for King's Great Western Powder Company. One of the Wilson families is arrayed here for the camera, from the carriage on the left to the rocking horse on the front porch.

Warren County Historical Society.

The town (and company) doctor also lived on King Avenue.

No word about the town would be complete without mention of the "Tin Whistle." This was a temporary factory set up at the lower edge of town to make cartridge shells after the explosion of 1890 devastated the fledgling cartridge-loading operation. This building was apparently thrown up hastily and had a covering of sheet metal. No doubt there was a whistle associated with the steam boiler that supported the operation, which evidently inspired the derisive name.

The "Tin Whistle" did not last long as a cartridge factory. That operation moved back across the river in 1892 or '93. It can be argued the operation was intended to be permanent but the

Site of the old "Tin Whistle" on the lower edge of town. Nothing is left of the old shell factory that stretched along the far side of the drive, parallel to–and nearly one block west of–King Avenue. This photo is from the same perspective as that of the Park Department Store, shown elsewhere, which later occupied the site. *Photo: Schiffer.*

inconvenience of trucking everything up and down the steep hill below town forced the move.

When the factory was moved back across the river, the front portion of the "Tin Whistle" was converted into commercial stores. The rear became apartments. A nearby building served the town as a gym until a new one replaced it in 1928.

The company mentioned there was fishing and swimming available in the Little Miami River. They did not mention the fish would bite best below where the cartridge factory sewer entered the river!

The swimming hole consisted of one of the deeper river 'holes,' complete with a rope swing suspended from an available sycamore.

There was also an opportunity for swimming, fishing and boating above the dam. This dam only raised the water level six or eight feet. The river was not navigable to boats larger than small pleasure boats—the type called into use when flood water swept away the bridge between the cartridge plant and Kings Mills.

The company did not mention in their catalog that, on occasion, there would be an explosion at the powder plant, an unforgettable experience for all concerned. Over the years, a number of workers were killed or injured. There was a big explosion July 15, 1890, caused by railroad negligence at the cartridge plant. The entire plant *(in its infant days)*, surrounding houses, the company office and the railroad depot were destroyed. Eight were killed. Aside from this notable incident, most deaths from explosions were at the powder factory, not the cartridge factory.

A first-person account of one such powder company explosion appeared in the Lebanon, Ohio *Western Star* of August 9, 1940:

"I was just at the top of the hill driving to work when I heard two sharp blasts and then the big explosion came. I jumped from my car in time to see a cloud of debris shoot skyward hundreds of feet in the air. A large 12" x 12" [timber] was carried several hundred feet upward and then it seemed to be held as if suspended for several seconds. The particles spread, began to open like a parachute and descend to the earth. I saw two of the bodies as they skyrocketed into space and seemed almost a minute until they fell to the ground."

Peters Cartridge Company explosions were isolated to the mixing and handling of priming compound. There was the double threat of explosions and mercury poisoning. Purposely, very few employees were exposed to this and the work was done in remote areas.

Explosions affected the village in several ways.

There was the dread of hearing that a loved one or neighbor had been killed or injured. Also, the force of the blast broke many windows in town. It has been said that one reason for closing the Peters Cartridge plant in 1944, was that every time King Powder had a blast, Peters, located closer to the powder line than the town, would have to replace 3000 windows! By 1934, Peters was no longer owned by the Kings.

Testimony varied as to whether the glass

A ROW ON COLLEGE STREET.

Typical residence on College Street. College Street ran parallel to King Avenue and one block west of it. This is in the King Powder part of town, the Peters part of town was farther west.
The King Powder Company, Illustrated 1896. *Courtesy of Bob and Betty Carter.*

The Kings Mill Band on parade in Lebanon, Ohio, March 8, 1913. Note the hearse, the early automobile and the IR&T street-car. The IR&T was the interurban line that ran through Kings Mills, to Cincinnati from Lebanon.   *Joseph Warren King II.*

was blown into the structures, or fell outside. It was stated that, if the blast was typical, the glass fell outside. If the explosion was particularly severe, it fell inside. Jane McDowell reported that when she and Steve ran the grocery store, the front window glass was once blown all the way to the meat case at the rear of the store! Fred Schwietert, who grew up in Kings Mills, mentioned another factor I never considered, that many homes heated and/or cooked with coal stoves. In the summer, many stoves and stovepipes were removed from the house for the season. The open flue in the wall or ceiling was then plugged with a special decorative sheet metal stopper. A nearby explosion caused the stopper to be violently sucked out of the wall, pulling a disgusting amount of black soot with it that would settle over the furnishings, rugs and walls!

Townsfolk were pretty philosophical about the

explosions and accepted them as part of their way of life. R. Eugene King indicated that they "paid their workers a little more" who were exposed to the hazardous operations. Women were not allowed to work at these hazardous jobs. An exception was during WWII when women were utilized to load powder into practice bombs and flares. A few were severely burned in one incident. However, no women ever worked on the powder line. In any event, the company evidently had little trouble recruiting workers.

There were many happy times; lawn fetes, athletic games (but not on Sunday), picture shows, and other such activity. There was a Kings Mills Band with members from both King and Peters. They were evidently of no mean talent, some of them having been associated with 'big bands.' A bandstand was provided (the old "jail") as a place to practice as well as perform. The grass around the bandstand

was covered with kids in summer, even when the band was only practicing.

There were trips to Coney Island, a local amusement park. Coney Island was subsequently closed in the 1970s, moved to Kings Mills and renamed Kings Island by the owners! These trips to "Old Coney" involved a train ride to Cincinnati (25 miles) and a steamboat trip to the park some ten miles up the Ohio River. There was a much-publicized baseball game between teams made up of workers in the various departments. There are those today who can tell you who won in 1939!

Edna Bowyer notes the town streets and sidewalks were subjected to a liberal dose of cinders, a by-product of the coal-fired boiler houses. As a result, knees and elbows of active children took on a "road rash" more severe than that occasioned by contact with mere concrete paving. Generations

YOUR ANNUAL OUTING Sponsored by FOREMEN'S CLUB

...OF...

PETERS CARTRIDGE DIVISION
Remington Arms Co.

9 p.m. — Fireworks Display — 9 p.m.

C O N E Y   I S L A N D

S A T U R D A Y

JULY 29

SEE YOUR FOREMAN FOR
TRANSPORTATION, ADMISSION AND SPECIAL LOW-PRICED
AMUSEMENT DEVICE AND REFRESHMENT TICKETS

🐂 **CONEY ISLAND TICKETS** 🐂

Admission tickets, by boat or auto, will be furnished by your Foreman. Special low-rate amusement device, refreshment and pool tickets will be handled as follows:

Your Foreman has strips of tickets at 30¢ per strip. There are ten stubs on each strip. These give you 50¢ worth of rides. One stub will be accepted on a five-cent ride; two on a ten-cent ride and three on a fifteen-cent ride. One entire strip will be accepted as admission to the pool. Children under 12 will be admitted for 6 stubs, equivalent to 18¢. Your Foreman also has refreshment tickets for 4 for 25¢. Get all these tickets you need in advance. NONE CAN BE SOLD AT THE PARK ON DAY OF OUTING.

🐂 **RAILROAD TRANSPORTATION** 🐂

We're going to Coney on a special train, which will take us direct to the steamer Island Queen. The round-trip fare will be only 70¢ for adults and 40¢ for children from 4 to 12 years old. We leave Coney Island immediately after the fireworks and our train will meet the boat when she docks at Cincinnati. The train schedule follows:

GOING:		RETURNING:
Leaves Morrow .... 9:00 A.M.		
" South Lebanon .. 9:10 A.M.	Boat leaves Coney Island 9:30 P.M.
" Kings Mills ...... 9:15 A.M.	Train leaves Cincinnati.. 10:30 P.M.
" Fosters .... 9:20 A.M.	Return trip to starting points
" Loveland .... 9:25 A.M.	approximately one hour.
Boat Leaves Cincinnati.. 11:00 A.M.	

SEE YOUR FOREMAN IMMEDIATELY FOR RAILROAD TICKETS.

FREE DANCING ON BOAT — FREE FLOOR SHOW IN MOONLITE GARDENS IN AFTERNOON.

Poster advertising the Peters annual outing to Coney Island, a Cincinnati area amusement park. The park owners sold it and, in 1972, built Kings Island, a large amusement park on land bought from the Kings– where Detonite used to be made.
Postmaster Ruth Fisher.

Chapter 11

The Kentucky Connection: KICO (King Powder Company) Plant in Wurtland, Kentucky

"...a place under the sun, walled in by the wind and the hills. ...it's just a place with four seasons - wind, sun, rain, snow - with scrub oaks and old log houses and new plank shacks - a place that's somewhere for some and nowhere for many.

"... In the spring you can hear the wind slushin around in the leaves. In the summer you can hear the wind and the corn blades parlyin around. ...The whole hollow looks lazy in the summer sun. And the sun always shines on W-Hollow in Kentucky. It never reaches some of it til noon. But it gets there.

"... For it is a place under the sun, walled in by the wind and the hills - nowhere for many - somewhere for some."

-Jesse Stuart

Aerial view of the KICO plant. The town of Wurtland is in the background. The scattered buildings in the foreground were part of the KICO operation. The largest building, *center/left*, was the combined washhouse-laundry. The airplane would have been over the hill separating the Route 23 from the black powder line.

Photo: Milton F. Lindsley, Jr. Courtesy of David Spencer.

After WWI, the King Powder Company opened a new powder manufacturing plant at a location other than Kings Mills. The *History of the Explosives Industry* stated this decision was driven by the need to reduce congestion at the Kings Mills operation. The new plant was to be nearer the customer's coalfields than the Kings Mills plant. The new plant was to make only blasting powder.

This was pretty much the same mixture invented by the Chinese in the 1300s. It was essentially the same powder that powered Daniel Boone's famous "old tick-licker" Kentucky long rifle. The only change was in the substitution of sodium nitrate for potassium nitrate.

The essential difference was that the soda powder did not have as long a "shelf-life" when exposed to atmospheric moisture; as when stored in a powder horn.

Potassium powder lasted indefinitely unless water got to it. Put up in a blasting powder keg and kept closed, soda powder did all right.

The use of black blasting powder was relatively easy to understand by the user. Misuse of black powder in firearms usually was not associated with serious consequences. This was because it developed relatively low pressures. Nitro powders would have opened up "old tick licker" like an umbrella!

It was this same relatively low pressure that endeared blasting powder to miners. It heaved the coal loose from the overburden and shale in large lumps, not tiny fragments and dust. On the other hand, it was the long flame duration associated with this soft explosion that caused the ignition of many secondary explosions in mines.

The coalfields of eastern Kentucky and West Virginia were certainly the largest users of King explosives in the time after WWI. Empty wooden blasting powder and dynamite cases were plentiful in the Manchester, Kentucky area during the mid-1950s. Blasting powder accounted for the largest tonnage of powder produced by King. In later years this was supplanted by shipments of specialized explosives to the Louisiana oil fields.

Common carriers could be counted on to be skittish about trucking explosives. For this reason, King Powder maintained some of its own trucks and drivers for delivering powder. Having a plant closer to the customer translated to lower costs, hence bigger profits. Much of this trucking originated at the Kentucky plant. The site location for the new plant was no doubt also driven by the need for rail service to obtain raw materials.

David Spencer, a foreman at the new Kentucky plant, related the following story about the prospective site: *"While riding on the C&O train ... he [George King] had just left the Riverton Depot at Greenup, heading for Russell.* [This would have been when passing through the area on his way to and from visiting customers] *While looking out the window of his coach, he noticed a large hollow and a steep mountain near the track.*

"At this period of time many men were making charcoal in Greenup County. It was source of income for many families. Although it was not the booming business as when the old iron furnaces were in operation, it still remained a source of livelihood for some, and the advent of the King Powder plant greatly revived the charcoal business."

An essential ingredient of blasting powder was charcoal. Here was a nearly dormant cottage industry waiting to be awakened. This was by no means the smallest or least important piece of the puzzle.

The King Powder Company acknowledged in the September, 1942, issue of *The Russell Times,* that: *"Another point in favor of this locality was the fact that it was possible to secure an adequate supply of efficient and conscientious workmen for the tasks assigned."*

Greenup County, Kentucky, was about a hundred miles nearer the coalfields than Kings Mills. The Ohio River navigation map shows it to be almost exactly one third of the way from Pittsburgh to the Mississippi

The King Powder Company had its own fleet of trucks.
Courtesy of Bob and Betty Carter.

River. Some hundred and thirty seven miles upstream from Cincinnati, less than 25 miles downstream from Huntington, just over the West Virginia border.

The county was no stranger to commerce at that time. The C&O Railroad ran along the river border with Ohio and had done so since the 1880s. The C&O had a junction at Riverton (now part of Greenup), with the little Eastern Kentucky Railway.

I asked Dr. Harris, who was raised in Greenup County, where an upcoming young man could work in the Greenup County area back then. Not entirely tongue-in-cheek he replied: *"Armco Steel, the railroads, assorted steel mills and blast furnaces across the Ohio River, a dairy, Ashland Oil, a coke plant...or he could make moonshine or go bootlegging!"*

Armco, now A-K Steel, can trace activity at Ashland *(a few miles up river from Wurtland)* to 1861. The moonshine may well date from the first corn crop. Alcohol was easier to take to market than corn! Who discovered you could drink it is not recorded. Bootlegging probably dates back to when government started regulating things! Dr. Harris also said that, danger aside, a young man could do far worse than to work for KICO.

The name KICO, a contraction of the words King Company was given to this new plant, and referred only to the Kentucky plant. Variously, the name is pronounced "key co," "kick o" and "ki co" as Dave Spencer pronounces it. The KICO plant was variously referred to in the King Company as Wurtland, Greenup, KICO and Riverton.

The county was bisected by the E-K Railroad, which dated from the Civil War (1865-1933). The E-K was thirty-seven miles long and was built to service the iron furnaces, bring out coal and the resulting pig iron. Cannel coal was mined along the E-K

and there had been a coal oil extraction facility in the county about 1850. Cannel coal contains a high percentage of volatile matter, which facilitates the production of coal oil [kerosene].

Jo Harris Brenner, historian and writer concerning Greenup County, stated the general area was no stranger to manufacturing potassium nitrate—the largest ingredient in black powder and the activity dated back to the gunpowder trade during the War of 1812. It was processed from bat guano from Swingle's cave and Saltpeter cave.

David Spencer *(left)* and James Gillespie on a field trip to the site in 2000. James, as a youth in the 1920s, supplied King with charcoal.

Eastern Kentucky (E.K.) Railroad (1865-1933) locomotive, northbound at Argillite about 1928. Argillite was only a mile or so south–and a bit west–of the KICO plant.   *Photo: G. C. Spencer. Courtesy of David Spencer.*

This is the *Southern Queen* which ran commuter service on the E. K. Railroad right-of-way after the roadbed became unsafe for regular train service in the late 1920s. It, and others like it, was powered with Model T Ford engines.

Eastern Kentucky Railway Historical Society. Courtesy of David Spencer.

Supplying potassium nitrate (saltpeter) from the caves did not extend to the KICO operation. It was too expensive. Brenner also stated that Daniel Boone's son, Jesse Boone, was long associated with making salt in the Greenup area. This was not saltpeter but table salt (sodium chloride), which was a very expensive commodity on the frontier.

The E-K Railway could, perhaps, make real money today, servicing tourists in season. It would be charming with its quaint locomotives, many tunnels and picturesque scenery as the roadbed winds its way through the hill country. There was also a "Blue Goose" and a "Southern Queen" on the E. K. These were passenger coaches with Model T engines to power them.

Poet Laureate of Kentucky, Jesse Stuart–whose lines opened this chapter–was from Greenup County. He also said: *"...the old E-K - Railroad, where the mail used to start out once a day and then twice a day, but if a tunnel fell in, there was no mail at all."*

For all this bustling commerce, the surrounding hills pretty much insulated the inhabitants from both the benefits and vices

thereof. While no insurmountable barrier to the engineer who wanted to get "from here to there," the hills were— and are yet—proof against casual trespass.

Jesse Stuart could say: *" My love is with my own soil and my own people and may I truly say the land is a land of log shacks and lonesome waters. ... I could run wild with the dogs over the hills now November-desolate and forsaken."*

Having viable quantities of coal and iron, and located on a main route of immigration to the "west" of the day, the Greenup County area bloomed early. However, richer coal and iron deposits, discovered and exploited elsewhere, diverted boom times to other parts of the country. The Kings found an area that had not fulfilled its early promise, and moved into it.

The Greenup County hills harbored–and sometimes sent forth–sons and daughters who became engineers, educators and poets like Jesse Stuart. Some, like David Spencer, with a high school education, utilized his talents via an ability to make other people's dreams happen– with baling wire and binder twine if necessary.

The Ohio River, throughout recorded history of the area, was one of the principal water transportation routes in the nation. However, little if any transportation use was made of it by the new powder mill. Sulfur, although one of the common barge-load bulk shipments made on the Ohio River, amounted to only about ten percent or so of the powder company's raw material requirements. It was delivered in boxcars.

The new plant was located in an area the Kings considered to be sufficiently remote. The nearest town, Wurtland, Kentucky, was far enough away that possible explosions were thought to be of no consequence to the people in the town.

On March 14, 1919, King Powder bought land from John and Hattie Harris and W.T. and Arminta Justice. These and subsequent purchases eventually amounted to nearly 900 acres. Both the C&O Railroad and Route 23 ran parallel to the Ohio River at this point. Route 23 was known at that time as the A&P Highway (for Atlantic and Pacific). It was an important artery for a nation slowly awakening to the potential of the automobile. The road lay in the relatively flat floodplain near the base of the surrounding hills. It was a little less than a half-mile from the river at this point, near the mouth of Deep Hill Branch. The mainline C&O railroad lay much nearer the river.

King constructed a railroad siding along the south side of the main C&O line, between it and Route 23, parallel to both the railroad and the highway. It was near the mouth of Deep Hill Branch, just west of Uhlen Hollow.

As a matter of historical interest and background, Jo Harris Brenner traced the ownership of Uhlen Hollow to Benjamin Ulin *(note different spelling; Jo found over a dozen different spellings of Uhlen used until ~ 1850! This is the spelling used on USGS map).*

Isaak Zane had adopted the owner, Ulin. Zane had been captured at age nine by the Wyandots and later married a daughter of Chief Crane. The Zanes were prominent frontiersmen. Ebenezer Zane, grandfather of Zane Grey, laid out Wheeling, West Virginia, and established Zanesville, Ohio. He also surveyed Zane's Trace from Wheeling to Maysville, Kentucky. Property contiguous to Ulin had belonged to members of U.S. president Zachary Taylor's family.

Near the mouth of Uhlen Hollow, the Kings built a hotel, residence houses for workers, stables for draft animals, storage houses, a company store, garages, gas pump, blacksmith shop, a soda house, charcoal house, sulfur house and a power house. These structures were strung out along this spur [see Dave Spencer's sketch of the area]. Buildings and mills completed, production of blasting powder at KICO was started in 1922.

The first superintendent of the Kentucky operation was Louis M. Dunn, who had worked at Kings Mills for some years. He retired in 1940 in favor of his son Virgil. Mr. T. F. "Shorty" McKee was office manager. The office was in the first floor (front) of the KICO hotel. The dining room and utilities were in the basement. The rest of the building was given over to rooms.

Notably absent, by today's standards, was a large parking lot. Workers lived on site for the most part, and walked or rode a horse there from nearby Wurtland. Automobiles were not that plentiful yet.

The KICO operation was a two-shift operation for the most part. First shift was during traditional daylight hours. Second shift was from 3:30 pm to 11:30 pm. There were watchmen who made clock rounds but no identification badges were worn. There were washhouses for cleanup after the work was done.

In later years coveralls were furnished and a laundry kept workers as free of powder residue as was practical. Powder-contaminated clothing was a real danger to the wearer, especially in a fire or explosion.

During good times, in more recent years, there were about 200 employees at this location. Dave Spencer lists names of some of the key employees, during his tenure at KICO, from 1948 forward. Dave makes clear his is not an all-inclusive list; it was not taken from any employee records—which probably no longer exist.

When KICO was first built, there was no electric power available. Accordingly, the Kings built the above-mentioned powerhouse, a coal-fired boiler, engine and generator. According to Jo Harris Brenner, the KICO power plant was later replaced when, around 1924 or 1925, Boyd County Electric ran power lines to the King Powder Company village and mill.

According to David Spencer, when no longer needed, the equipment KICO had used to generate electricity was sold. The vacated powerhouse was subsequently used for storage and a can shop operation. The building itself burned in the early 1950s.

A narrow-gauge tramway crossed Route 23 from the hotel area and extended back into the hollow to connect this area to the strung-out powder mills. These buildings were kept remote from this housing area—and sufficiently remote from each other to prevent explosions from wrecking the entire operation.

If you travel toward Ashland along Route 23 today, the C&O Railroad siding would be on your left. The siding and almost all the buildings are gone now. The tramway would have crossed Route 23 at grade, turned left to parallel your progress along the right side of the road for a few hundred feet and then taken a right turn and disappeared back into Deep Hill Branch Hollow. Along the strip roughly parallel to Route 23, three wheel mills, the washhouse and a boiler house were on the near side of the tramway. The largest part of the blasting powder manufacturing line was in the

This scene, looking south-west, includes the combination hotel and office of the KICO operation. The houses to the right were for supervisory employees. Route 23 was located on the other side of the office and houses.
Greenup County (Kentucky) Historical Society. Courtesy of Dorothy Griffith.

Aerial view of part of the KICO operation at the mouth of the hollow. The building at the lower left was No. 1 Warehouse, then No. 2 Warehouse, the Paint and Can Shop, the Paper Shell Machine House and, at the far right, the ammonia pump. The two small buildings beyond were laboratories; the one to the right housed lab stock. The larger building beyond it was the combination washhouse and laundry. The one to the left of the bathhouse was a test bunker, soon abandoned because of proximity to town.

Photo: Milton F. Lindsley, Jr.
Courtesy of David Spencer.

hollow, out of sight. All of the mills were connected by the tramway with the exception of the few connected by conveyor.

Draft animals powered the KICO tramway in the early years. They were supplemented later, but not replaced, by two gasoline-powered units not unlike the small electric-powered "mules" of the mines. These locomotives—or the animals—pulled cars like those used at the Kings Mills operation. Dave Spencer states mules were not used at KICO while he was there, only horses and the locomotives. Like Kings Mills, these animals were shod with bronze shoes held on with copper nails.

The tramway track was laid to a three-foot gauge and the crossties were spaced consistent with the stride of the horses. The tramway transported the raw materials through the successive steps, from start to finish. Flat cars, hopper cars and stock cars were all used on the tramway by which, ultimately, the finished

powder was carried to the storage magazines. A return track again crossed Route 23 at the mouth of the hollow. In later years, a C&O spur and a new tramline ran up the eastern branch of the hollow to service the new "white" [Detonite] production line.

A long pole was used by the locomotives to push or pull cars in and out of mill buildings that housed hazardous operations. The pole was fitted with hooked ends, which connected the locomotive with the car.

One of the locomotives had a four-cylinder engine, the other a six. The engine exhaust was piped into a can of water mounted on the locomotive to arrest any spark or backfire, which might initiate a fire or explosion. David Spencer said these had to be filled with water every morning; he also said these were commercial locomotives, not 'homemade' ones.

Another conveyance used at KICO was a Georgia buggy. This

was a smaller hand-pushed cart. It could be carried on the flat cars of the tramway and was used to convey the unfinished powder the relatively short distance from the tram into some of the mills, and back.

The magazines at KICO stored products made at Kings Mills, as well as KICO's products. Sporting powders, dynamite, blasting supplies etc.–in short, everything King Powder made or sold–was staged here for distribution. The KICO hourly employees were organized as Local #50 of the United Mine Workers. This was likely driven by the fact that the UMW also organized many of the King Powder Company's customers.

David Spencer stated the union struck the company one time for 25 cents an hour, but they settled for a dime. He did not mention any protracted labor strife. Spencer also stated he was the highest-paid hourly employee at $1.20 per hour. There were no paid vacations, but as Doc Lee indicated earlier, the local community considered jobs at KICO good work.

Life around the KICO operation was likely very much similar to that in Kings Mills, Ohio. Farming, hunting, fishing, boating, churching—and moonshining—were available, not necessarily in that order. Greenup County was a Methodist Church stronghold, but Jesse Stuart mentions there were both "Free-Willed Baptists" and "Forty-Gallon Baptists" in that area.

Although a copy of the KICO plant work rules is not available, it is reasonable to assume they were similar to those issued in Kings Mills. Safety was a subject of genuine concern by management and workers alike. If KICO management was callous about the danger to their employee's lives, research does not reveal it. Since the biggest threat was the volatile explosiveness of the powder, that was, of course, the focal point of the safety rules. Aside from the humane factor,

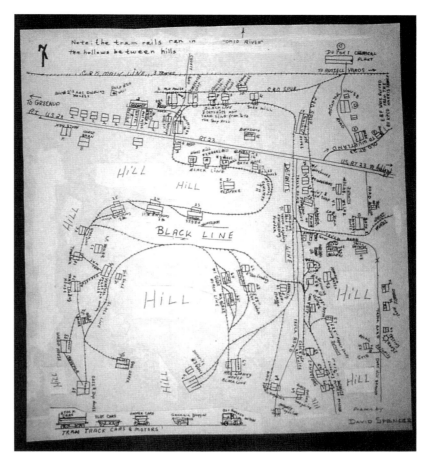

KICO plant layout.

This is a photo of the KICO bargaining unit. They are *(front, seated left to right)*: Clyde Webb, president of United Mine Workers Local No.50, Milton F. Lindsley Jr., Local No. 50 representative, "Shorty" McKee, KICO office manager. Back row *(left to right)*: unknown, Mr. Johnson, George Coffee, Chris Messer, unknown, unknown, all committeemen and Joe McMahon, superintendent of the Detonite line.

Courtesy of Joe Quillen.

explosions were a no-win situation for both the company and the employees.

The loss of plant and equipment, business, powder, good will–as well as the loss of trained, experienced employees–was expensive. Some workers simply quit when their friends got killed - and sometimes when there was no injury at all. Many a powder company was literally blown out of the business.

David Spencer noted that when he worked at KICO, he observed some unsafe acts and conditions. In this observation, Dave refers to the more conventional safety subjects—such as unguarded shafts, belts and pulleys, use of personal protective equipment, hot work permits, confined space entry etc.–not those things uniquely associated with powder manufacture. Violations like these would result in fines from OSHA today and would, if not corrected, eventually shut down the operation. No doubt Dave's observations are accurate. However, there has been great change in our culture with regard to safety in just the past twenty years or so. Just as we are appalled by some of the sanitation practices of our forefathers, our attitude regarding on-the-job-safety has changed, too. Hot work permits, confined space entry, etc., were likely unheard-of by most employees in that day.

In past years, survival of new and young employees in a forest of unguarded shafting, belting and pulleys–and general life among similar workplace hazards–was considered a rite of passage; the inept simply not making it. A sort of grim humor was associated with surviving within the hazards, a certain pride exhibited by those who were skillful and/or lucky enough to avoid injury or worse. Most would argue today's changes are all for the better and trot out lower operational cost figures to prove it. Others would argue the modern safety rules simply

assure us of more fools in the workplace. We'll not get into a debate on that subject here.

The man in charge of all of King's operations during Dave Spencer's tenure, and for many years before that, was Milton F. Lindsley Jr., the inventor of Detonite and, perhaps as importantly, developer of the means and methods for manufacturing it. Milt pretty much stayed in Ohio at the Kings Mills operation and many, if not most, of the KICO workers liked it that way!

Lindsley owned his own airplane and flew it to KICO on occasion, buzzing the plant and landing at an airport in nearby Worthington. Someone would then drive over and pick him up. In this way, he could go down to KICO, transact business and depart the same day.

Milton F. Lindsley was without doubt very talented, a graduate mechanical engineer from Ohio State University. According to Dave, Milt seldom admitted he was wrong about anything. After all, his father had been *the* Milton F. Lindsley who had worked with Dittmar, who had worked with Nobel. Old Milt had not only been one of the pioneers in smokeless powder, but had also invented and commercialized both Smokeless and Semi-Smokeless powders for the King Powder Company.

Both Lindsleys may well have been descended from a Major Joseph Lindsley who erected a powder mill near Morristown, New Jersey. According to the *History of the Explosives Industry,* they made "a considerable quantity of powder for the Continental Army" there during the Revolution, as early as 1775.

David Spencer has indicated that if Milt had any humble feelings about his own importance, he had difficulty in exhibiting them. Fred Pott, Milt's brother-in-law (Lindsley was married to Fred's sister, Daisy), noted that for all that, Milt took care of his own and saw to it that

they had what they needed. Fred knew Milt well and kindly sent me a layout of the KICO operation that he found in Lindsley's attic after his widow, Daisy, died.

The KICO plant was first set up to make only blasting powder. This was "B" blasting powder, or soda powder. That is to say, the powder was made with sodium nitrate rather than the potassium nitrate used in sporting powders. The process of making blasting powder at KICO was substantially the same as it had been at Kings Mills. Reference to that chapter can be made for details. Perusal of David Spencer's diagram of the KICO layout, in this chapter, will show the similarity.

The blasting powder (black powder) line at KICO was called the "black line," or sometimes the "black patch." The Detonite line was called the "white line." These were in-house terms and were not generally used outside the plants.

According to a September, 1942, article in the *Russell Times,* pellet powder had been added to KICO's product line in 1928. Pellet powder consisted of a series of two-inch long compressed pellets of black blasting powder loaded nose to tail into a two-inch, or inch and a quarter-diameter cartridge, eight inches long. They had the usual quarter-inch hole down through the middle of the eight-inch stick to accommodate the fuze or cap. Pellet powder was a very slow-burning powder used to heave coal loose in large lumps.

Since David was recruited to help build the new "white line" at KICO, we know that Detonite was introduced at the Kentucky plant about 1948. This explosive had been initially introduced at the Kings Mills operation and had been manufactured at that place for over a decade. It may well have been at this time the newer C&O siding was run into the hollow to bring tank cars of ammonia and nitric acid to the new operation.

you hear about. When the techniques for initiating the detonation of ammonium nitrate were generally understood, much of the market for dynamite *and* Detonite evaporated.

Couple this with the fact that the use of blasting powder was outlawed in mines in the early 1950s. Blasting powder dropped from 31 perecent of the explosives market in 1925 to less than 1 percent in 1955, according to Marks' *Mechanical Engineer's Handbook.* Since Detonite and blasting powder had been the backbone of King's business, there was little to do but close the operation.

And close it they did in July, 1958.

It is perhaps ironic that the only manufacturer of dynamite in this country–as this is written–is owned by Dynamit Nobel, the successor to the Hercules Powder Company. David Spencer stayed on to close the KICO operation. The contaminated buildings were burned and the metals remaining were scrapped, and when David was through and the place was safe for casual entry, the scrapping operation was turned over to a Cincinnati firm.

Jo Harris Brenner says that in June 1960, the King Powder Company conveyed 857.80 acres to the Franklin Real Estate Company, a Pennsylvania corporation with offices in Newark, Ohio. The King Powder company had six months to remove buildings and improvements, with the exception of the standard-gauge railroad siding (C&O siding). When this was done, KICO, along with the King Powder Company, no longer existed.

This mishap shows that Detonite is relatively insensitive to rough handling. Over the years, two truck wrecks scattered Detonite boxes over the roadway like this, with no explosion.

Bob and Betty Carter.

It could be said that the land reverted to:

"...a place under the sun, walled in by the wind and the hills - nowhere for many - somewhere for some...[Where] I could run wild with the dogs over the hills now November-desolate and forsaken."

Author's note: I visited the site in April of 2000 with Dave Spencer as guide. I found his description of the geography was pinpoint accurate. There had been a crew harvesting the timber off the site and I find my use of Jesse Stuart's lines in ending this chapter all too apt.

This chapter could not have been written without the help of David Spencer, a native of Argillite, Greenup County. Argillite was just a few miles over the hills from KICO. David worked at the Kentucky plant of the King Powder Company from 1948 past the closing in 1958. He stayed on to work at making the KICO area safe for other uses.

David had been a soldier in WWII. He was the first sergeant of a rifle company in the Battle of the Bulge in 1944. Thirty-five men of his 193-man Company F died there. Returning home, David worked here and there until he was recruited by Virgil Dunn, superintendent of the Detonite line, to help build the KICO Detonite line in 1948. David stayed on as head of the Detonite line maintenance.

Detailed technical information used in this book is due to David's mechanical and observational skills that included the ability to design and build automated can-filling equipment and other automated technical innovations when he worked for King Powder. Skills that allowed him to recreate a detailed schematic of the KICO layout - from memory! Standing in evidence of these skills are various scale models of iron furnaces to be found in museums and historical societies, including the Kentucky Historical Society. These models were made and donated by David Spencer.

David Spencer was also, and still is, a prolific writer on various subjects over the years, including a newspaper column called *Another Time and Place.* David also has built working models of automobiles large

Two ex-King employees, Joe Quillen and David Spencer, in front of Joe's filling station. Joe was a truck driver for King and David was in charge of maintenance on the Detonite line. Joe's office is a gathering spot for King employees.

enough to ride in, and a working alcohol still to produce auto fuel. He is licensed to run this still but he wouldn't let me sample it - motor fuel only. Sounds like something the government would come up with!

Mrs. Jo Harris Brenner was raised near the KICO site and the Kings purchased a key part of the land from her family. The Harris home was just on the edge of the KICO complex. She published a family history called *Dear Mother*, which is rich in information about the land the Kings purchased and other

peripheral details. Her book is the source of information on land acquisition and many other personal notes on the area.

Jo Harris Brenner suggested contacting Dr. Harry Lee Harris, M. D., who was raised in the Greenup County area, now retired and living in Oregon. The good doctor had recollections of many who worked at KICO or were associated with the plant in some way. It was an excellent suggestion.

Jesse Stuart, author of the opening lines of this chapter, was designated poet laureate of

Kentucky in 1954. Hearing of his proximity to the Kentucky plant, he was contacted through mutual friend Randy Cochran shortly before Jesse died. He sent word back to come up and talk about the King operation. Jesse was very knowledgeable about KICO from the remote view of a neighbor and the more intimate view of knowing many of the local people who worked there. However, Jesse died before an interview could be scheduled.

There are some gleanings to be had from Jesse's well-known book *Head o' W-Hollow*. These gleanings are about the Greenup County, Kentucky, area and are relevant to this chapter. Jesse had an unabashed affection for W-Hollow, his home in Greenup County and the country and people surrounding it.

Jesse Stuart's W-Hollow was the next hollow west of the King operation. KICO was only a couple of miles away. Can't say Jesse liked the mills–there were other mills in the area also. But all were in some way a part of his home. While the area was remote from what many would call the centers of commerce, there had been coalmines and iron furnaces dating from the Civil War, and a coal oil extraction facility within the county. For all that, Greenup County people were independent and self-reliant.

Jo Harris Brenner mentioned that the Grasselli Chemical Plant was nearby on the north (*river*) side of the C&O railroad tracks. Brenner's records indicate the Grasselli plant was constructed in 1927. King's office, hotel, etc. was located on the other (*south*) side of the railroad tracks and between them and Route 23. The *History of the Explosives Industry* has much to say about Grasselli. That it was founded in 1839; one of the oldest chemical companies in the country. The Grasselli Chemical Company made acids for the manufacture of nitroglycerine.

There was also a Grasselli Powder Company (*not at*

Wurtland), part of which was the old Burton Powder Company that made black powder. However, *History of the Explosives Industry* is mute about a Grasselli, Kentucky, location. This is no doubt due to the fact the book was published in 1927. The book mentions the existence of the KICO operation but gives no other information. Jo Harris Brenner dug up the fact that, in 1929, Grasselli was taken over by Du Pont. Grasselli was in the business of making nitroglycerine and dynamite, elsewhere.

The Grasselli plant was a chemical plant; making sulfuric acid to support their dynamite operations at the other location. They probably also sold acids to the trade. Doctor Lee Harris said they made pickle liquor for the Armco steel mill in Ashland. It may well have been in King's mind to use nearby Grasselli to supply acid to make dynamite themselves at the new site. They never did.

The McConnell House was the closest non-company residence to the KICO operation, being between it and Wurtland. The house combines history with charm. It was home to Jo Harris Brenner who remembered the KICO operation from childhood.

Chapter 12

Exhibition Shooters and Promoters

TRICK AND FANCY exhibition shooting became a national spectator sport during the last two decades of the 1800s. The Buffalo Bill Wild West Show's William F. (Doc) Carver, Annie Oakley and her husband Frank Butler, all became world famous performing as exhibition shooters. As has been mentioned elsewhere in this book, Peters employed trick shooters. Other cartridge companies did as well. This was in addition to other promotional shooters who were hired or in some way subsidized to keep the Peters name in front of the public.

Exhibition shooters were different, however. They had a bag of spectacular tricks that were used to entertain and impress the shooting public. These men and women sometimes had an advance man to go around the country to set up the exhibitions. Most of them

probably did their own advance work, working through the local dealers and/or agents. They secured a date, some advance publicity and a place to exhibit their wares and show.

Peters was just a cartridge company, so they had no allegiance to any particular make of gun, rifle or pistol. At least, that was true until they slid under the Remington umbrella in 1934. These shooters were generally of the Annie Oakley stamp. That is to say that they were showmen, rather than practical shooters. That is not to say they were not capable of practical field shooting, it simply means that in order for the crowd to see the spectacular effects, there was some compromise in practicality.

The ability to hit marbles thrown in the air at a relatively short distance has little to recommend it in the game fields.

A well-known shooter and writer just before the turn of the century was A. C. Gould, who had little use for such activity and was vocal in denouncing it. Be that as it may, trick shooters were a popular draw. Here was a mini-circus that usually cost nothing in the way of an admission charge. Indeed, the sponsors were anxious that attendance be good. It was a spectacular and, evidently, effective showcase for their products.

Peters engaged a number of them over the years. The two best known and longest in the field were Capt. A. H. Hardy and Gus Peret. Hardy was the earlier of the two and there was some overlap. Hardy had performed since shortly after 1900. Peret survived into the mid-1940s and was both an exhibition shooter and a great photographer. As a result, he branched out into other fields of endeavor for his sponsors, producing advertising copy concerning hunting experiences and other shooting activities.

The following is from *The Sportsman's Review*, published in Cincinnati on January 21, 1905:

"Mr. Frank L. Carter is a very fine expert in rifle shooting, having had an extended experience of over twenty years in the Rocky Mountains hunting large game. He carries a novel watch charm, which is a bullet with which two antelope were killed while running at full speed at a distance of over 200 yards. The opportunity of securing such shots is very rare indeed and making them still more rare. Some years ago in a team match between Montana and Colorado trap shooters [they might have been trap shooters, but they were

Exhibition shooters were well established before Peters was started in 1887. Two of the best known, Frank Butler and Annie Oakley, are shown here. Annie is shooting and Frank is pulling the strings, releasing the clay birds.

Annie Oakley Foundation. Courtesy of Bess Edwards.

movie camera. He illustrated many magazine articles and later began writing for *Outdoor Life* and other outdoor magazines. He was an avid hunter in the U.S., Alaska *(which was not then a state)* and Africa. Applegate credits Peret for being responsible for the Peters Belted Bullet. And, that later his designs and sketches resulted in Remington's production of the well-known Core-Lokt big-game bullet.

Peret and a contractor friend went on safari to Africa in 1931 to hunt and photograph wildlife. The following account quoting Peret is from the *Morning Oregonian*, December 10, 1931:

"We had been on the Serengeti Plains, the greatest big-game country in the world, several days. [We] had not been able to sleep any at night on account of the roaring of lions all around our camp. They did a lot of killing within a few yards of us and when we went out at night in our camera truck to take pictures of them, they were around us everywhere.

"Several times we came very close to groups of three to ten of them in the shade of trees. They didn't notice us part of the time, and again they would get up and move into the brush. But a day or two before the accident we saw a very large, beautiful lion with a lioness resting by a tree. And I want to tell you right here that the lionesses are the ones that make the most trouble. We took some pictures of the two, but the lioness began to get mean. I could see there was going to be a row.

"Up through the brush came another very large lion with his harem of two. When the two males met, they had a terrific battle, rearing up on their hind legs and biting and clawing to beat the devil. I was in a lucky spot and got wonderful moving pictures of this fight. Well, in a few minutes the lion we first sighted got the best of the fight and the other one ran away.

"It was in this neighborhood a day or two later that Bill and I saw a very large beautiful lion with a lioness. I am sure as anything that this was the one that we had seen fighting. He acted very surly, seeming to be suffering. I had the .405 Winchester then, and seeing that the brute was looking for trouble I let drive. I hit him in the right shoulder, and as he started away I hit him again in the body. He fell over.

"We ran up to him and I put the rifle between his eyes, intending to finish the job, for the beast was still alive. A live wounded lion is always dangerous.

"'Don't shoot Gus, let's take a picture of his head!' yelled Bill, so I let the rifle down. The lion lay very still but his eyes were glittering.

"Here Peret explained that he handed the rifle to Herren, as the camera had to be refilled. This was done quickly, and Peret, 40 feet away, began filming the wonderful head. With his sights on the animal, Gus couldn't see what Herren was doing. The main object of the expedition was to

get pictures of wild game, and this was the first lion that had been shot on the trip.

"Suddenly I saw the lion, which was the maddest I ever saw an animal, jump up from near the tree where he had tumbled when shot, and start to charge. I was getting a wonderful picture but was all set to run, because when the lion first began to get up he was looking directly at me. I knew I could outrun him, and, anyway, Bill had the rifle and I was sure he could stop him. Bill said to me "Gus, are you all right?" I yelled I was, and that I could run away from him if he came toward me.

"But the lion turned away. Then I heard a muffled shot, but Bill didn't yell, neither did the native gun bearer standing back of us. I didn't know there was danger until I heard the words, 'Gus, he's got me.'

"I had the camera strapped to my wrist, but I jerked loose instantly. About 40 feet behind me was a native carrying a shotgun. ...I grabbed the gun, knowing it had at least one charge of buckshot in it. As I ran toward Bill... I put a dozen buckshot into its heart but that didn't kill the enraged animal and I had Bill get his Winchester off his arm, and then I grabbed it and shot the lion through an eye, when it dropped dead.

"Bill didn't seem badly injured. He had the rifle strap around his arm and was fighting the lion with his fists, having one of

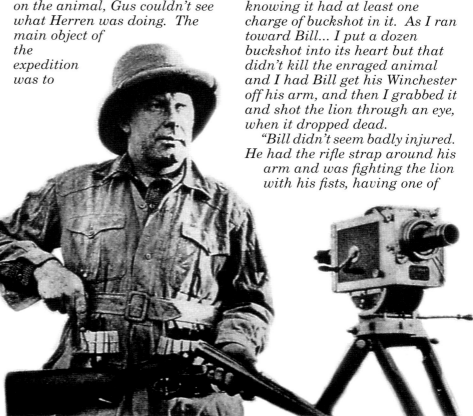

Gus Peret in his safari garb and movie camera.   *Stephen Farfaro.*

This illustrates Gus' versatility in doing "portraits."   *Dick Baldwin.*

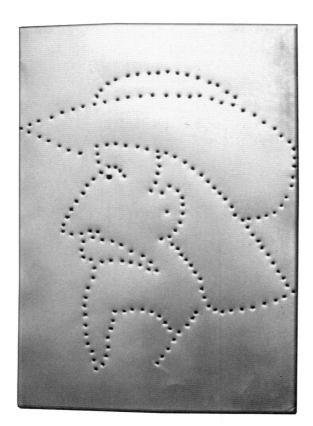

Gus Peret's "Buffalo Bill."   *Photo: Schiffer.*
Courtesy of Stephen Farfaro.

them crammed into the animal's throat. Bill was on his back, his right leg up and being bitten below the knee. There were a number of teeth marks in the leg. No bones were broken and neither of us thought the wounds were dangerous.

"I got him to camp, having wrapped my undershirt about his wounds and took a turn in it just below the knee. We dressed the leg in camp, then I had him in the hospital at Musoma within an hour and 15 minutes. There two doctors treated him, and then we started for a larger hospital. "...The hospital doctors explained that the wounds were not dangerous and that the patient would be out in 40 days. "Forty days," said Bill, looking up from the table where they had gone over his injuries, 'you say I can get out in 40 days? Say, I'll be hunting elephants long before that!' He died before we got into Mwanza from the poison engendered by the lion's dirty teeth.

"The game on the Serengeti plains is so plentiful that it looks as if it will never be driven out if the killings by lions are stopped. A lion will kill more game in a short time than all the hunters in a year."

Peret started exhibition shooting for Peters before WWI and after Peters became a division of Remington in 1934, Gus represented both. The heyday of his exhibition shooting was between the two world wars. During WWII, Gus was called in from the field to the Bridgeport plant. It was here that Dick Baldwin and his father came to know Peret well. Baldwin remembers that many times Gus came home with Dick's father and was a genuine character. He had stories to tell of great adventures and hunting trips. Gus had been hunting in Alaska over twenty times.

Peret considered himself a Westerner and sometimes his habits attracted a bit of attention on the East Coast. Dick remembers Gus once attended a private Christmas party held in the back room of a Danbury, Connecticut, restaurant. Peret entered into a disagreement with one of the other guests with some enthusiasm, and a fight erupted. "It looked like the barroom fight scene out of a John Wayne movie," stated Baldwin and took some $1,500 to put the room back together.

When WWII was over, exhibition shooting was about done. Ken Beagle did an exhibition shoot for Remington in about 1950. Herb Parsons was still shooting for Winchester but that was about the end of the trail for this form of promotion. By 1950, Gus was retired.

Colonel Applegate remarked that:

"The writer (Applegate) had an opportunity to witness the performances of many of Gus' contemporary exhibition shooters such as Dave Flannigan, Billy Hill, Rush Rezee, Milt Hicks of Remington, Herb Parsons and Claude Parmalee of Winchester,

Annie Oakley drew a crowd nearly anywhere that she shot. Here she is entertaining a crowd in Philadelphia, some spectators standing on the roof.

Annie Oakley Foundation. Courtesy of Bess Edwards.

and Henry Fitzgerald of Colt. From an admittedly biased viewpoint, Gus Peret's all-around expertise and abilities as a shooter, hunter, photographer and entertainment personality topped them all."

Walter J. Keenan was a first vice president of the fledgling National Muzzle Loading Rifle Association (NMLRA) in the 1930s. Walter had been a "boy wonder" trap shooter in his youth. He was understudy to the legendary Rollo Heikes, who later was the winner of the first Grand American Handicap, as we know it, in 1900. Walter tells this story in the April 1941 issue of *Muzzle Blasts*:

"...Rollo Heiks, who was in his prime [as a shooter] conceived the idea of renting [a Dayton, Ohio] rink for the winter and turning it into a trap shooting building...He

invited many shooters to come and see Annie Oakley shoot and also to participate in the target shooting from the five traps he ingeniously placed in the rink. .. with the five traps sitting on a slight curve. .. They were very deceiving and many of the well-known shots fell down badly in their scores.

"Annie Oakley at first had trouble hitting all of them...and towards the latter part of the week Rollo Heikes came to me and said that he had put up $100 on me to beat her on a 25 clay pigeon race, and that she had accepted. So the public... having heard so much about Annie Oakley, the star attraction, when she was advertised to... shoot a race against [a] Dayton boy, who was a youngster then, but who had gained a prominent place in shooting by accompanying Heikes all over Ohio and beating the best

of them in shooting, the public came in throngs to witness the match.

"Shorty Webb said: 'Is your gun in first class shape and have your shells been properly checked?' (I used nothing but Peters shells and King's Semi-Smokeless powder and Colonel George King... had presented me with several cases of his fine ammunition and I knew they were O.K.). 'You know this match is to be for blood and nothing must go wrong,' said Webb. Mr. Butler looked after Annie's affairs and I can see them now sitting on the seats waiting to be called for the shoot.

"Annie stepped up firmly to the shooting post, shot her five Blue Rocks from one position and broke four out of five; then came the writer and I missed one out of five. Then the next lot she broke four again and I broke five straight; we kept this up, both having settled down, and then she missed one more target, breaking 22 out of 25, and I missed one later in the match but managed to break 23 out of 25. I had won the match and the bet of $100. She was one of the first to come over and congratulate me on my wonderful shooting and I received the plaudits of the audience because I had beaten the great Annie Oakley."

As noted in the chapter on the Grand American, Annie used UMC shells exclusively. We will always have to wonder what would have happened if Annie had used Peters shells.

Dick Baldwin sent the following poem to me. It is attributed to Neaf Apgar, shooter for the Peters Cartridge Company and East Coast representative about a century ago. There was no doubt in Neaf's mind:

Pasting Them With Peters

When you start out on a program
And your nerves both twitch and
    twinge
When your trigger pull is jumpy
And you catch one in the fringe -
Then you settle down to business
And forget your flinchy spells
As you sock 'em in the center
When you're shootin' Peters
    Shells

When a head wind kicks them
    upward
Or a tail wind bears them down
When the lefts are rising smartly
and the rights most hit the
    ground -
Then you smack 'em as you see
    'em
And your "confidence" it swells
As you smoke 'em in the middle
When you're shootin' Peters
    Shells.

Perhaps you favor Em Ex
Or maybe you chose Red Dot
Again you may be satisfied
With anything behind the shot -
The thing that's most important
Is the tale the scoreboard tells
And the story's never bitter
When you're shootin' Peters
    Shells.

Why fritter all your efforts
With a load not tried and true
Because someone broke a
    hundred
With the stuff when it was new
If you want real satisfaction -
Every single doubt it quells -
You'll be pasting them with
    Peters
Those "Peerless Peters" shells.

One of the boys
that shoots "em"

Neaf Apgar as he appeared in a group of Peters shooters, promoters and salesmen in 1905.
The Sportsman's Review.
Courtesy of Trapshooter's Hall of Fame and Museum.

Chapter 13

Collectibles

I **HAVE STATED** that King's Great Western Powder Company, its successor, the King Powder Company and their offspring, the Peters Cartridge Company, influenced their respective trades far above their market share. As a corollary to that, collectors revere artifacts associated with these enterprises in like manner. Peters and King materials often command a premium above "rarer" items from another mill with a "bigger" name.

Anything identifiable to the King or Peters operation, their workers or their products can be considered a collectable. These fill many categories. Most collectors stay pretty much within one or two categories. The items can range from things as small as a .22 BB cap cartridge to a house. One collector actually acquired the A. King mansion and housed his collection inside! Another has an original steam engine (Peters asset No.3074) from the Peters powerhouse and Milton F. Lindsley's own '03 sporting rifle serial No. 3304117 (Remington).

This chapter will describe and illustrate some of the collectibles, rare and not so rare, which have come to my notice. You will find many photos of these in the color section. Shown with them is a price range. The pricing represents the opinion of experts in their respective fields of collecting. Pricing is a two-edged sword. It not only affects what you get for an item, but it also affects what you have to pay for it. Pricing, while subject to change over time, gives you an evaluation of both rarity and desirability. Be aware that prices are affected by region, condition–and simply how

badly someone feels they need a given item. There are times when you might gladly give ten dollars for a drink of water, but that hardly establishes the going price for water. The price of shotshell boxes is based on excellent condition empty boxes. Expect to pay a premium for full, sealed boxes. The price of metallic cartridge boxes is for full boxes in excellent condition. Calendar pricing is based on their being in excellent condition, original (not reproduction), not torn, faded or foxed–and with the calendar pad intact.

Wooden powder kegs with their labels intact, and in sound condition, are not easy to find. Remember that the predecessor of the King operation at Kings Mills was the factory at Goes Station, the Miami Powder Company on the Little Miami Railroad, and Little Miami River about six miles north of Xenia, Ohio. The keg that I have seen is marked: "FRONTIER RIFLE POWDER, wheel mill manufactory, Xenia, Ohio, 1859". It is of typical tongue-and-groove staves bound by four split-wood hoops on one end and three on the other; one hoop band appears to be missing.

At one time I entertained the notion that there were *no* wooden kegs associated with the King Powder Company at Kings Mills. It has been stated that the Wilsons were recruited by the Kings to make metal kegs for King's Great Western Powder Company at an early date in King Powder history. Regardless, there is a wooden keg at the Warren County Historical Society in Lebanon, Ohio. Edna Bowyer, secretary at King's, donated it along with powder tins and other

memorabilia from King and Peters. What is left of the label on this wooden keg is torn, faded and shellacked over, but a very careful examination will reveal its "Great Western" parentage. I believe such wooden kegs are rare, not only because of normal attrition, but because they were replaced by metal at the King operation at an early date.

Kegs, tins and other labels marked **King's Great Western Powder Company,** in use from the beginning to 1889, are considered more rare than **The King Powder Company** labels, which came later. King's Great Western Powder Company's "Far Killing Duck Powder" tin falls into that "early" category. Having said that, it is probable that there are *no* wooden powder kegs marked "The King Powder Company" simply because, by 1889, they were already using metal kegs.

The King Powder Company employed a label featuring a close-up of a duck, probably introduced when the name was changed in 1889. The hunter is seen in the background, along with his retriever. Some posters advertise Quick Shot powder, introduced in 1886, yet the logo in the corner uses the name adopted in 1889, "The King Powder Company."

This "Busted Duck" poster, as some collectors call it, is a close approximation to a can label used by the American Powder Mills of Boston and may well have been a 'knockoff' by King. A. O. Fay, of the Miami Powder Company, came from the American Powder Mills and was King's rival and chief competitor. King Powder used the "busted duck" on both can labels and posters and it is uncommon on either item. As a poster, it can be seen in the photo of the trade show shown elsewhere.

The most common label of the King Powder Company is the one depicting a crown with the granulation shown in an oval beneath the crown. A banner beneath that proclaims the product contained, such as Quick Shot, Semi-Smokeless or Smokeless. Early cans feature this label silk-screened right on the can in colors. Later, labels were printed on paper and pasted in place. While both were in circular motif, early ones were die-cut round, whereas the later ones were printed on a square piece of paper. You will sometimes see a paper label pasted over a silk-screened label indicating a different product than the can was originally intended for. There are instances where paper labels are pasted over paper labels. The variety is seemingly without end.

You will see differences in the cans made before the arrival of Wilson to the King operation in 1884. But there are the odd cans out of time sequence, such as the use of soldered cans for odd lots of powder long after the introduction of Wilson's double seam can. There is a can of Semi-Smokeless in a soldered can that has to date from late 1895, when it was first made, until shortly after January 17, 1899, when their "patent applied for" was issued. The label on this can looks to be a keg label pasted on, the last "S" in the name is wrapped around the edge of the can out of sight! The powder company, like the cartridge company, wasted nothing. It makes life very interesting for the collector.

There are half-pound tins and tiny salesmen's samples, 6 1/4-pound kegs, 12 1/2-pound kegs and, of course, 25-pound kegs. Expect to find blasting, as well as sporting powder in their many granulations. The collector may find packing cases for Detonite and Dynamite as well as blasting

fuze, caps, blasting machines, blasting wire and squibs. There were advertising items such as match books, trade cards, pencils, yard sticks, pins and who knows what else.

Although canister lots of King's Smokeless powder were sold, they are scarce, whereas Semi-Smokeless powder was sold until 1958. It would seem that the Smokeless line was not competitive with that of Du Pont and other mills and disappeared before WWI. It was withdrawn as a load in Peters' Ideal Shells before 1907. On the other hand, King's Semi-Smokeless was said to have no competition until 1911 when Du Pont's Lesmok Powder was introduced. Semi-Smokeless lasted as long as King did and, most likely, King could sell some today.

Photos of the grounds and personnel are rare but do exist. Brass or bronze horse shoes and mule shoes *(quite different from each other)*, copper horse shoe nails, narrow-gauge track, wooden shovels, leather and brass "booties" for horse's hoofs, and the various kinds of paper goods such as letterheads, letters, stock tags, catalogues, warehouse receipts, invoices, bills of lading, etc., can still be found. And there *are* red-hot collectors after them!

A study of the photos will give you an idea of what is authentic. While there is no guarantee that everything shown is authentic, I believe that it is. The reason for such confidence is that much of the material shown here belongs to people who acquired it during the days when it was still being produced at the King Powder Company. Non-sparking tools like wooden shovels and brass or bronze horseshoes were used by other firms, as well as King. Non-sparking tools are used today. If you would convince someone that an expensive object came from King, you had better have documentation.

As this is written, it is still possible to find empty cases, boxes and other memorabilia at

antique stores and flea markets in the southern Ohio and northern Kentucky area. However, the word has gotten around; don't expect to find many bargains.

In 1995, an innocent and unknowing auctioneer (yeah, it happens!) knocked down a totally *empty* Peters cartridge box (12 gauge), of the type made back in the '30s, for $275. He wanted to know when the bidding was over "what was *in* that box?!!" If you think stories like that are kept quiet, think again! Dealers who know that something might be valuable, but don't know the true value, can be very difficult to deal with. But there *are* artifacts still to be found here and there–and you never know when you will find a "sleeper."

Much the same goes for Peters memorabilia. Many collectors collect both King and Peters. It seems that the King interest is more intense locally, while the Peters interest is more universal. Don't underestimate the interest.

Now, let's look at some Peters material. As noted elsewhere, in 1887, Peters began loading new, empty, primed paper shells with shot and wads bought outside the company. It was an attempt to capitalize on the Peters-invented cartridge-loading machine, and have an outlet for King's powder production.

Peters Cartridge collectors can be placed into three rough categories: Shotshell, .22 Rimfire and Metallic–four, if you count Military. Rimfire .22 boxes of equal rarity will command a bigger price than a box of other metallic cartridges. A premium generally follows a cartridge in a "pretty" box, or one that has nice graphics on it. Military cartridges are often put up in drab packaging.

In addition to the common roll crimp for loaded shot shells, Peters utilized a unique and patented "stab" crimp and termed them "indented cartridges." You will find the earliest Peters loaded shotgun cartridges in "STAR" brand shell cases of UMC, U.S. Cartridge or Winchester; depending on whose empty shells they were buying. Those with the unique indented crimp give them away as being Peters. Those with the standard roll crimp, termed "Peters Crimped Cartridges", can be identified if separated from their packaging by the top wad, as it was distinctive. Study the photos in the color section to see what it should look like.

Collector William Paul Smith cites *Iron Age* of May 1888, pp. 828-829: *"Peters Cartridges for trap and skeet shooting... are loaded in Star, Rival or Club Climax shells... the "Popular" Cartridge... the Quickshot Cartridge in 10 and 12... the Ducking Cartridge... in 12 gauge."* As indicated here, the head-stamp does not reflect what cartridge is in the box. If the cartridges are head-stamped "QUICKSHOT", "VICTOR" or "PRIZE", you know that they were loaded after December of 1889, when Peters started manufacturing their own shells. Early cartridges and boxes are extremely rare and keenly sought.

In addition to the regular box of 25 loaded shells, Peters sold 100 shell boxes that contained empty shells only. The early shell boxes consisted of two pieces–a bottom and a lid–sealed with a label wrapped around the box. This type of box lasted until nearly the end of civilian production. There is no precise documentation as to when this introduction was made, it being introduced at different times within each product line.

One of the most desired boxes is the so-called Christmas Box, containing 100 empty shotshells. That many loaded shotshells in one box would be quite heavy. The label graphics, as well as rarity, being the driving force in the higher priced boxes.

I believe indented shells were abandoned about the time Peters went back into production after the July 1890 explosion, probably early 1891. The candy-stripe shells were probably produced in this next period. I believe all cartridges loaded in 1891, and thereafter, were in shells made by Peters.

The next big product step was the introduction of metallic cartridges. This was during a period of rapid change. Rimfire cartridges were no doubt introduced first. The Cincinnati City Directory and company literature tells us 1895 was the date of introduction.

The first metallic cartridges were loaded with *Quick Shot* powder or *King's Extra Quality Black Powder*. Catalog information in 1896 used the term *King's Extra Quality Black Powder*. Keep in mind that *Quick Shot* was not only a brand name for one of King's Powders, introduced in 1886, it was a name used by Peters for early metallic cartridges, a brand of empty paper shotshells so head-stamped and a brand of shotgun cartridges! I believe the earliest metallic cartridges marketed by Peters were in yellow boxes, branded *Quickshot*.

As early as March 1896, King's *Smokeless* was also loaded in rimfire and centerfire cartridges. Since Milton F. Lindsley had come to Peters in 1895, it was obvious they had wasted little time setting up smokeless powder mills and making smokeless powder.

A big collector's item is Peters advertising calendars. They appeared in 1897 and spanned the years until 1931, inclusive. Their colorful and interesting motifs put them in great demand among collectors and their popularity and scarcity place them in a fairly pricey market. Interest in them has created a market for reprints of some of them.

As you might suspect, the reprints are worth less than a tenth as much as good originals. How do you tell the difference? The original had a metal tab at the top to hang it, whereas the reprint's tabs are plastic and of a bit different shape. Some people have been known to cut the plastic off the reproductions and replace it with metal. All the original calendars I have examined have brass-colored bands at the top and bottom. The reproductions have painted steel bands. An experienced eye with a good pocket glass can see differences in the dot patterns of the old and the new. Another telltale to the reproduction calendars is that the originals sometimes copied for the reprint had tears or flaws in them that, with careful search, can be spotted in the reproduction. My advice is not to pay big money for a calendar if the seller will not let you examine it closely. As with all expensive paper goods, it pays to have them properly framed with acid-free materials to protect them. However, if you are interested in buying one already framed, be aware that tears, trimming and tabs may be hidden. Most collectors know that torn, trimmed, foxed or otherwise-altered paper goods may be severely discounted in price. It is a rare, desirable and expensive piece of art indeed that will demand any price if trimmed or otherwise cut, torn or defaced.

King's *Semi-Smokeless* Powder was introduced as early as 1896 and by July 1, 1897 was used–for sure–in metallic cartridges when Peters started to work toward the slogan *"not a grain of black powder is used behind a single ball, slug or bullet."* Just when this became fact, I do not know. However, it was definitely true before the April 15, 1901, catalog was published.

1898 was the year that Peters is said to have made its first government contract for .45-70 cartridges. The head-stamp on these cartridges is unknown to me. It would presumably be dated with the month and year and contractor identification such as "PC". I have not seen, or heard of, a specimen.

A separate chronology is provided to help the collector

date items in question. It is simple to use and features a reference to the source of the information.

Jim Sones, an avid collector of information on Peters and other cartridge companies, has kindly provided a listing of Peters and King copyrights and trade marks with their dates of introduction. These will be found in Appendix 9.

No one is known to have all of the catalogs of Peters, let alone King. A comprehensive listing of Peters cartridges alone would occupy a book larger than this. To give you some idea of the scope of their activity, consider this quote from a 1906 brochure *Talking Points for salesmen of Peters Goods*: *"[Our] list of loaded shells embraces 637 varieties of standard length, one kind of shot and one kind of powder. But taking all the combinations it regularly loads of different lengths, of soft and chilled shot and of all powders, black, smokeless and semi-smokeless the number extends to over 20,000. [We are] now making for revolvers, pistols and rifles, 223 different styles of cartridges. [We] make 85 sizes and qualities of wads, 9 different styles of primers and 31 kinds of empty shells."* If you add to this all the different varieties of boxes in which the same cartridges were shipped over the years you will get some idea of the magnitude of their operation in 1906.

With any expensive collector's item, get the advice of an expert before purchasing, or buy from a professional who will give you a bill of sale. It is the professional's duty to know whether the item offered is authentic. The professional should also make good on any item that later proves to be a fake. A key word here is *proves*... this determination may not be easy or inexpensive.

There is no substitute for long hours of research, and simply looking at known authentic items. It has taken me more years than I care to admit to gather the data for this book. Even so, collectors freely shared a lot of the information. Most of the photos, while taken by me, were of items in private collections.

The biggest value of this book to collectors is the information about the companies and people who *produced* the collectables. While the chronology is valuable for dating items, the text provides a whole new dimension and life to the mute items one collects. There are many differing reasons for collecting. Perhaps one of the best reasons to collect, is to honor the long line of people—some of them ordinary and some extraordinary—who toiled to give this country some of the essentials needed for securing its place in the family of nations.

Nice graphics on old booklet. Price: N/A.

This "Busted Duck" poster hung in the King Powder Office in Cincinnati for many years. $1,500 - $3,500 if untrimmed. This one has been trimmed.

Colorful graphics on a die-cut store card. Price: N/A.

A Peters Tradecard. This fellow appears on a Christmas box of Peters Shells. $300 - $500.

King's Great Western Powder Co.
Office,
XENIA, OHIO.
MILLS, SOUTH LEBANON, OHIO.

L.C. EARLE

Rare early King cartoon advertisement. Price N/A.

Rare early King cartoon advertisement. Price N/A.

George King Estate.

This original painting hung in King's Cincinnati, Ohio office. Price: N/A.

Ron Willoughby Collection.

Resulting 20" x 30" poster. $1400 - $1700.

George King Estate.

Original art which hung in King's Cincinnati, Ohio office. Price: N/A.

Jim Eckler Collection.

Resulting 1918 calendar. $600-900.

Only one known. $5,000 - $6,000.

Jack Malloy Collection. Photo: Mike Sayers.

Rare. $4,000 - $6,000.

Ron Willoughby Collection. Photo: Schiffer.

Rare. $4,000 - $6,000.

Ron Willoughby Collection. Photo: Schiffer.

Jack Malloy Collection. Photo: Mike Sayers.

Scarce. $2,000 - $3,000.

Jack Malloy Collection. Photo: Mike Sayers.

Scarce. $1,800 - $2,500.

Ron Willoughby Collection. Photo: Schiffer.

Rare. $2,500 - $3,500.

Jack Malloy Collection. Photo: Mike Sayers.

Rare. $1,800 - $2,500.

Jack Malloy Collection. Photo: Mike Sayers.

Scarce. $900 - $1,500.

Jack Malloy Collection. Photo: Mike Sayers.

Scarce. $800 - $1,200.

Scarce. $900 - $1,400.

**Fairly common.
$600 - $900.**

**Fairly rare.
$1,800 - $2,500.**

Scarce. $600 - $900.

Common. $600 - $900.

Common. $600 - $900.

Scarce. $600 - $900.

Common. $600 - $900.

Common. $600 - $900.

Common. $500 - $700.

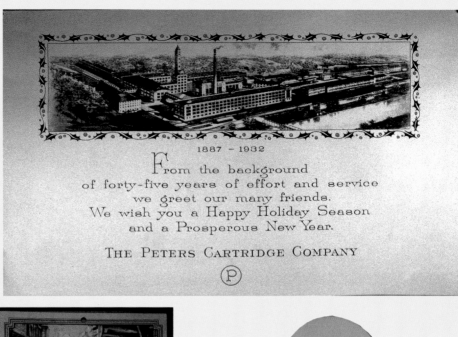

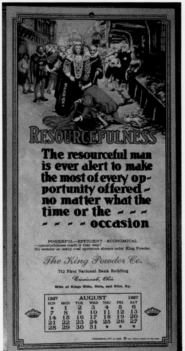

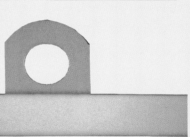

Plastic hanger on reproduction.

Brass on original.

Magnified "dots" forming reproduction calendar.

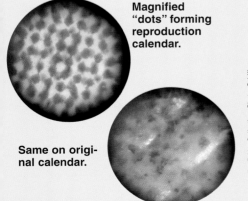

Same on origi-nal calendar.

Calendars were usually given as greetings of the sea-son. Here is another form. Price N/A.

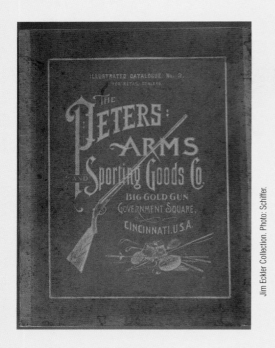

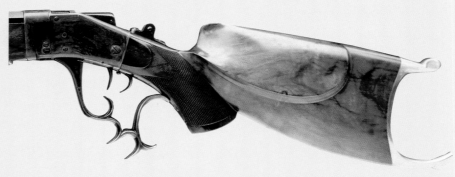

Note the distinctive Zischang-Style butt plate on this Peters Arms Company rifle.

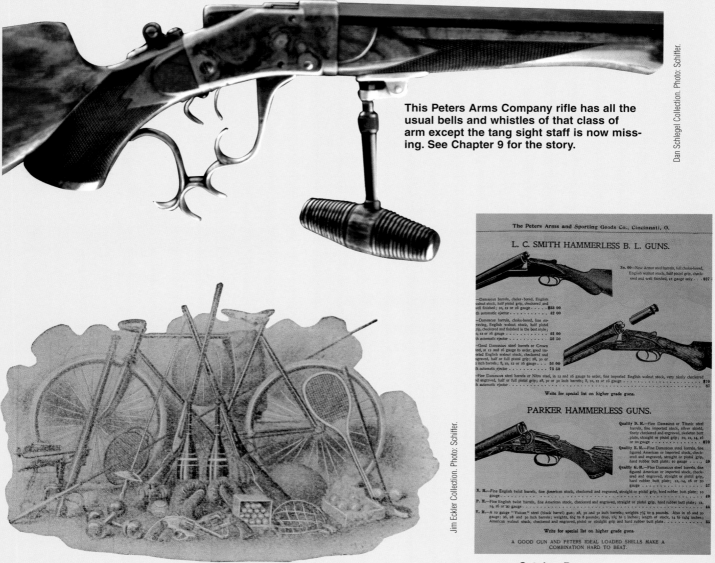

This Peters Arms Company rifle has all the usual bells and whistles of that class of arm except the tang sight staff is now missing. See Chapter 9 for the story.

Catalog Page.

This is a closeup of the engraving on a different Peters Arms Company schuetzen rifle.

This is the same rifle shown on the opposite page. This view of the left side shows the modeling of the cheekpiece and other details.

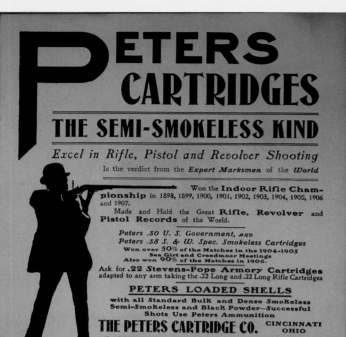

Both boxes $125 - $175.

Top to bottom, left to right:
$50-$75; $20-$25; $125; $75;
$300-$400; $50-$75; $600-$800;
$300-$400.

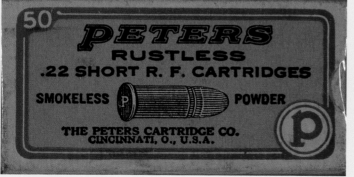

$300 - $400.

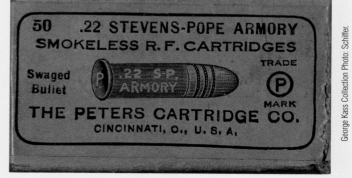

$300 - $400.

Price: N/A.

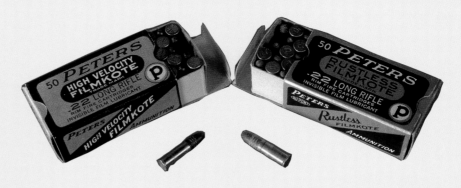

Each: $20 - $25.

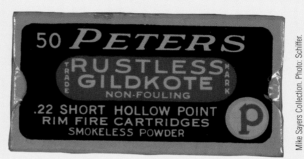

$50 - $75.

$25.

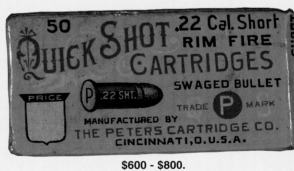

$600 - $800.

Each: $30 - $50.

Peters .22 Short—Giant of its kind

This grouping shows some rare and not so rare cans and kegs. The keg is from Miami Powder Company, where King got his start in the powder business. The Hercules can represents later ownership of that mill. Price: N/A.

$800 - $1000.

$75 - $125.

$125 - $175.

$75 - $125.

2 oz. Sample Can
$800 - $900.

$75 - $150.

Front
$100 - $150.

Back
$100 - $150.

$300 - $400.

2 oz. Sample Can
$800 - $900.

Sample Bottle. 1 3/4"
High.

Part of the King Powder line, early 1900s.

Each: $75 - $100.

Three Pound Can

One Pound Bulk Can

$800 - $900.

$400 - $600.

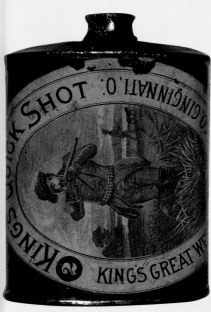

$600 - $800.

$400 - $600.

KING EXPLOSIVES

FROM THE YEAR 1878

Price: N/A.

THE
KING POWDER CO.

KING
EXPLOSIVES

TRADE MARK
CINCINNATI, O.

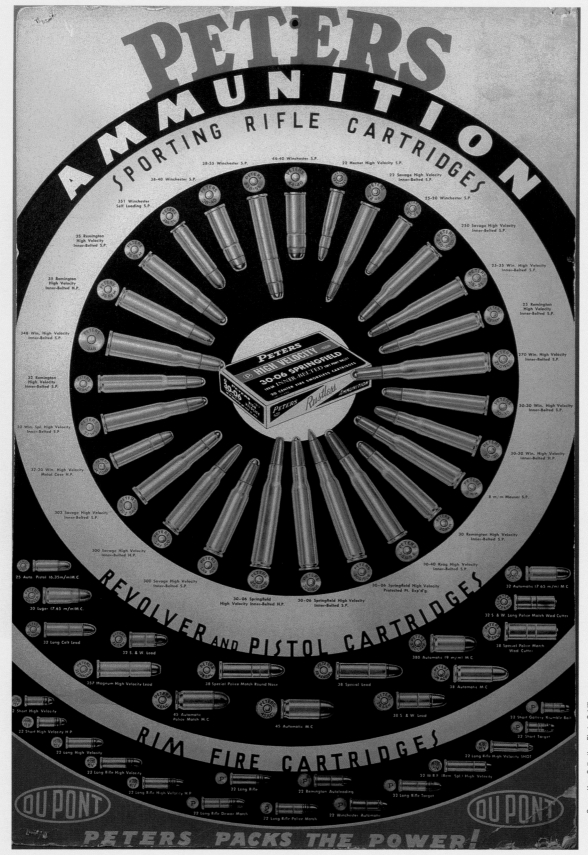

George Kass Collection. Photo: Schiffer.

Price: N/A.

$30 - $45.

$30 - $45.

$25 - $40.

$60 - $75.

$75 - $85.

$100 - $125.

Mick McLaughlin Collection. Photo: Schiffer.

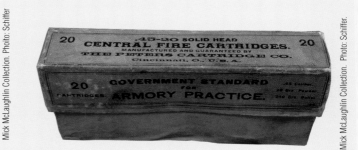

Top to bottom, left to right: $45 - $60; $50 - $60; $100 - $125.

Mick McLaughlin Collection. Photo Schiffer.

Top to bottom, left to right: $75 - $85; $75 - $85; $40 - $50.

$150 - $175.

Mick McLaughlin Collection. Photo: Schiffer.

Mick McLaughlin Collection. Photo: Schiffer.

Top to bottom: $100 - $125; $110 - $140.

$15 - $20.

Mick McLaughlin Collection. Photo: Schiffer.

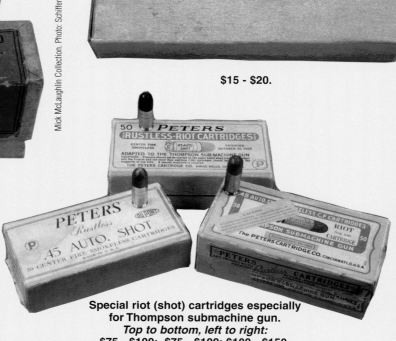

Special riot (shot) cartridges especially for Thompson submachine gun.
Top to bottom, left to right:
$75 - $100; $75 - $100; $100 - $150.

Mick McLaughlin Collection. Photo: Schiffer.

Blank cartridges. *Top to bottom, left to right:* $3 - $5; $5 - $7; $5 - $7; $5 - $7; $5 - $7.

5-In 1 Blanks. $1.50

Boxes of bullets only. *Top to bottom, left to right:* $25 - $35 each

Pistol cartridges. *Top to bottom, left to right:* $20 - $30; $25 - $35; $35 - $50.

$35 - $50, each.

$35 - $50, ($45 - $60, with paster)

$20 - $45.

$10 - $15.

Thompson gun with special shot cartridges shown (red tip) on near side of magazine; ball cartridge in front of magazine.

$15 - $20.

Top to bottom, left to right: $25 - $35; $25 - $35; $25 - $40.

.32 Rimfire.
$25 - $35.

$50 - $75.

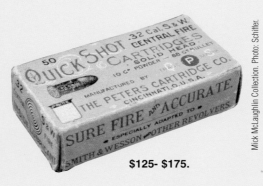

$125- $175.

$25 - $35.

$2 - $5, each; with embossed lid, $20 - $25.

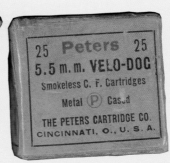

$100 - $150, each

Windy Klinect Collection. Photo: Schiffer.

Indent detail.

Windy Klinect Collection. Photo: Schiffer.

The only thing rarer than this would be an indented crimp cartridge with the earlier two indents. None are known to me. These two cartridges with three indented crimps are the only ones known. Price: N/A.

Head detail of the indented cartridges.

Windy Klinect Collection. Photo: Schiffer.

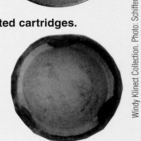

Crimp end of the indented cartridges.

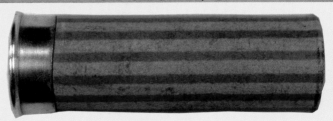

Author's collection.

The Sportman's Review advertisement. Photo: Schiffer.

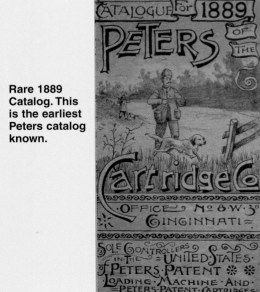

Rare 1889 Catalog. This is the earliest Peters catalog known.

Ted Bacyk Collection. Photo: Schiffer.

Rare Peters candy stripe shell. Price: $125 - $175.

Candy stripe shell headstamp.

Author's collection.

Detail of candy stripe shell top wad.

Author's collection.

$1,800 - $2,200.

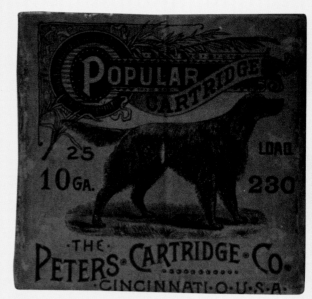

$1,500 - $2,000.

$150 - $225.

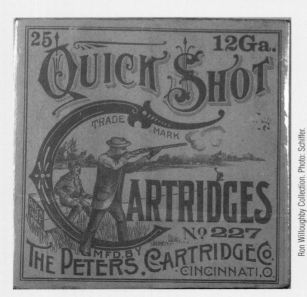

$1,400 - $1,800.

$1,400 - $1,800.

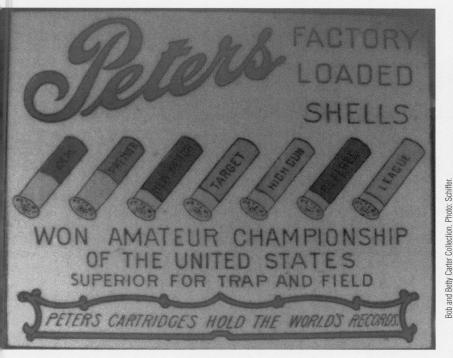

Counter Felt
$350 - $500.

$300 - $500.

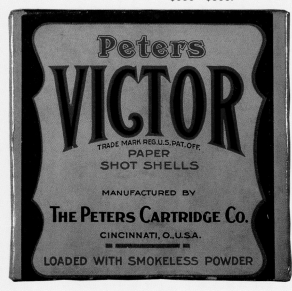

$50 - $100.

$400 - $600.

Price: N/A.

$125.

Price: N/A.

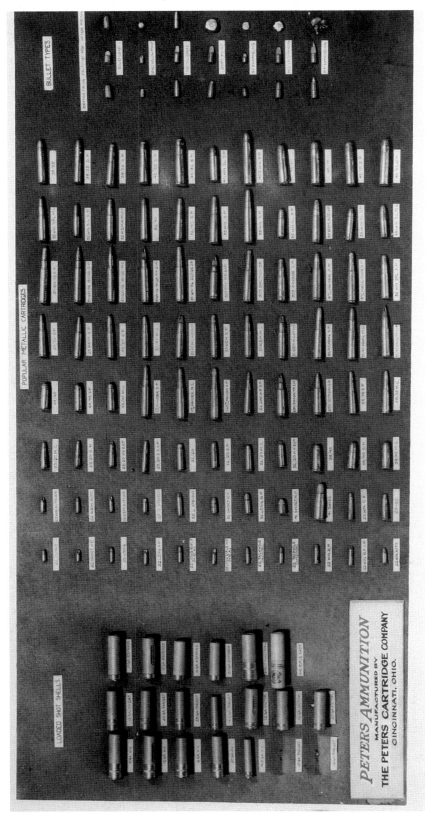

This cartridge board was sent by the Peters Cartridge Company to the Smithsonian in 1927 *(per Smithsonian files)* to commemorate Peters' fiftieth anniversary. It is the only Peters cartridge board known *(prior to association with Remington)* that has actual dummy cartridges attached to it. The cartridge board on the preceding page was entirely lithographed, cartridges and all. *Smithsonian collection, courtesy of Harry Hunter.*

Chapter 14

Epilogue

AS THIS PROJECT matured over the years, I saw there would be cracks in the mirror. There are things I have not been able to discover; others, there is no room to include. Yet I am amazed at the rich tapestry that has emerged, thanks to the scores of people who have shared their memories, their artifacts, their opinions and their time to advance this work.

I certainly hope this is the definitive work on the subjects included here. But I also know new information will emerge after this book is printed and gets into the hands of shooters, collectors and historians–and those interested in a good story. Constructive commentary is certainly invited.

I wish this work to be a monument to those people, ordinary and extraordinary (not unlike the author and the reader), who made these things happen–people who were just looking for their own place in the sun. They made these things happen in a rough-and-tumble economy; through war and peace, economic depression and boom times. A result of their efforts

Peters .22 Short—Giant of its kind

was the furtherance of the shooting sports, the definition of some and, more importantly, a real contribution toward spiking the guns of tyranny that emerged in their lifetime.

The venue of most of these efforts, Kings Mills, is now rapidly becoming a bedroom community to a growing greater Cincinnati. I hope that the valley that once echoed to the factory whistle and the wail of the locomotive will now be a safe haven to those who choose to live there. And that those same people will, in their daily comings and goings, occasionally pause to reflect on the sometimes-dramatic events that took place within sight and sound of their homes.

To the collector who carefully places a new acquisition into his or her collection, or reflects on those already there; to the hunter and shooting sportsman who casually thumbs a cartridge into his or her firearm: Be mindful that we inherited all this. The fact that you are reading this is eloquent evidence of that.

They built better than they knew. We would do well indeed, to do as well.

Appendices

Lawsuits involving Peters

Standard Cartridge Company v Peters Cartridge Company

G. M. Peters invented a round table or rotary cartridge-loading machine. One Charles Hisey worked on said machine. Cincinnati Screw and Tap Company had employed him in the summer of 1887 for that purpose. George Ligowsky was there, saw Peters' machine and conceived the idea of an endless belt machine instead of a round table machine. Making sketches, Ligowsky showed them to Hisey and others. Hisey subsequently applied for letters patent for the invention, as did Ligowsky and Peters. The patent office declared an interference between the three. The interference was subsequently decided in favor of Ligowsky. On appeal, it was decided in favor of Hisey. Another appeal found priority in Ligowsky. A rehearing stretched the case to November 17, 1891, again finding for Ligowsky. At some time in this controversy, Hisey sold his patent to Standard Cartridge of Chicago.

Tuttle, an officer of Peters, some years later stated that G. M. Peters had initially conceived an endless belt machine before he abandoned that idea and went on to invent the round-table machine. He abandoned the endless belt idea because he anticipated that it would suffer inaccuracy due to wear. The patent office probably decided against Peters' priority because he had abandoned the idea. If this view is accepted, in the initial concept of an endless belt machine, Peters was undoubtedly prior to both Hisey and Ligowsky.

Standard Cartridge sued Peters and not Ligowsky because, by this time, Peters had obtained the right, title and interest in the straight-line machine patent from Ligowsky. The question to be decided was, who held the valid patent on the straight-line machine.

It must be presumed that Peters and Standard Cartridge were both using the endless belt machine patent to load shotshells. I have found no other evidence that Peters ever did. Harold Himes, an ex-employee of Peters, in an interview by me in February 1999, insisted that there were only round-table machines used by Peters to load shotshells in 1929 when he worked there, loading shotshells.

Sage, who issued the opinion for the Circuit Court, S. D. Ohio, W. D. noted that..."*The total number of octavo pages of printed matter in the case, exclusive of letters patent, and of certain other exhibits, is 4,022.*"

The above is cited to show that the actions, appeals and defenses were drawn out and bitterly contested. These were, no doubt, very expensive proceedings. Sage found on July 15, 1895, again in favor of Ligowsky (*by extension, Peters*), saying:

"*The opinion of this court, after having heard the arguments of counsel, examined their briefs and the record, and considered the whole case, is that, independently of the rule as to the burden of proof, the decision of the commissioner of patents is right, that Ligowsky was the inventor, and that the attempt of Hisey to appropriate the invention was fraudulent. For reasons stated in his opinions, the conclusion of the court is that the equity of this cause is with the defendant [Peters]. The bill will be dismissed, at the costs of the complainants [Standard].*"

Still not satisfied, Standard Cartridge Company appealed. Thus we see this final appeal:

December 8, 1896

Appeal from the Circuit Court of the United States for the Western Division of the Southern District of Ohio.

COUNSEL: Robert H. Parkenson for appellants.

Frank T. Brown, for appellee.

OPINION BY: LURTON

OPINION [*632] Before TAFT and LURTON, Circuit Judges and HAMMOND, J.

The following is from the appeal document listed above. The appeal itself is very pertinent to this book in giving insight into happenings within the Peters Cartridge Company at a very critical time in their corporate life, their very beginning. Very little of a detailed nature is to be found from other sources between Peters' incorporation and the explosion of 1890.

This appeal is a name-dropper's dream. There are characters well known within the shooting fraternity of that day. Ligowsky, inventor of the clay bird and trap; Chamberlin, called as an expert witness, was the inventor of the first rotary (hand powered) loading machine; G. M. Peters, inventor of an automatic loading machine which improved upon Chamberlin's patent and carried Peters into the cartridge business; and lastly, we have the Standard Cartridge Company of Chicago.

On a more general level, we have the Cincinnati Screw and Tap Co. that later became known as Cincinnati Milling Machine Company and is now Cincinnati Milacron. We have William Howard Taft, later President of the United States, and later yet, Chief Justice of the U. S. Supreme Court, as one of the judges. Cited as precedent in the case is a reference to the McCormick Reaper case, which starred Edwin M. Stanton, later (*than the McCormick case*) Secretary of War under Abraham Lincoln, and Abraham Lincoln himself as lawyers in that celebrated case.

Here are some of the interesting facts revealed (*from Lurton's opinion*):

"*In 1887, and prior to that time, G. M. Peters, of the Peters Cartridge Company, had been engaged in the perfecting of certain improvements upon the old round table type of machine, for which he obtained a patent March 29, 1887, upon an application filed March 26, 1886. That patent is numbered 360,043. The device thus patented related to improvements in machines for loading cartridge shells, and was described as consisting, "primarily, of a circular table peculiarly actuated, and revolving within a stationary table, the revolving table being provided with the shell holding cases [shell holders], the filling devices being supported by the stationary table." Two machines built under the claims of this patent were in use in the summer of 1887, at the mills of the Peters Cartridge Company. These machines did not work satisfactorily. To remedy their defects, and improve their mechanism, they were sent to the shops of the Cincinnati Screw and Tap Company in the summer of 1887. Hisey was a mechanic employed by the company to overhaul them and make them operative. That job gave Hisey his first acquaintance with such machines and was also the occasion for Ligowsky's becoming interested in that line of invention. After the overhauling of the two old machines, the same company was employed to build two new Peters machines, and Hisey was again selected for this work. Certain improvements were made in the mechanism of these machines, which Hisey subsequently claimed credit for as an inventor. These improvements in no wise involved a change in the type, for the new machines constructed for the Peters Company were round table machines, constructed under the G. M. Peters patent, with certain improvements not involving the endless belt carrier idea in the remotest degree. The improvements in these machines were claimed by Hisey as his own conception, and Ligowsky credited this claim. Subsequently, these improvements, or certain of them, became the subject of controversy between G. M. Peters, the patentee of the Peters cartridge loading machines, and Hisey, and became the subject of a heated interference contest between them, the issue being decided in favor of Peters, to whom the patent was issued. Precisely how wide the claims*" made by Hisey were does not definitely appear. Certain it is that when one Armin Tenner, a German manufacturer, visited this country in the winter of 1887-1888, he was introduced to Hisey by Ligowsky as the inventor of improved cartridge loading machinery. So much impressed was Tenner with Hisey's claims that he entered into a contact with Hisey, dated February 17, 1888, in which it was recited that Charles S. Hisey "has invented a certain novel and useful automatic shotgun cartridge loading machine, for which he was desirous of securing patents in the European countries." By this contract, Hisey authorized and empowered Tenner to apply and obtain letters patent in Great Britain, the German Empire, and such other European countries as he may deem advisable; and Hisey agreed to furnish complete sketches of the machine embodying his invention, and such information as should be necessary or desirable for the use of the patent solicitors, or in securing such patents; and Tenner agreed "to apply for, and if possible, obtain, at his own expense, letters patent of Great Britain and of the German Empire, and to use his best endeavors to dispose of said letters patent by sale, license, or otherwise, on advantageous terms and to pay Hisey one-half the entire proceeds from sale of said letters patent in European countries." At the time Hisey was making his broad claims to improvements — claims broad enough, in his judgement, to justify describing himself as the inventor of "a certain novel and useful automatic shotgun loading machine," he had not, according to his own admission, conceived the endless belt carrier idea. That invention, he admits, was not made until April 1888. That Ligowsky should refer to the machine claimed by Hisey, and which

Tenner was to aid in pushing, as a "great success" or a "great invention" and as "Hisey's machine," or, "Hisey's new machine," is quite probable and altogether natural. In the face of the strong independent evidence that Ligowsky, in 1887, claimed to have himself made the endless belt carrier invention, and that he disclosed that invention to Hisey and others during that year, it is clear that no declaration by Ligowsky, made in 1888, whether oral or written, should be regarded as conflicting with his claim to be the inventor of the endless belt idea, which do not specifically attribute that idea to Hisey.

"...There are many inexplicable things tending to cast a doubt as to who is the first inventor. Some of them we have stated, and others have not been specifically referred to. On the whole case, however, we lean to the correctness of the judgement of the circuit court, and of the action of the patent office. This mental attitude is one that requires that the decree of the circuit court shall stand. It is therefore affirmed, with costs."

The costs were, of course, not stated, but it took eight and a half years to get this far! By now, Ligowsky was dead. The lights of the Standard Cartridge Company flickered and went out for good about the time of this verdict. It is not hard to speculate that this litigation had a lot to do with Standard's demise.

As contentious as the above had to be for all concerned, it gives us an insight into the Peters Cartridge Company and the times that cannot be gotten from looking at ever-so-many cartridge boxes, cartridges or advertising.

Winchester v Peters Cartridge Co.

The first out-and-out litigation Peters was involved in was another convoluted case involving a third party. The complainant was Winchester Repeating Arms Co. It started as a patent infringement suit against another party, American Buckle and Cartridge (A B & C) of West Haven, Connecticut. This case is of interest because it tells how Peters got into the paper shell manufacturing business and how Peters, probably quite innocently, got to be in infringement of Winchester's patent.

West Haven is part of greater New Haven and A B & C was thusly in the same town as Winchester. A B & C entered the business of making paper shotshells. Winchester confronted A B & C about infringing Winchester's wad winding patent.

In Circuit Court, D. Connecticut, March 10, 1893, Judge Shipman wrote the following in his opinion:

"In May 1889, the Complainant [Winchester] brought a bill in equity for an injunction against the defendant's [A B & C's] alleged infringement of the wad-winding patent. And on May 24, 1889, [A B & C] sold [Winchester], all its machinery and tools which were used in the paper and brass cartridge shell business, and its partially made shells to be completed by [A B & C], and its stock of paper, but not its patents. [Winchester] agreed, upon the complete execution of the contract of sale, to withdraw the suit, and waive damages for the previous infringement of the patent. The machinery so sold, consisting of three wad winding, two priming, and two assembling machines, was retained for a time by [A B & C] in order to complete the shells, which were being finished under the [Winchester's] inspection, and on August 23, 1889, was delivered to [Winchester]. On July 3, 1889, [A B & C] sold its patents to the Peters Cartridge Company of Ohio, and also thereupon secretly manufactured for [Peters] two full sets of machines for making shells, including two wad winding, two assembling and two priming machines, which were, in substance, duplicates of the machines sold to [Winchester], and in November, 1889, sent them to the factory of [Peters] in Kings Mills, Ohio where they were set up by the [A B & C's] workmen. [A B & C] also sent the Peters Company, at the same time, its drawings and patterns of these machines, and [A B & C] has not

since engaged in the manufacture of paper shell machinery. The machines were destroyed by fire about July 1, 1890, [it was July 15, 1890]. [Winchester], when it examined the assembling and priming machines which it purchased of [A B & C], was of the opinion that they infringed [two other of complainant's patents]. These suits were brought in October 1890. About May 1, 1892, [Winchester] brought suits in the United States Circuit Court for the Southern District of Ohio against the Peters Cartridge Company for infringement by use of the machines it had purchased."

In this case, Shipman said: "Let a decree be entered for and injunction against [A B & C's] infringement of [various claims of] letters patent No. 181,309 [priming machine], No. 232907 [cartridge assembling machine] and No. 237605 [wad winder] and for an accounting in each of said cases."

Williamson, in his book, Winchester, tells the story of the above litigation as follows, having had access to the Winchester company records:

"On March 18, 1892, Winchester brought suit against Peters Cartridge Company alleging patent infringement on one of the [types of] machines [wad winder] sold to Peters by the American Buckle and Cartridge Company.

"...The case, which dragged on for a number of years, was bitterly fought. Winchester finally won the case in March 1900, and was subsequently paid damages of $1,000 [In an opinion filed on March 24, 1900, "Not to be Reported" by Judge Thompson]. By this time the patent under controversy had run out and there was no question about Peter's right to use the machinery under dispute.

"While the suit was being carried on Peters had been able to continue its manufacture of shot shells using machinery that did not infringe any existing patents. [Peters] had [developed during this interim] an exclusive agreement with its paper supplier, made its own shot, and developed its own facilities for the manufacture of primers, and wads.

"Peters seems to have built up its sales outlets during the period when it was loading empty shells purchased from the association [Ammunition Manufacturers' Association]. These outlets remained with [Peters] after its break with that organization."

Peters Cartridge Company v Winchester
Decided June 3, 1907

This was a trademark suit. Peters opposed the granting of the trademark "Self Loading" to Winchester as it applied to cartridges. Peters held that a trademarked name could not consist of merely descriptive words. If it could, the trademark registration would preclude any

competitor from marketing such a product and telling the consumer on the label what its purpose was.

The Court of Appeals of the District of Columbia upheld the above decision on the grounds stated. The decision was made on March 3, 1908, and announced on June 23, 1908.

Winchester v Peters Cartridge Company

Opinion dated January 9, 1911

After smokeless powder was introduced, greater internal pressures were generated within the shotshells. Among other problems was that of "cutoff." Cutoff was a term used to designate the occasional separation of the paper tube from the brass head, in the gun chamber, upon firing.

The brass head itself, with its substantial rim, would be readily extracted, leaving the paper tube within the gun. When this occurred, the shooter was forced to remove the cut-off paper tube from the chamber of the gun with no tools, and under field conditions. The gun barrel subsequently could not be used until the paper tube was removed.

Winchester met this problem by embossing that part of the brass head that held the paper. This was done in a circular manner such that the brass had somewhat of a "bellows" effect. That is to say that it gave the brass head a freedom to elongate upon firing such that it would not concentrate all the stretch in the paper tube, occasionally wringing one off. Winchester patented this.

When the Winchester patent was presented to the Patent Commissioners, they rejected it on the basis that the claims were too broad. The patentee had tried to claim that many kinds of embossing on the side of the head might accomplish the same goal. The patentee subsequently narrowed his claims to continuous circumferential embossing. The patent was granted on that basis.

Peters meanwhile had recognized the same problem and, whether influenced by Winchester's solution or not, introduced embossing on the head of their Ideal shell to avoid cutoff. Unlike Winchester's, Peters' embossing took the form of a series of diagonal hash marks running around the circumference of the shell head. There is evidence that Peters recognized that they might be in infringement of Winchester's patent and changed their advertising accordingly. The courts found, however that the Peters embossing was not of a continuous nature and found no infringement on the part of Peters. In this the court acknowledged that the Patent Office probably erred in their initial rejection of Winchester's patent. However, the court held that Winchester had rejected its opportunity to appeal this ruling but instead elected to narrow their claim.

Coxe, circuit judge, wrote the following opinion:

"In our view the question is a simple one. The patentee in order to secure the patent, acquiesced in the decision of the Patent Office that broad claims could not be allowed, in view of the prior art. He accepted claims substantially limited to the precise structure shown in the drawing and described in the specification. The defendant's structure is not within these claims unless a construction be given them which the law does not permit."

Taylor v The Industrial Commission of Ohio

Opinion dated June 19, 1920

This case is primarily of interest in that it set the precedent that an employee is still held *(in Ohio)* to be an employee, even while on break or at lunch.

Hamilton, in his opinion stated:

...Taylor, the deceased, was a night watchman at the Peters Cartridge Company's factory at Kings Mills, Ohio, and was on duty on the night the injury was claimed to have occurred; that he went on duty at 5:11 pm and worked until 6:02 am, approximately 13 hours. With the sanction of the employer, about 12 o'clock an hour for lunch, rest and recreation was taken. On the night in question, during the recreation hour, Taylor, who at the time appeared all right, stepped out of the company's shop on to the company's property to smoke. In going out he passed down some concrete steps leading from the shop. In a very brief period of time, approximately two minutes, he returned, holding his back and seemingly in pain, and immediately stated to other workmen, as testified by them, that in going out he had fallen on the concrete steps and injured his spine. Taylor continued to suffer and died three weeks later. There was medical evidence of injury to the spine.

The Industrial Commission denied widow Gussie Taylor's petition for Workman's Compensation on the basis that Taylor was at his own business when injured and there was no evidence of injury; testimony of his fellow workers was not admissible, being hearsay.

Hamilton found that statements made immediately after an injury, and in the presence of the person testifying, were "...*lacking the usual grounds of untrustworthiness, and therefore admissible.*"

Hamilton also found: *"The procuring of food or other refreshments by an employee, although personal in character, is considered so far incidental to the employee's work that injuries received while procuring such food and refreshments may be found to arise out of and in the course of the employment, provided the employee acts in a reasonable and prudent manner, and the injuries occur while he is upon the employer's premises."*

Gussie got paid!

(The author's indebted to George Kass who initially opened the door on the lawsuit involving A B & C. Mike Pynn, then a law student, provided copies of the opinions on all but the case involving trademarks, which came from Jim Sones. Sones shared his findings on that case, and the ones involving Standard and A B & C.)

Kings Mills Ordnance Plant (KMOP)

The information here was obtained from the files of the Cincinnati Historical Society. The author/s are unknown, but it was obviously a product of the Ordnance Department itself. It is included here for the interesting and little-known information it contains, and as a tribute to the unique contribution this "shoestring" organization made toward the successful conclusion of WWII.

Author.

"Industrial Preparedness

Procurement Planning

"Not until the last few weeks have the great majority of people in this country heard of the term 'Industrial Preparedness' or 'Industrial Mobilization'; however, it is a term that is twenty years old and known to *practically all of the large manufacturing concerns of the Cincinnati District.*

"Few people other than the manufacturers, have ever heard of the Cincinnati Ordnance District, yet there is located in the Enquirer Building of this city a unit of the War Department known as the Cincinnati Ordnance District Office.

"The history of the Cincinnati Ordnance District is divided into two definite periods, the first from March 1918 until the fall of 1920, during which time a total of 1,016 war contracts for ordnance material amounting to $220,000,000, and claims approaching $100,000,000 were handled. During this period the Cincinnati Ordnance District was in charge of the late Mr. C. L. Harrison. The second period started in December 1922, when the Cincinnati Ordnance District was re-established by the War Department with Mr. C. L. Harrison again appointed District Chief. A regular Army Ordnance Officer, Lieut.

Charles E. Lex, Jr. Ordnance Dept U. S. A., was detailed assistant to the District Chief. Mr. Harrison served until his death in December 1936.

"In May, 1937, Mr. E. A. Muller, President of the King Machine Tool Company was appointed Chief of the Cincinnati Ordnance District at a salary of $1.00 per year. Mr. Fredrick V. Geier, President of the Cincinnati Milling Machine Company was appointed Assistant District Chief, Major Fred. A. McMahon, Ord. Dept. U. S. A. is the present regular army Executive Assistant to the District Chief.

"The mission of the Cincinnati Ordnance District is to locate industrial plants in the southern section of Ohio, and Indiana, and the entire state of Kentucky and Tennessee capable of producing such ordnance items as ammunition, guns, recoil mechanisms, combat cars, fire control equipment, gauges, flares, machine tools, etc. which would be required in large quantities in time of war. After locating industrial facilities capable and willing to do such work in the event of a national emergency, to request the Assistant Secretary of War to allocate that plant to the Ordnance Department for such use. After a plant is allocated, the management is presented with a schedule of production of the article, which the management in conference with a member of the Cincinnati District Ordnance Office agrees could best manufacture in time of war. The management then signs the 'schedule of production'. This 'accepted schedule of production' has no legal status and is not binding on either the Government or the Industrial plant. It simply means that the industrial plant has cooperated with the Government in studying and analyzing the war load that may be placed upon it, and is prepared to carry this load in war.

"Industry, after accepting a schedule of production, then proceeds to make a factory plan or production analysis, for most items. Here industry is not so well prepared to assume the load, since it is unfamiliar with the product required, and the manufacturing activities involved are of a character entirely dissimilar to those used under peacetime production. These plans are prepared by industry at no expense to the Government.

"There is one problem in this scheme of National Defense which greatly concerns the War Department and which cannot [be solved] in any District except the Cincinnati Ordnance District and that is the procurement of Machine Tools in the event of a national emergency. It will be necessary to get the largest number of machine tools in the shortest possible time. These machine tools will be needed by plants throughout the United States who will be engaged in the production of munitions. This problem is being given careful study at the present time by the War Department and the Machine Tool Builders of the Cincinnati Ordnance District.

"Recently, Congress passed the so-called Educational Order Bill which will allow the War Department to [place] orders for articles of ordnance with certain selected industrial concerns to enable them to obtain the necessary machine tools, dies, jigs, fixtures, and gauges to accomplish their war orders. Those plants receiving educational orders will be better able **when war comes** [emphasis the author's; note it does not say if war comes] to start off on their war program. Much of the confusion and delay will be eliminated. The 'educational order' program is to cover a period of five years [this written in 1938].

"At the present time there are one hundred and forty-three (143) industrial plants allocated to the Cincinnati Ordnance District, most of which have accepted schedules of production placed with them. In addition to the list of manufacturing plants already allocated there is being prepared a comprehensive file of manufacturers in the district that could be used as sub-contractors in the event of an emergency.

"Another function of the Cincinnati District Ordnance Office is to procure in time of peace suitable qualified personnel for commission as Reserve Officers. At the present time there are forty Reserve Officers assigned to this office. These officers have been chosen because of their special adaptability to ordnance work. These are the officers who in time of war will actually run the affairs of the Cincinnati Ordnance District. These officers, with certain key civilians, will fill the executive positions in the Ordnance District. In time of peace, as funds permit, these officers are sent for two weeks training at Aberdeen's Proving Ground, Maryland, or to one of the manufacturing arsenals, or to the District Office, where they become acquainted with their duties as Ordnance Officers in time of war."

November 16, 1938

"PROCUREMENT SERVICE

"PLANNING DIVISION   1/21/42

"The main function of the Planning Division of Procurement Service

is to locate manufacturing facilities in this District capable of producing Ordnance items and to plan for the use of these facilities most useful to the Ordnance Department.

"To accomplish this purpose practically all metal working plants of any appreciable size, and any other miscellaneous types of facilities, have been surveyed by engineers from this Division. Information obtained by survey includes a complete list of all machine tool equipment and various information pertaining to type of buildings, handling and shipping facilities, power supply, normal products, previous experience in Ordnance work, number of employees, financial condition, and especially the abilities of the management and engineering staff. By analysis of the Report of Survey it is determined which items procured by this office are best adapted to the manufacture in each plant and estimates are made of the capacity for the production of the selected items.

"Of course, this capacity varies from time to time as the companies obtain contracts for various Ordnance items or items for other Government Agencies, but this office attempts to keep records of available capacity up-to-date from week to week. Records are also maintained of the available working hours on each critical machine tool in each plant. These records also must be changed from time-to-time in order to be of any real value.

"When Ordnance Production Programs are to be established by the Chief of Ordnance, the Planning Division immediately begins to determine in advance the companies best suited for the manufacture of each item on the Program and reports available capacity for each of these items to Washington. On the basis of these reports the District office is alloted [sic] a portion of the items to procure and the Planning Division, which includes those companies that have been determined as capable of producing the required item, makes up a bidder's list. As far as possible, companies given invitations to bid are limited to those facilities already having the necessary equipment. Where equipment is not available, companies are selected which have the necessary engineering staff, management and experience to handle the particular type of manufacture.

"The planning Division in connection with the Contract Distribution Division of OPM also assists in locating subcontractors to more efficiently produce the item or to speed up production schedules.

"In order to assist prospective manufacturers a suggested list of operations, machines required, and plant lay-outs have been prepared for several typical Ordnance items and they are furnished to interested facilities.

"Any other additional assistance possible is rendered to companies desiring to began production for the Ordnance Department. Possibly the most helpful aid in this respect is the display room which is maintained as part of the Planning Division. In this display is attempted to have samples of all types of Ordnance items and pictures or sketches of those items which it is impossible to display or obtain."

CDOO (Cincinnati District Ordnance Office) issued "CDOO 687-5" which listed the following:

"The Cincinnati Ordnance District has the following
Sub-offices:

Dayton, Ohio

Springfield, Ohio

Indianapolis, Indiana

Muncie, Indiana

Louisville, Kentucky

Chattanooga, Tennessee

Cincinnati, Ohio

Evansville, Indiana

Memphis, Tennessee

Frigidaire Ordnance Plant

Kings Mills, Ordnance Plant

The following was taken from CDOO 685-6. It relates to instructions to inspectors who will represent the Ordnance Department in inspecting to determine conformance with specifications:

"Basic Fundamental NO. 4

"Basic Fundamental NO. 4
"Relations With Contractor.
"The importance of pleasant relations with contractors cannot be stressed too often. There never was and never will be a good inspector who lacks the ability to successfully meet corporation officials, from the superintendent down to the foremen and the men directly under him. This statement should not be interpreted to mean that a good inspector must have a gift of gab. A very unassuming person, who is thoroughly familiar with the basic fundamentals mentioned, will have taken a long step in acquiring the necessary confidence and poise to command respect of Company officials necessary to enable him to conduct his inspection in a thorough and workmanlike manner. A surly, overbearing, or to mention another extreme, a person not sure of himself and afraid to say "no", will not in any case make a patch on a good inspector's overcoat."

Reminiscences of Mrs. Betsey Kendall King (Mrs. Joseph Warren King I)

While the subject of this biography had no input to this story as a direct participant, she was the wife of "Old J. W." (Joseph Warren King) who, together with his nephew Ahimaaz King, founded the King's Great Western Powder Company. That the wives of important men are too little recognized is all too well known. It is rare that one of them leaves *any* memoir. Betsey did, albeit of a fragmentary and incomplete nature. It was dictated to her daughter in 1896.

The writer is including it with no apology whatsoever. Betsey's story gives us an insight into frontier Ohio at a time when Ohio was indeed that. It also lends a flavor of the times to the story of the founding of King's Great Western Powder Company, that this writer's feeble fingers could not possibly provide.

Betsey Kendall was born, with a twin sister, Rebecca, on October 3, 1812. They were descended from William Bradford who came over on the Mayflower. Their place of birth was Suffield Connecticut. They were educated, to use her words, in the *"little red schoolhouse."* In this institution the *"winter fuel was supplied by the patrons of the school in turn; if by chance any belated farmer was not on time with his load of wood, his children were promptly dismissed from the school...*

"The course of study was not extended; the three Rs received special attention...dire doom awaited her of being seated in open disgrace upon the bench with the boys."

Betsey's twin sister Rebecca died when she was ten, after a week of serious illness.

Betsey told of routine daylong preaching on Sunday; of Sabbath observation beginning at sundown on Saturday. Indeed, in her experience, a preacher was dismissed for *"immoral conduct"* consequent to his *"having suffered his hired man to drive an ox team with a load of hay from his farm 'after sundown of a Saturday night.'"*

"Christmas was studiously ignored. ...Thanksgiving was, par excellence, the feast day of New England. ...After church service, at which the Governor's Proclamation was always read, came dinner, fragrant with odors of chicken pie, and mince pie and pumpkin pie, and of the delicious spiced, baked Indian pudding. ... In the evening of Thanksgiving Day we had games - - blind man's bluff, for the children, and fox and geese and Twelve Men Morris for the elders, interspersed with popcorn, nuts, cider and grog.

"I note since that early day a remarkable change in public sentiment regarding the temperance question. In my day, cider - - sweet or hard - - was a favorite beverage, and the brewing of beer was as much a part of the regular duties of the New England housewife as is the preserving of fruit at the present day [January 11, 1896]. At barn-raisings, liquor was always served, and in haying time the jug of rum was always passed around with the noon luncheon. At my own simple wedding wine was served to the guests, and when the parson made his parochial call it would have been highly inhospitable - - not to say discourteous - - to neglect to offer him the customary glass of wine or toddy. Yet, with all this, in my opinion, men controlled their appetites far better then than now, and though the habit of drinking may have been more universal then, I believe that more liquor is drunk now-a-days - - there is certainly more open drunkenness. ...

"My married life was begun in Ohio, married in the evening of an August day [8-23-1838], I left my home the next morning to begin the long journey to a State far removed - - as was then thought - - from the border-land of civilization. It seemed a great and perilous undertaking, and when - - in response to her question - - my husband assured my mother that in three years at most I should come home for a visit, she was consoled- - only three years! Traveling would surely be easier and safer by that time - - possibly there might be a railroad - - part of the way at least - - who could tell?

"Our wedding journey began with a drive to Hartford, Conn., sixteen miles distant, where we took the boat for New York - - a conveyance considered extremely comfortable and commodious, but vastly different from the floating palaces of today. At New York, we crossed the city in a stage - - this being before the days of the streetcars - - and took a Hudson River boat for Albany. Here we took the canal boat for Buffalo. We traversed the entire length of the Erie Canal at the rate of four miles an hour, and as we were two weeks in reaching Buffalo, this part of our journey, while not eventful, was restful and pleasant.

"Sometimes when the boat stopped for freight we would relieve the monotony of the ride by walking along the towpath. There were no staterooms on the canal boat - - only double berths in a long, public cabin - - and the lack of privacy was doubtless as keenly felt by the three other brides aboard as myself. At Buffalo, we took the lake steamer for Cleveland, at which point we took the canal again to Akron, which was at that time a thriving little village. A few miles out from Akron lived a cousin of my mother, with whom we stopped a few days to wait for our buggy, which we were to meet there. When it came, we drove through the Indian Reservation of the Wyandots, over a corduroy road through the woods, stopping for dinner at a tavern kept by a half-breed Indian. Everything about the place was scrupulously neat, and it was here that I saw for the first time in my life a puncheon floor. As we drove through the woods deer fled at our approach and the forests seemed full of smaller game. We finally reached our home, Westfield, Medina County - - a rude hamlet of scarce twenty houses - - and began our housekeeping in a house of four rooms, partly frame but mostly log cabin. I did my cooking over the fireplace, and on washdays the water was heated in great kettles in the yard. In case of illness the neighbors were mutually dependent, our doctor being a mile away, and the trained nurse an unknown quantity.

"There was little social life outside our home, which perhaps made the Sunday services more appreciated. There was no need to urge people to come to church, for the weekly opportunity for social intercourse - - to say nothing of spiritual needs - - was too highly prized to be neglected. People would come on Sunday from far and near, in wagons, on horseback (riding double), the men in top boots, the women in sunbonnets, and sit the service through on rough, backless benches - - a striking contrast to the luxurious modern church.

"I well remember the stir occasioned by my new cook stove, which was not only the first one I had ever seen, but the first one ever brought to Westfield. It was a "rotary" stove, the top being of sheet iron, and turned with a crank so as to bring the pots and kettles directly over the holes beneath; on top was a tin oven with reflectors; it was a great curiosity, and scarcely a day passed that some one did not come to our home to inspect the working of the new stove. After a stay of three years in Westfield, my husband decided to change his location, and I seized this opportunity, long coveted, to visit my New England home and exhibit to my parents their first grandchild, my oldest daughter.

"I left in March [1842], in the company of two cousins from Elyria, who were to make the journey east at that time to buy goods. Navigation being suspended, we went by stage from Cleveland to Albany over such roads as the present generation can have no conception of - - mud to the hubs and over; often the driver and male passengers would have to bring rails and pry the stage out of the mud, from which our four horses could not extricate it; occasionally an ox team would be pressed into service to pull out the floundering horses. I have said that we went by stage from Cleveland to Albany, but I think that fully half the journey was made in great lumber-box wagons pulled by six horses!

"We traveled day and night, except that once we stopped over Sunday at Batavia, N. Y., as both my cousins and myself had conscientious scruples regarding travel on that day. At Albany, we reached a new - - and short - - railroad, and I had my first glimpse of and ride on a railway train. I do not recall at what point we left the train, nor where we crossed to the other side of the Hudson River, but the rest of the journey to my native village of Suffield was made by stage. When I reached my old home, I had been traveling day and night for two weeks and one day, during which time I had had my clothes off only once. I had carried my baby in my arms all the way, and the chafing of my skirt-bands had left a broad stripe around my waist where the skin was almost entirely rubbed off! However these discomforts were soon forgotten in the pleasure of once more being in the company of my friends, and when - - in the fall - - my husband came for me, I was quite ready to return with him to my adopted state. Our new location was at Lima, Ohio, which was our home for twelve years [until 1854], and from there we removed to Xenia, where

I have spent the best years of my life in the companionship of my family and friends, and where I hope to spend my remaining days.

"Born when the century was but twelve years old, I have lived to within four years of its close. I have seen the wilderness vanish under the refining influence of civilization; the pathless forests have given way to broad highways and prosperous cities with beautiful homes.

"I have seen the introduction of steam railways, of the telegraph and telephone, of street cars and the postal service; I have witnessed the introduction of the sewing machine, the substitution of the cook stove and the furnace for the fireplace, and of gas and electricity for the tallow and dip.

"My life has not always been free from care and anxiety; I have had some dark days as well as sunny; yet from the vantage point of more than four score years I can say with a thankful heart, 'Goodness and mercy have followed me all the days of my life.'"

The above was dictated to one of Mrs King's daughters "E. C. K." (probably Miss Emma King) and was read to the Catherine Greene Chapter of the N.S.D.A.R. on January 11, 1896. Betsey King, who was regent of this D.A.R. chapter, died less than two months later on March 3, 1896. It was Betsey King who presented the Baptist Church to the town of Kings Mills in honor of her husband who died in 1885. The dates in brackets above are mine, calculated from Betsey's narrative from her certain marriage date of August 23, 1838.

James Q. du Pont

James Q. du Pont was the Project Engineering Supervisor for the Kings Mills Ordnance Plant from late 1942 to April 15, 1943. In this capacity it was his job to wrap up the considerable number of loose ends created by building a functioning ordnance plant.

A native of Johnstown, Pennsylvania, he was a graduate of MIT in electrical engineering. He was in business for himself for a number of years. In 1940 he joined the E. I. Du Pont Company and was associated with building a cellophane plant in Clinton, Iowa. He served there as project engineer upon completion of the plant. He was next assigned to Kings Mills Remington (Peters) plant in Kings Mills, Ohio.

Mr. du Pont left Kings Mills suddenly to work in Tennessee. It later became known that he was associated with the Manhattan Project, which produced the atomic bomb. He worked at Oak Ridge, Chicago, and Hanford Engineer Works in Washington, on that project.

After 1946, du Pont moved to Wilmington where he served in the Du Pont public relations department. In later years, he was a roving goodwill

ambassador for Du Pont. He crossed the United States, Canada, Mexico and Cuba in that capacity.

He married Helen Louise Rodgers in 1938; they had four children: Helen Quinn, Deborah, Pierre Coleman, and James Bidermann.

A review of James Q. du Pont's monthly reports, a couple of his expense accounts and internal memos while at Kings Mills, reveal a remarkable man. It was evident that he was a hard worker, possessed great energy, enthusiasm, wit, warmth, good will and not a little engineering ability. He was the great great grandson of E. I. du Pont de Nemours, founder of the Du Pont Company, and a nephew of T. Coleman du Pont, president from 1902 to 1915.

The above information was abstracted from a biography and other papers, courtesy of Marjorie G. McNinch of the Hagley Museum and Library.

Philip Quayle

Philip Quayle brought spark photography ['Sparkography,' as he named it] to Peters Cartridge Company. This was the first technology to "stop" bullets and shot in flight. While the idea was not new, the successful use of it was. Quayle brought this technology to Peters from the U.S. Bureau of Standards. Until the mid-Twenties, this technology was all but unknown. After Peters introduced it, other companies had to follow suit some years later. It was Quayle's work that led Edgerton to invent the strobe light. Edgerton himself credited Quayle's contribution toward that invention. Ironically, Quayle's sparkographs were more useful ballistically than the later strobe light in that the sparkographs clearly showed the shock waves which resulted from the discharge of firearms.

Quayle was also involved in work for Auto Ordnance in the mid-Twenties that slowed the cyclic rate of the Thompson submachine gun, or "Tommy Gun", making it a more tractable and effective weapon. Peters' production of special cartridges for the Thompson gun was likely a result of this connection.

The July, 1928, issue of The American Rifleman (TAR) had this to say about a unique man:

"A handsome medal of honor has been awarded by the Royal Photographic society of Great Britain to Capt. Philip P. Quayle, Chief of the Physical Laboratory of the Peters Cartridge Co.

"This medal was tendered for the remarkable pictures that Captain Quayle has produced by means of spark photography, and is in recognition of his services in advancing this branch of photographic art.

"Captain Quayle has been a pioneer on the photography of projectiles in the air, and is the first man to successfully photograph a shot string in flight. Some idea of his accomplishment can be realized when the infinitesimal accuracy required is revealed. In the series of photographs of shot in flight, for which the award was made, the shot strings were moving at the rate of 1,000 feet per second, and the time of exposure needed was only two one-millionths of a second.

The April, 1931, issue of TAR contained a terse announcement of Quayle death.

The May, 1931, May issue of TAR had this to say: "Readers of our April issue will have seen on page 26 a notice of the sudden death of Captain Quayle. This information reached us just as we were going to press, and owing to the consequent lack of time and space we were unable at that time to express fully our feelings as to the great loss that the rifle-shooting world has suffered in the death of this distinguished investigator.

"Captain Quayle was first and foremost a most highly educated and talented scientist, and fortunately for the shooting fraternity, he devoted his unusual ability almost exclusively to firearms.

"For some years Captain Quayle was employed as a physicist at the Bureau of Standards in Washington where he devoted his attention to the subject of spark photography. He developed a system of taking photographs by the light of an electric spark lasting only a millionth of a second so he was able to take pictures showing many things hither to unknown regarding the discharge of firearms and the flight of bullets.

"For example, he has photographed the air coming out of the barrel ahead of the bullet; the powder gas escaping past the bullet and coming out of the gun before the bullet has reached the muzzle; the bullet just appearing; the bullet just out of the barrel, with the gas mushrooming out past the bullet's base; the bullet in flight with sound waves forming. The

bullet in flight passing into solid objects and emerging from them and in fact, every phase of ballistics that could conceivably be photographed.

"Readers of the Rifleman are familiar with many of Captain Quayle's articles that have appeared in the past. In our May issue, some of his work is included in Mr. Cline's article.

"During the past several years Captain Quayle was chief physicist of the Peters Cartridge Co., where he was accomplishing work of a revolutionary nature. His death was due to a supposedly simple operation, from which unexpected complications developed. Captain Quayle's work forms a contribution to ballistics science which will remain forever a monument to his memory."

◆ ◆ ◆

W. A. Tewes

Bill Tewes appears several times over the years in the Peters story. He was important as a shooter, representative of and, later, technical director of the company.

Tewes was born on June 27, 1872, in New Jersey.*

1898 - W. A. Tewes was president of the Zettler Rifle Club (*Shooting And Fishing* article shown in Smith book, *The Story of Pope's Barrels*).

Excellent target shot by Tewes shown in Peters' *Score Book* - fifty shots at 75 feet (*circa 1900*).

1905 - Tewes won the Wimbledon Cup with a .30-40 Krag. *

~ 1906 - "*This was about the time (actually 1907 **) when Bill Tewes, captain of the 1928 Dewar Team, then of New York, made his famous 100-shot indoor world's record at Grand Rapids, Mich. His score was 2,481 out of a possible 2,500 on the 1/4-inch ring target. This score was beaten several years later by Arthur Hubalek, who made 2,484 in Zettler's Gallery, New York, that still stands as the 75-foot offhand world's record in 100 shots. Prone shooting was not practiced at all in those days, only offhand free rifles with telescopes, set triggers etc., being used*" The American Rifleman (*TAR*), January, 1929, pp 7. C. T. Westergaard.

1907 – Tewes, member of Palma Team setting new world record, Tewes shot in the middle of the pack (4 higher, three lower) 800, 900 & 1000 yds. Rockcliff range Ottawa. The great Dr. Hudson was also on team (3rd). In 1912 Tewes was third in breaking world record score. *TAR* Dec 1927, Maj. L. W. T. Waller pp 574 (10) *et seq*.

1909 - Tewes was on the first Dewar International Team.*

1910 - Tewes won the Sea Girt Championship.**

1913 - Tewes took over the duties as coach of the U.S. Free Rifle Team.**

1913 - Tewes, W. A. Jersey City, New Jersey Bullet U.S. Patent No. 1,072,880 Sept 9***

At Sea Girt-1926 - 11th in Eastern Individual; 33rd in two man; 13 in Spencer; 2nd in Camp Perry Spl.; 4th in grand agg; *TAR*, Aug 1, 1926 Jack Rohan pp73 (9) *et seq*.

1925 - Tewes was coach of the U.S. Palma Team.**

1926 - Tewes won the Swiss Match.**

1926 - Oct. 1 photo of Hessian (Hessian was a technical man for Winchester - and a fine rifleman), Lee and Tewes coaching Dewar at Sea Girt. *TAR*, Oct 1, 1926 pp 199 (7) *et seq*.

1927 - Tewes was coach of the U. S. Dewar Team.**

1927, January 8 - Montvale N. J. Letter and target in Peters ad showing one hole group at 75 feet in prone position. (all inside 10s) signed Tewes; referred to in the ad as Col. Wm. A. Tewes.

1928 - *TAR* June pp 7 W. A. Tewes article on Dewar candidates. Called by the TAR staff: ... "a man who himself ranks as one of the greatest shots and greatest coaches that this country has ever produced"

1928 - Tewes was Captain of the U. S. Dewar Team**

1929 - Tewes was Captain of the U. S. Dewar Team**

1930 - Tewes was Captain of the U. S. Dewar Team**

March 24, 1976 - letter [Elmer] Keith to Schiffer (Note: letter reproduced using Keith's spelling):

"... *Col Bill Twees* [Tewes] *headed Peters Cartridge back in the early thirties when I loade and fired 1000 rounds of my 173 grain bullet backed by 10 grains No 80 through heavy duty 5" S & W 38-44 and this made Doug Wesson decide to bring ouyt the 357 and I sent Twees 100 rounds loaded and he chronographed (th-am pressure tested) th-am at 42,000 psi and gave me hell over it though the 45 frame S & W handled th-em perfectly. And Wesson decided to bring out a 357 and I cast sized and lubed 200 of my 173 grain for his initial experiments and Remington would no[t] load them but Winchester did and that was the start of the 357 magnum.*

In t-he late 20s I had some Peters 32 Win Spl that would not shoot in my hat at 50 yards, Pulled some and the bullets had slant bases, so sent them back to Peters Ctg co with my compliments. Then they improved their ammo until it was very good epecially shot shells.

Sincerely

Keith

1932 - Tewes was coach of the U.S. Olympic Team. *

1932 - Bill Tewes was Technical Director of Peters, not Plant Manager as Keith suggests above. Tewes' name is on correspondence with the Chief of Ordnance dated August 8, 1930. He signed for Peters as "W. A. Tewes, Technical Section" [National Archives].

1934; May 23 - W. A. Tewes signed an advertising letter as Technical Director of "Peters Ballistic Institute".

1943 - Tewes retired from the "Remington-Peters complex of arms and ammunition companies."*

Tewes wrote two articles on coaching high-power rifle teams. Considered by Nordquist and Brennan to be among the very best pieces of firearms writing in the (20th) century." These appeared in the February and July, 1948, issues of *TAR*.

Tewes was active in the New Jersey National Guard, rising to the rank of Lt. Col. He died in Florida on February 22, 1953. Buried in George Washington Memorial Park, in Paramus, New Jersey.*

W. A. Tewes was selected as one of the "Fifty Greatest Competitive Shooters of the 20th Century" by the staff of *Shooting Sports USA*, which is a publication of the National Rifle Association. Tewes is said therein to have topped the ranks of riflemen for 37 years. **

* Information from September, 1998, issue of *Precision Shooting* (with two photos). "The Last Post" pp52, by Paul Norquist of Alexandria, Virginia.

** Shooting Sports USA, Vol 13, No.2, February, 2000, pp14.

*** U. S. Patent Gazette.

◆ ◆ ◆

Lammot du Pont

The following is abstracted from the book *Du Pont, One Hundred and Forty Years*, by William S. Dutton:

April 13, 1831-March 29, 1884. Lammot was the second son of Alfred Victor du Pont. He was graduated from the University of Pennsylvania at 18 as a chemist. "*Six feet two, lanky and big-boned, he

had his mother's dark brown hair and a chin, mouth and cool grey eyes as determined as those of his Uncle Henry.*"

Practical experience in the mill, plus technical schooling and natural ability caused his Uncle Henry (*aka* General du Pont, or simply "The General"), to defer to him in questions of powder making in the

Du Pont firm. He was sent to Europe in 1858 to study powder-making methods.

Lammot developed a method, using sodium nitrate, to make blasting powder or "soda powder." It was patented on May 19, 1857, and called "B" blasting powder. The coal fields and iron fields rapidly adopted B blasting powder. It used refined sodium nitrate and was the first notable change in gunpowder manufacturing in 600 years.

At the age of thirty, Lammot was the nation's leading authority on explosives chemistry. He worked with Rodman, developing Mammoth Powder for large artillery pieces.

It was Lammot who went to London in November of 1861 to get saltpeter for the Union. He arrived there in the middle of the notorious Trent Affair that almost caused the deal to fall through. He ultimately secured 2,000 tons of critical saltpeter, said to provide the Union armies powder sufficient for a year of the war.

Lammot, alone at Du Pont, was interested in the new dynamite invented by Nobel. Uncle Henry would have none of it for some years yet. Indeed, a decade later, Lammot tricked the General into investing in a dynamite plant that the General thought was making black powder. Later, Lammot built the giant Repauno Works in New Jersey to make White Hercules, a form of dynamite. This new works was controlled by Du Pont but was not exclusively owned by them.

April, 1872, Du Pont, Laflin and Rand, Hazard and several smaller mills formed the Gunpowder Trade Association of the United States. Lammot was elected president. The plan was to set prices among the members. If someone outside the Association undercut their pricing, members of the association would pool their resources to undercut them until they were out of business or brought into line.

The story is told of Lammot that, asleep in a small hotel, with his paymaster's payroll for the mill under the bed, he detected someone entering his room. Swooping down on the would-be burglar, he threw the bedclothes over him, carried him to the top of the stairs and threw him into the lobby. Taking bedclothes from an adjacent vacant room, Lammot returned to sleep. The next day, the owner of the hotel was unaccountably missing! Lammot continued to stay at the hotel, but the owner would disappear when Lammot showed up on his monthly visit!

An explosion at the mill killed Lammot, like Alexis du Pont whom he succeeded in the Du Pont Company. Black powder killed Alexis while he was helping move a large powder-contaminated bin. But it was nitroglycerine at the Repauno works that killed Lammot. He was killed as he attempted to halt a runaway reaction in a vat of nitroglycerine.

These nineteenth century du Ponts were accustomed to working in the mills and knowing the business from the ground up. They were formidable business adversaries. It was the Gunpowder Trade Association's president, Lammot du Pont, with whom Joseph Warren King contested.

Helen Hooven Santmyer, on the King Family

Betsey King made her home in Xenia at 'The Kingdom,' a mansion built during the Civil War by her husband. Helen Hooven Santmyer, author of the bestseller *...And Ladies of the Club*, also was raised in Xenia. Ms. Santmyer relates that her grandmother grew up with Betsey King's daughters. Betsey's daughter, Ella, was bridesmaid at Ms. Santmyer's grandmother's wedding.

Both "The Kingdom" mansion and three of Betsey's four daughters were described in some detail in Ms. Santmyer's delightful book, *Ohio Town*. Ms. Santmyer had this to say about 'The Kingdom:'

"The King house is on the Main Street corner; it is set far back from its iron fence and, except at the gate, is concealed by shrubbery from the passer-by. "Old J. W." was not only a banker but a manufacturer of gunpowder as well; he built 'The Kingdom' during the Civil War. The house is rather more elaborate than the ante bellum houses [in Xenia]: its pillars are larger, and the roofline rises in a curve over the central windows above the porch; inside, the carved walnut woodwork is dark and massive. Old J. W. would have done well to wait until the war ended to build his house. His great prosperity confirmed the suspicion (just or unjust, who knows now?) that he was selling gunpowder to the Rebels as well as to his own side. When the new mansion had been finished in every detail, and the family was ready to move in, some of his fellow townsmen hauled a cannon up Main Street, warned everyone in the neighborhood to open his windows, and let go with a blast that shattered every piece of glass in 'The Kingdom.' I never heard this story from anyone except my grandmother; she was never so in awe of the Kings as to think any shadow of scandal touching them should be forgotten, and in spite of her long and devoted friendship with J. W.'s daughter Ella, she told it with some relish. (Perhaps Grandma was sufficiently envious of great wealth to suspect the means of acquisition.) ...And now [1962] the King family has long been gone. When Grandma was a girl and visited them, before she married and came to town to live, the King's daughters were young and pretty and gay, but only one of them had children and died while they were still small. So the young son and daughter came home to live with their aunts. With that daughter [,] Mother went to school and romped in the King house and climbed every tree in the yard. But her children did not grow up there; they married and established themselves elsewhere before their parents came home to keep an eye on the aunt who had been left alone. After the mother died, they and the son's children gave 'The Kingdom' to the American Legion. ...

"I cannot remember that I ever saw Miss Elouisa King in the flesh, but she was a person in my mind from my earliest childhood, never just a name. After having been accepted for years as one of the town's old maids, she married and went to live in a neighboring county. To the end of her days, she was a friend kept lively by Grandma's memory. As 'Ella King' she appears in Grandma's diary: they were classmates and summer visitors in each other's towns. One particular visit of Grandma's to Ella's house, after their graduation, is recorded in minute-by-minute detail. Grandpa had been honorably discharged from the army in the spring of 1864, physically unfit; his family lived in our town (Xenia) where Grandma had gone to school and Ella lived. Grandpa doesn't sound so awfully sick, in the diary: there were picnics, fairs, band concerts, Sunday evening calls. In the February following, Ella returned the visit and was bridesmaid at Grandma's wedding. We have a daguerreotype of Ella King among our old photographs: tiny and dark, with sleek hair and black eyes like saucers– composed and grave–there is nothing in the picture to suggest the fire of life the was in her. ...

"Miss Emma and Miss Issie [Isadora] King, Ella's younger sisters, stayed on in their father's big house, with the big yard, up on Main Street. Richer than anyone else in town, in their old age interested in the DAR to the exclusion of all else, the Misses King grew so retiring and aloof that few outside that organization could claim to know them well. They appeared together - and after Miss Issie died, Miss Emma appeared alone - at important functions; but toward the end they had few, if any, intimate friends. The town was chiefly interested in their cars, for they were seen in our streets only in their cars. First, long ago, they had a little electric which they drove themselves until the day it took them over the curb, up the bank steps and down again, with Miss Emma helpless at the steering bar–but unflustered and stately as only so small a woman could be. After that they got a larger car and a chauffeur and, year after year, still larger cars–none of them with so much as a scratch to mar its polish. Miss Emma was almost blind toward the end of her life, and her last automobile was a spectacular limousine, painted half sky-blue, half cobalt, so she could find it at the curb when she came out of a shop. Poor Miss Emma! She lived alone for many years in her big square-pillared mansion, at the far end of a lawn whose every blade of grass was in place, behind an iron fence which barred from the street all consciousness of what was beyond it. She lived there blind and dependent on a retired school teacher hired, by the day, to read books aloud to her, and on her niece and her husband, who came back to town and bought a house across the street from 'The Kingdom' to be close at hand when needed."

It should be noted that Ms. Santmyer does not chronicle the most important daughter to this narrative. That being Mary King, who married a Baptist preacher, Gershom Moore Peters. Mary King Peters, as the wife of the preacher of the First Baptist Church, lived in Penn Yan, New York, until 1881 when her husband went to work for King's Great Western Powder Company in Xenia. They subsequently moved to Cincinnati from Xenia in 1887, when the office was moved there.

Trademark Introduction Dates

Jim Sones of Denver, Colorado, has been a tireless investigator of patents and copyrights related to cartridge companies, in the government files. He has gathered the following data and also a listing of unregistered trademarks that Peters used. This data can be used as an aid in dating some of both Peters' and King's products. Jim reports that Peters was better than most loading companies in that they copyrighted a large percentage of their products. It is appended here with Jim's permission:

Unregistered Peters Paper Shotshell Trademarks

PRIZE	Chain around primer-advertised in October 1890. Shown with indented crimp. For black or nitro powders. Came in Peters "Popular" boxes and was probably their first headstamped shotshell. Green, brown, or blue paper tubes.
NITRO	Chain around primer. Early to mid 90s period. Probably discontinued almost immediately after introduction. Tan paper tube.
FIELD	Chain around primer. Same period as NITRO above, a violation of UMC's registered trademark "Field" (1892) so immediately dropped after introduction. Black paper tube.
HSB&Co. Ajax	Chain around primer. For Hibbard, Spencer, Blanchard & Co. Contract load.
NEW VICTOR	Chain around primer. Green paper tube with low brass & copper primer. Used with Kings (bulk) smokeless powder in pink or brown paper tubes also. Introduced before 1897 (*Shooting & Fishing* ad) and dropped before 1905 (pricelist).
REINFORCED	Chain around primer. Green tube in 12Ga and maroon tube in 10Ga. In use by at least Dec. 1895 (*Shooting & Fishing* ad). Best quality Peters shotshell in 1896.
PETERS No 10 CT'GE C<u>O</u>	No chain around primer. Light brown paper tube.
TARGET	Apparently introduced between Dec. 1903 & Dec. 1904, definitely in use by 1914 through the 1930s. Green or red paper tubes. Medium height, knurled brass head. Loaded with DuPont; Kings; Hazard, E.C. Improved; and New Schultze smokeless powders (same as powders used in "IDEAL" rounds).
DELUXE TARGET	Brown or green paper tubes.
HV	Blue paper tube. In use in mid-30s into 1950's. The same as the "HIGH VELOCITY" registered trademark of Jan. 16, 1925.
SKEET LOAD	Orange paper tube. Spreader loads use red paper tube. First ad in May 1933.
TRAP LOAD	Orange paper tube. In use in mid-30s. First ad May 1933.
The "FIELD" & "NITRO" may have been internal marketing projects which were never marketed to the public.	

King's Great Western Powder Company, Xenia and Cincinnati, OH

13,293 May 11, 1886	The words "Quick Shot"	Gunpowder. Used since Jan. 1, 1878.

The King Powder Company, Cincinnati, OH

31,005 Dec. 21, 1897		Gunpowder, ordnance powder and blasting powder. Used since Oct. 29, 1895.
31,138 Jan. 11, 1898		Gun, ordnance and blasting powder. Used since Oct. 29, 1895.
62,497 May 7, 1907	*SEMI-SMOKELESS*	Gunpowder. Used at least 10 years.
63,959 July 16, 1907	*QUICK SHOT*	Gunpowder, and particularly black sporting powder. Used at least ten years. See King's Great Western Powder Co. entry above.
503,416 Oct. 26, 1948		For black powder, both potassium nitrate and sodium nitrate base, high explosives, blasting caps, and electric blasting caps. Claims use since Jan. 18, 1884.

The Peters Cartridge Company, Cincinnati, OH

16,152 Jan. 8, 1889	The word "Shotless"	Used since Aug. 1, 1888.
16,153 Jan. 8, 1889	The representation of a shot-gun shell and the words "Shot Gun Blanks" printed thereon.	Used since Aug. 1, 1888.
16,190 Jan. 15, 1889	A red label bearing the words "Ducking Cartridges"	Used since Jan. 1, 1888.
16,191 Jan. 15, 1889	The words "Peters Popular"	Used since Jan. 1, 1888.
16,192 Jan. 15, 1889	The representation of a blank cartridge resting on a shotgun with the words "Blank Shot Gun Cartridges"	
16,193 Jan. 15, 1889	The words "Quick Shot Cartridges"	For ammunition. Used since Jan. 1, 1888.
24,609 Apr. 24, 1894	*VICTOR*	For ammunition. Used since Mar. 1894.

1873	**UMC produces their first paper shells–probably** the first paper shells given wide currency. *The Rifle In America*, Sharpe, pp 296.
1877	**Kings** (Joseph Warren and Ahimaaz) leave **Miami Powder Co.** *Hist. of Exp. Ind.. pp 273,*
1877	**G. M. Peters** and brothers Alvin L. Peters and Orrin E. Peters, patent an anti-friction journal box. *Sones.*
1878 (*spring*)	**Dittmar** starts an explosive plant in Binghamton, N. Y. (Note: this is where **Milton F. Lindsley** became associated with Dittmar). *Hist. of Exp. Ind., pp 619 & 788.*
1878, Aug 8	**King's Great Western Powder Co.** incorporated in Ohio "for the purpose of **manufacturing gun powder**, powder kegs and other purposes… shall be located in Warren County on the Miami River and the Little Miami Rail Road equal distance from South Lebanon & Fosters crossing at a place called Kings Station. With offices at Xenia… & also at the manufactory and in Cincinnati. The Capital Stock … two hundred and fifty thousand dollars…" *Office of the Secretary of State of Ohio.*
1878	**King's Great Western Powder Company** capacity 100 **kegs per day** (2500#). *Leading Manufacturers of Cincinnati 1886.*
1880 (*about*)	**King** Powder Co. suffers an **explosion**; three killed. *Western Star, July 24, 1890 quoted J. H. Mc Kibben, secretary to both Peters and King: "With regard to the eighteen explosions referred to in yesterday's paper, only one had fatal results. That was about ten years ago and three men were killed in it."*
1880	James **Wilson** migrated from Delaware; Started tin keg mill in South Lebanon, later moved keg mill to King's powder line. James Wilson was patentee for double-seam can or keg and patentee for machinery to fabricate it. Constance Witt's 1981 book, *Families.*
1881	Capt. **Bogardus** and Dr. W. F. **Carver** toured the U.S. to **introduce the Ligowsky clay pigeon** and trap (first successful saucer-shaped clay bird sprung from a trap with a skimming motion). *Arms and the Man*, 12-4-1918.
1881	**King's** Great Western Powder Co. required a "carload of sheet metal each week to make powder cans." *History of Southwestern Ohio, pp 285.*
1881	**Gershom Moore Peters** joins **the King Powder Company.** *History of Southwestern Ohio, pp 398.*
1883, Feb. 28	**King's** Great Western Powder Company **increases capitalization** "from two hundred & fifty thousand **to three hundred & twenty five thousand dollars.**" *Office of Secretary of State of Ohio.*
1884, Jan. 18	Copyright No. 503,416 for King Powder Company for crown-shaped **logo** with name KING inside, not copyrighted until October 26, 1948. (see) *Sones.*
1884	**King's Great Western Powder Co.** conveys lots to Wilsons in Kings Mills. *From deeds displayed by Wilson heirs (6-25-98).*
1884, April 17	Franklin L. Chamberlin, Cleveland, Ohio. **Patent # 295980**, automatic shotshell **loading machine**. Note this was prior to the Peters Patent. Chamberlin was a competitor to Peters. The Peters patent was for a much faster and more sophisticated loading machine. *Kass.*
1884, April 29	Peters, G. M. **Patent #297712.** Mfg. of cartridge shells from paper pulp. *Sones.*
1884, May 27	G. M. Peters **Patent #299162** unique top **wad crimp** (2 triangular). *Sones.*
1885, July 7	G. M. Peters, **Patents #321848 & #321849.** Mfg. of cartridge shells of paper or wood pulp. *Sones.*
1885, July 8	**Death of Joseph Warren King**. *Robinson's History of Greene County*, pp 612.
1885	The **King** Powder Company **moves its office** from Xenia, O. to Cincinnati, O.; *Cincinnati Enquirer of October 6, 1919* (obituary of G. M. Peters).
1886, March 1	Dry house containing **50, 000 # of powder** explodes at **Miami Powder Co**, Goes Station (Mill with which King was first associated; left in 1877). *Howe's Hist. Coll. of Ohio, pp 702.*
1886, March 15	**Post Office** established **at Kings Mills**, William C. White appointed Postmaster. *Interview with Paul E. Harbaugh, postmaster at Kings Mills in 1976, verbal History, pp 18.*
1886, March 26	**Gershom Moore Peters** applies for loading machine patent. **Patent No. 360,043** was issued March 29, 1887.
1886	The **King Powder Company** had a **capacity** of 1000 kegs (**25,000#**) per day; 400 acres of land, two miles along river; largest powder concern west of the Allegheny Mountains. *Leading Manufacturers of Cincinnati, 1886.*
1886	Introduction of **Quick Shot** powder (brand of black powder. Note: **Popular Sporting** was evidently another black powder in the line; date of introduction unknown). *Hints to Sportsmen on Semi-Smokeless & Peters' Cartridges, pp 2*; also *Leading Manufacturers of Cincinnati 1886.*
1886, May 11	Copyright No. 13293, the name ***Quick Shot*** for gunpowder by Kings Great Western Powder Company, Xenia, Ohio, in use since January 1, 1878. *Sones.*
1886	Terrible **flood at Xenia** (J. W. King's home town). Note: Xenia is located on the same river as Kings Mills. *Howe's Hist. Coll. of Ohio, pp 703.*

1886	**Gershom. M. Peters** reluctantly becomes member of **Gunpowder Trade Assn**. *Himes.*
1886 (or early 1887)	Peters has **first loading machinery** made by **J. M. Robinson & Co.** (229 W. Second, Cincinnati, Ohio). *William Paul Smith, collector.*
1887	**A. King builds mansion** in Kings Mills. *Bob Wilson, long-time resident of Kings Mills (6-25-98).*
1887, Jan. 18	The **Peters Cartridge Company**, **organized** in State of Ohio; capitalization **$50,000**; Principal office in Cincinnati, Ohio. *Office of the Secretary of State of Ohio.*
1887, Jan. 28, 11 AM	The books of The **Peters Cartridge Company** are opened for subscriptions to the capital stock; *Office of the Secretary of State for Ohio*
1887	**Peters Cartridge Co.** announces **plans to build cartridge factory**. *Himes.*
1887, March 29	**Gershom Moore Peters patents** a dial face cartridge **loading** machine, **Patent # 360043**. *TDS.*
1887	**Baptist Church built** at Kings Mills in honor of the late Joseph Warren King by his widow, Betsy Kendall King. *Plaque in the church and Jean Wilson Heinke photo in verbal hist. 1976.*
1887, *Summer*	**First two machines** under G. M. Peters **Patent No. 360043** were in use at Peters factory. They were **not satisfactory**. Sent to Cincinnati Screw and Tap for modification. *Standard Cartridge Company v Peters, Dec 8, 1896 pp 7.*
1887, Dec. 15	Cincinnati Screw and Tap Co. and Peters Cartridge Company agree to a **modify two shotshell loading machines**–one in 12 gauge and the other in 10 gauge–before March 10, 1888, Peters to furnish drawings and patterns; also had **two new machines** made by Cincinnati Screw and Tap. *Sones.*
1888, July 5	"*The cartridge companies are now putting up their paper shot shells in fancy boxes*" (USCC, Winchester and UMC). *Shooting and Fishing,* successors to *The Rifle, July 5, 1888 pp12.*
1888, (*about*)	**Completed** most of powder **buildings and village** of **Kings Mills**. *Himes.*
1888	**Peters Cartridge Co.** issues first catalog. *Jim Sones, IAAI Journal issue 392.*
1888, April 10	G. M Peters **Indented crimp** (three) **Patent #380689**. *Sones.*
1888, June 5	**Paten**t #383905, **G. M. Peters**, cartridge loading machine. *This still used the indented crimp but modified some of the original (Patent # 360043) design. Sones.*
1888, Nov. 20	**Patent #393028, William B. Place** (assignor to American Buckle and Cartridge Co), wad winder. Note: this was one of the patents Peters bought of AB&C; subject to an infringement suit by Winchester. *Sones.*
1888, Dec. 13	**"Peters" cartridges used at Walnut Hill** (Mass) range. *(First record I have found of use of Peters Cartridges in competition).* Wheeler, of Marlboro, lost to Dickey 93 to 78 at clays. Both used ten-gauge guns. Wheeler took first place in some of the other matches that day. *Shooting and Fishing, Dec. 20, 1888, pp 16.*
1889, Feb. 11	**American Shooting Organization organized.** King and Peters charter members. *Shooting and Fishing, Feb. 14, 1889, pp 1.*
1889, Feb. 20	**Name change** from **King's Great Western Powder Company** to the **King Powder Company**. *Records of Ohio Secretary of State.*
1889, Feb. 26	**Patent #398650, G. M. Peters,** cartridge-loading machine. Two new machines–12 gauge and 10 gauge– were built under this patent and # 398651 by Cincinnati Screw and Tap in spring of 1888. *Per Sones, refinements of Patent #360043.*
1889, Feb. 26	**Patent #398651, G. M. Peters,** automatic shell feed for cartridge loading machine. *Per Sones, further modification to Patent #360043.*
1889, May	**Winchester** brings injunction against **American Buckle And Cartridge** of West Haven, Conn. for infringement of Winchester's cartridge *shell-making* machinery patents (#181309, #232907 and # 237605). A B & C settled with Winchester on May 24 by selling all its paper and brass shell-making equipment and work in process to Winchester (did not include AB & C's patents on shotgun shell making equipment). Winchester thereupon would agree to withdraw any suit and waive damages (Note: this action sets in motion a series of events culminating in a finding on March 24, 1900). *US Circuit Court of Connecticut, Winchester vs. American Buckle and Cartridge, March 10, 1893. Pynn.*
1889, June	**American Buckle and Cartridge** offers its patents to **Peters Cartridge Co.** *US Circuit Court Southern District of Ohio, Western Division. Pynn*
1889, July 3	**Peters Cartridge Co.** agrees to purchase **American Buckle and Cartridge Company's** patents and two sets of machinery based on these patents for $21000.00. This done through Peters attorney I. H. Mc Donald. Francis X. Dunn, machinist, built the machinery under supt. William B. Place. Both went to Peters to set up machinery, stayed on as employees of Peters, Place as supt. at Peters. *Williamson, also Winchester vs. Peters. US Circuit Court, Connecticut: Winchester v American Buckle and Cartridge, March 10 1893. Sones/Frederickson/Pynn.*

1889, Aug. 23	**American Buckle and Cartridge** completes the agreement with Winchester to finish goods in process and **delivered** them and the ***shell making*** machinery on this date **to Winchester** (sold to Winchester on May 21). Winchester thereupon inspected the machines and reaffirmed infringement of three of its patents (#181309, #232907 and #237605). **Winchester** evidently, subsequently, **learned** that **AB&C** secretly **manufactured** two sets of this ***infringing shell making*** machinery and **sold** them **to Peters**. *US Circuit Court Connecticut, Winchester v American Buckle and Cartridge March 10, 1893. Pynn.*
1889, Sept. 25	The **Peters** Cartridge Company **increases** its **capitalization** from $50,000.00 to **$100,000.00** (no doubt to pay for the machinery bought from American Buckle and Cartridge and erect such buildings and machinery to support its operation). *Office of The Secretary of State of Ohio.*
1889, Dec.	As result of the July 3 contract, **American Buckle & Cartridge** construct, **deliver (November) and have running,** by December of 1890, the two sets of ***shell-making*** machinery at **Peters Cartridge Co** at Kings Mills, Ohio; *US Circuit Court of Southern District of Ohio. Western Division. Pynn.*
1889	**Sherman Anti Trust Act** becomes law. *Williamson.*
1889, Dec.	Peters **operates new *shell- making* factory**; name of shell (shotgun cartridge) was likely "**PRIZE**"; (July 15 1890 explosion destroyed new shell factory qv). *Information gleaned from Dec 2, 1891 letterhead in the Ohio Secretary of State's office*; shows **PRIZE** shells thereon.
1890, Jan 22	**The King Powder Company** capitalization increased to **$500,000** from $325,000. *Records of Ohio Secretary of State.*
1890, July 10	Issue of *Shooting and Fishing* shows perhaps **Winchester's** first ad for **loaded** Star and Rival **paper shot-shells.** *S&F, pp 20.*
1890, July 15	**Great explosion** and fire caused by railroad negligence; **destroys Peters Cartridge Company's** production facilities almost completely–plus **The King Powder Co.** office (did not damage King's powder mills located on the other side of the river); *Hist. of Exp. Ind., pp 278; also 1903 Atlas Warren County pp 105; The Western Star, Thursday July 17, 1890.*
1890 Sept 20	**King** Powder Co and **Peters** Cartridge Company **file suit** in "superior court of Cincinnati" for damages resulting from the July 15, 1890 explosion. Defendant is the Pittsburgh, Cincinnati, Chicago and St Louis Railway. Peters for over $117,000.00 and King for over $49,000.00, *The Lebanon Gazette*, Sept 25, 1890.
1890 July	Warren County **Coroner issues his findings**: "...I find that the (July 15) explosion was caused by the too-rapid run of the soda cars on the spur switch at King's Station...from local freight train No.75 in the charge of Engineer Charles Keck and conductor James McDermott.... I further find... that there was no negligence on the part of the Peters Cartridge Company nor on the part of the King Powder Company." *The Western Star, July 31, 1890.*
1890, Oct.	**Winchester** sues **American Buckle and Cartridge** for patent infringement (#181309, #232907 and # 237605). *US Circuit Court Connecticut March 10, 1893. Pynn.*
1891, Dec 2	The **Peters** Cartridge Co **changed** its **incorporation** papers from: "the loading of shells to be used in firearms and the sale of same" to "the object shall be the mfg and sale of ctgs. for blasting purposes and for use in firearms; and also the mfg. and sale of material entering into same together with the transaction of any and all business incident thereto." *Office of Secretary of State of Ohio.*
1891	Patent #464833, **Ligowsky,** cartridge-loading machine. *Per Sones, an in-line endless belt type; not the dial face of Patent #360043; Note: this patent subject to litigation. Sones.*
1892	**Sir Charles Boys publishes photo** of bullet traveling at 2,000 ft/sec. Used Leyden jars (electrical condensers to store the charge). See Philip Quayle work for Peters in 1920's and following, *Electronic Flash, Lou Jacobs Jr.*; American Photographic Book Publishing Co., New York, 1962.
1892, March 18	**Winchester** brings suit against **Peters** Cartridge Company **for infringing patents** owned by Winchester (#181309, #232907 and #237605) by using the machinery Peters bought from American Buckle and Cartridge (see July 3, 1889 entry). *US Circuit Court, Connecticut March 10, 1893. Pynn.*
1892, Oct. 27	**Announcing the first "Grand American Handicap"** April 5, 6 and 7, 1893 by the Interstate Manufacturers and Dealers Association. Entries to be received at...[various locations listed including:]..."Mr. M. F. Lindsley of the American Wood Powder Company, 59 Wall Street." *Shooting and Fishing*, November 3, 1892, pp7.
1892 (*about*)	Deductions from an article in *The Primer* would indicate Peters abandoned the **"Tin Whistle"** factory (in the town itself) of Kings Mills to move into what was later known as Building R6 near the site of the 1890 explosion. Shipping difficulties were cited as being the reason for this. *The Primer, February 1943; Article about long-time employee Bill Schneider.*
1893, April 5, 6 and 7	**First Grand American Handicap held** at Dexter Park, Jamaica Plank Road, Long Island, New York [erroneously called the "Great" American Handicap here]. *Shooting and Fishing*, April 13, 1893, *pp13.*
1893, Panic of	Drove machinists and skilled workers out of Cincinnati and other urban centers to **Peters Cartridge Co** plant; *Between the Miamis; Himes, pp 105.*
1893, Panic of	Said to have driven **Dittmar** out of business; **Milton F. Lindsley** left Dittmar. Sharpe, *Complete Guide to Handloading.*

1894	"**Winchester** first offered empty paper shotshells in 1877. **Loaded shells** were **not** offered until **1894**" (Note: Author has seen ads for loaded Winchester shotshells as early as July 10, 1890). *Ronald Stadt, Winchester Shotguns and Shotshells; pp 3 (photo caption). On pp 6, Stadt notes "Star Shells were made (by Winchester) from 1884 to 1894."*
1894, Jan. 25	The **Peters** Cartridge Company **increases its** capitalization from $100,000.00 **to $300,000.00**. *Office of the Secretary of State of Ohio.*
1894, Sept. 25	The **King** Powder Company **changes its articles of incorporation** from "...for the purpose of manufacturing gunpowder, powder kegs and other purposes," to "...for the manufacture and sale of explosives and materials for same and for holding, leasing and using of property necessary or incident thereto." *Office of the Secretary of State of Ohio.*
1895	**Milton F. Lindsley** joins the **King** Powder Company. *Hist. of Exp. Ind.,* pp 281. According to a newspaper clipping in the files of Edna Bowyer, the date was July 1, 1895.
1895	**Peters** "Was obliged to go into the **manufacture of metallic ammunition** for rifles and revolvers. This last departure was made in **1895.**" *Talking points for Salesmen of Peters Goods pp 11; ca 1905.*
1895	First graduating class **Kings Mills High School**. *History of the Kings Mills School System; J. W. King, president of the school Board, 9/9/60.*
1895, May 28	Patent #540221, G. M. **Peters,** crimper. *This is for usual style of rolled-over crimp (not the indented type). Sones.*
1895, Oct.	**King** Powder Co. introduces **smokeless powder**. *King Powder brochure, 1896, pp 29.*
1895	**Peters** Cartridge Co. **built** "fine **shot tower** which dominated Miami Valley" (this is the wooden shot tower); F.C. Tuttle; *Remington Arms in American History, Alden Hatch. (Information from Dick Dietz of Remington Arms, 1-31-74.)*
1896	Introduction by King of "**Retriever**" brand black powder; *King Powder Company illustrated brochure, pp 22.*
1896, Feb. 9	Joe Mills at age 11 was working as a .22 caliber cup draw operator. This is one of the **earliest references** I have found of **workers actually making metallic ammunition** (see 1895 above). *The Primer, issue of December 1943, pp 1.*
1896, March 3	Patent #555734, G. M. **Peters**, cartridge-loading machine. *(A circular table rotating-format shotshell loading machine having a fault notification alarm and capable of loading pinfire shotshells.) Sones.*
1896, April 20	Peters Price List mentions Peters "Reinforced **Shells** and **metallic** cartridges loaded with **Kings Smokeless Powder** (Semi-Smokeless powder not yet mentioned. Still mentions black powder metallic loads). *Peters Price List. Klinect.*
1896	**Little Miami River flood** covered Pennsylvania railroad tracks at Oregonia (a few miles upriver from Kings Mills). *The Western Star, 3/23/61.*
1896	Patent #561029, G. M. **Peters,** cartridge-loading machine. *An in-line endless belt-type designed to cut top wads from a continuous strip. Sones.*
1896	**Peters** .22 Short rimfire loaded with **smokeless** powder; *Advertisement in the September 24 issue of Shooting and Fishing. Sones/Dutcher.*
1896	First use of **Semi-Smokeless Powder** (in cartridges). *Hints on Semi-Smokeless powder and Peters Cartridges.*
1896, Dec. 8	**Final appeal** -- Standard Cartridge Company vs. Peters **finding in favor of Peters** [Ligowsky Patent No. 464,883 assigned to Peters for "endless belt" or straight-line loading machine]. *Standard Cartridge Company v Peters, opinion this date by Judge Lurton, pp 19. Pynn/Sones.*
1897	Worst flood in history (to that date; **Little Miami River**). *Talking Points for Salesmen ca 1906, pp 8.*
1897	Advertisement for Kings **Smokeless** powder and an endorsement by F. C. Ross for .22 Short rimfire cartridges loaded with **Quick Shot** (black) powder. *Shooting and Fishing, April 8, 1897. Sones/Dutcher.*
1897, May	*"King's **Semi-Smokeless** has been under the most careful, searching and scientific investigation **for the past year** and is now offered for the **first time to the trade**", King Powder brochure dated May 1897. James Tillinghast.*
1897, July 1	Peters Price list mentions that the "**New King's Semi-Smokeless**" powder being loaded **in metallic cartridges and shotshells.** *Price list – Klinect.*
1897, Aug. 3	**Robert Eugene King born**, president of King Powder Company 1939-1957. *History of Southwestern Ohio, pp 397.*
1897, Nov. 11	The **Peters** Cartridge Company **increases** its capitalization from $300,000.00 **to $500,000.00**. *Office of the Secretary of State of Ohio.*
1897, Dec. 21	Copyright No. 31005 for a **trade label** (banner superimposed over circles) for The King Powder Company, for gunpowder, ordnance powder and blasting powder. Used since October 29 1895. *Sones.*

1898, Jan. 11	Copyright No.31138 for **logo** for the King Powder Company (a banner within a crown within a dark cartouche), for gun, ordnance and blasting powders. Used since October 29 1895. *Sones.*
1898, Feb. 15	**Battleship Maine blown up** in harbor of Havana, Cuba. *Random House Dictionary of English Language.*
1898	Brief **War** between Spain and the U.S. *Webster's New World Encyclopedia.*
1898	**Explosion at King** Powder, foreign agents suspected; **smokeless powder made for government** destroyed. Undated clipping from Cincinnati Post.
1898, June 7	**Patent** #605258, G. M. **Peters**, wad-placing mechanism for cartridge machine. *Sones.*
1898, June 7	**Patent** #605339, **William B. Place**, machine for priming heads of cartridges. *Sone.s*
1898, June 7	**Patent** #605340, **William B. Place**, machine for assembling heads of cartridge shells. *Sones.*
1898	**Peters** Cartridge Company received its **first** United States Army **Ordnance contract**... (for) .45-70 cartridges; *The Primer, October 1942 (this is the story of Frank E. Hoff, fifty-year Peters employee who went to work there in July 1893; contract was "five years later"). National Archives index refers to a contract of June 25, 1898 for " cal 45 and cal. .38 ball;" on June 27, 1898 "in reference to 3,000,000, r b (rifle, ball?) Cal 45 etc.;" on July 5, 1898 they refer to a "contract for 45/70 cartridges." There is also reference on June 1, 1898 to "45 Colt USA ammunition." TDS.*
1899, Jan. 17	G. M. **Peters**, **Patent #617766, Semi-Smokeless Powder** *(Note: Semi-Smokeless powder was always said to be Milton F. Lindsley's development, however his name does not appear on the patent). (Applied for 4-30-96). TDS.*
1899, Feb. 21	**Patent** #619787, **William B. Place**, Machine for making cartridge shells; *Description of wad winder. Sones.*
1899, June 7	**Patent** #605338, **William B. Place**, machine for heading shotshells. *Sones.*
1900, March 24	**Judge Thompson** opinion filed this date **finds in favor of Winchester** (infringement of **Patent #237605**; Winchester to recover damages and profits for past infringement - $1,000 according to Williamson) but requires Winchester to pay half the court costs. (Note: **patent #237605 had** since **expired; suit was result of American Buckle and Cartridge sale of shell-making equipment to Peters, and Peters' subsequent use**). *United States Circuit Court, Southern District of Ohio, Western Division, Winchester Repeating Arms vs. The Peters Cartridge Company et al, March 24. 1900. Pynn.*
1900	**Peters** produces the **first crimped .22 Long Rifle cartridge**; known as the Smith & Wesson Long. *Cartridges, Logan; pp10.*
1901	**King** agrees to sell all output to **Gunpowder Trade Association** for 25 yrs. *Himes.*
1901, March 12	**Patent** #699734; **William Place**, cartridge shell wad winder. *It was modification of Patent #619787. Sones.*
1901, June 18	**Patent** #676472; G. M. **Peters**, safety appliance for cartridge loading machine; *It was to separate the powder supply from the loading machine to prevent explosion of one powder charge from communicating to the large reserve supply. Sones.*
1901, Oct. 22	**Patent** #684861; G. M. **Peters**, apparatus for packing cartridges in boxes; *Uses a head-to-toe format. Sones.*
1901, Oct. 22	**Patent** 684862; G. M. **Peters**. *The same as Patent # 684861 except head-to-head format. Sones.*
1902, Jan.	**Explosion at King** Powder, One worker killed; four injured. *A History of Miami Land, Himes; 1990.*
1902, Jan. 22	The **King** Powder Company **increases** its **capitalization** from $500,000.00 to **$750,000.00**. *Office of the Secretary of State of Ohio.*
1902, Feb. 5	The **Peters** Cartridge Company increases its capitalization from $500,000.00 to $1,000,000.00. *Office of The Secretary of State of Ohio.*
1902, June 10	**Patent** #702151, G. M. **Peters**, metallic cartridge loading machine. *Appears to be a machine for loading metallic cartridges as blanks or with shot. Sones*
1902, June 30	**Death of "Wanda"**–Etta Butts Lindsley, wife of Milton F. Lindsley, of chronic interstitial nephritis, at Roanoke Flats in Cincinnati. *Death certificate, Hamilton County, Ohio.*
1903	**Colonel King's home** in Kings Mills **completed**; per *Bob Wilson, long-time resident of Kings Mills (6-25-98).*
1903	1,000 HP hydroelectric 500-foot dam, sprinklers @ 65 *psi;* nearly **1000** men, boys and girls **employed**. 10,000# sporting, 40,000# blasting and 5,000# smokeless. *1903 Atlas of Warren County, pp 105.*
1903	By this date the **Interurban** Railway and Terminal's Rapid Division was **complete** from between 4th and 5th Streets on Sycamore St. in Cincinnati to Lebanon, Ohio (went through Kings Mills). *Cincinnati Streetcars, Wagner and Wright; pp 210.*
1904, Feb. 5	The **Peters** Cartridge Company **increased capitalization** from $1,000,000.00 to **$1.500,000.00**. *Office of the Secretary of State of Ohio.*

1907	**Building R-21 constructed**. This was the shotshell-loading department. Probably the last of the post and beam construction for a major building. *Remington real estate listing 1944. George Kass.*
1907	**Du Pont** caught up in **anti-trust** violation suit. *Between the Miamis; Himes, pp 108.*
1907/1908	**Building R-3,** (Machine Shop) **erected;** postcard showing turn of the century Peters plant dated 12/3/07; postmarked Kings Mills, Dec 4, 1907;" *we are putting up another Building for this Co-400 x 60..."* signed: Philo S. Polly. Description fits existing machine shop building. *Note: Pat Miller, Chief (stationary) Engineer, told the author in 1974 that he thought the machine shop started up about 1910; that's pretty close.*
1907, March 1	**First Peters price list** which **does not** list a **King's Smokeless Powder** load in their Ideal brand shells. *Peters price list – Klinect.*
1907, May 7	**Copyright** No. 62,497 for King Powder Company, for name **SEMI-SMOKELESS** in hollow Roman letters printed in an arc, for gunpowder. Used at least ten years prior. *Sones.*
1907	**Mary Terwilliger Smith killed in explosion**. Does not specify whether she was a King or Peters employee [probably Peters; King did not hire women in powder work]. *Mason Journal July 4, 1974.*
1907, July 16	Copyright No. 63,959 for King Powder Company, for name **QUICK SHOT** in hollow Roman letters arranged in an arc: for gunpowder–particularly black sporting powder. Used at least ten years prior. *Sones.*
1908, Jan. 7	**Patent** #875762, Henry E, **Winans** & Fred **Sinnock**, spreader for shells; *a shot-spreading device to give larger shot patterns. Sones.*
1908, June 23	**Peters prevails** in their protest to Winchester's trademarking of the name "self loading". The trademarking prevented Peters or any company other than Winchester to market cartridges in this chambering. *Peters Cartridge Company v Winchester, US Court of Appeals, District of Columbia. Sones.*
1908, Dec. 1	**Patent** #905358, G. M. **Peters,** shotshell. *It covers a metallic lining of the base wad hole for the primer flash (steel where steel belongs?). Sones.*
1909, April 23	**Ahimaaz King's** death. *Hist of Exp Ind, pp 280.*
1909, June 1	**Patent** #923552, Anton **Mill,** tube machine. *A machine designed to cut paper tubes to length. Sones*
1909, June 1	**Patent** #923553, Anton **Mill,** tube-rolling machine. *A machine designed to roll paper tubes. Sones*
1909, June 1	**Patent** #923554, Anton **Mill,** tube-cutting machine. *A machine designed to cut paper tubes to length. Sones*
1909, Aug. 31	**Patent** # 932562, George A. **Muenzenmair**, shell. *A shotshell with a battery cup primer with a cap cover to prevent primer leaks. Sones*
1910, Nov. 1	Peters **Patent** #974418, **Muenzenmair** & Frank M. **See,** for a bullet. *TDS.*
1910, Sept. 6	**Patent** #969186, **Peters**, blasting. *TDS.*
1911, Jan. 11	**Peters found not in infringement** of Winchester patent for the embossing of shotgun shell heads to prevent cutoff. *Judge Platt opinion in Winchester Repeating Arms vs. Peters Cartridge Company, pp 6. Pynn.*
1911	**G. M. Peters** resigned; **Geo King** elected president of the King Powder Co. *Hist. of Exp. Ind.; pp 280.*
1911, April 4	**Patent** #988590, **Peters/Lindsley,** explosive. *TDS.*
1911, May 2	**Patent** #991238, **Peters/Lindsley,** explosive. *TDS.*
1911, June 6	**Patent** #994273, **Peters/Lindsley,** safety powder for blasting (67% ammonium nitrate, 20% table salt, 10% nitro-cellulose, 2% Mirbane oil and asphalt). Note: this was likely King's first successful "permissible" explosive.
1911, Aug. 1	**Patent** #999396, **Peters/Lindsley,** device used in mfg. of blasting cartridges. *TDS.*
1911, Dec.	**Patent** #1011238, **Peters/Lindsley,** for an explosive. *TDS.*
1913	**Flood** (worst ever; **Little Miami River**). *Between the Miamis; Himes, pp107.*
1913	**Building R-6** (bullet manufacture) constructed; *Remington real estate listing, 1944. George Kass.*
1913	Ammunition orders for **Russia** and **England**. *Between the Miamis; Himes pp 112*
1913, Sept. 29	**Patent** # 1072880, **Tewes**, for a bullet. *TDS.*
1914	Heir to Austrian throne **assassinated** at Sarajevo. **Starts WWI.**
1914, July 28	**Patent** # 1104923, G. M. **Peters**, for railway rail: *TDS.*
1915, May 7	**Lusitania,** ship of British registry with many U.S. citizens on board**,** sunk by German submarine.
1915, April 18	**King and Peters** said to **employ nearly 900** employees per diary entry of Herb Koch, Cincinnati Historical Society.

1916	No date specified. **Outright purchase of Fosdick** Machine Tool Company in Cincinnati to manufacture badly needed new equipment for **Peters** for war work. *Cincinnati Enquirer, July 12, 1927.* Note: in later years, R. K. LeBlond acquired Fosdick.
1916	**Building R-1 constructed** (*main building stands today*–paper shell and metallic cartridge mfg, cafeteria, offices, hospital, stores, etc; three floors and basement, 120,000 square feet). *Remington real estate listing, 1944. George Kass.*
1916	**Peters has contract with British** government for .303 British Mark VII ammunition. Headstamp "P16" at 12 o'clock; "VII" at 6 o'clock. *Cartridge Headstamp Guide,* H. P. White and B.D. Munhall, 1963.
1916	*Peters, Pioneer in Ammunition of Quality; How to Demonstrate;* refers to "our **new shot tower**" Note: this replaced the wooden shot tower erected in 1895.
1917	**Building R-19 Power House constructed**; produced DC power only, AC power bought from Cincinnati Gas and Electric. *Remington real estate listing, 1944, George Kass.*
1917	**Peters Cartridge Co.** payroll headcount **increases** from less than **1,000** to **3,000**; **1,000** were women; 1.5 million ctgs./ day. *Between the Miamis; Himes, pp 113.*
1917, March 25	The **King** Powder Company amend the Articles of Incorporation to **change the "location** and place where the principal business of the Company is transacted and its principal office location **from Cincinnati**, Hamilton County Ohio, **to Kings Mills**, Deerfield Township, Warren County, Ohio." *Office of the Secretary of State of Ohio.*
1917, March 29	The **Peters** Cartridge Company amend the articles of incorporation..."to **change the location** and place where the principal business of the Company is transacted and its principal office located **from Cincinnati**, Hamilton County, Ohio, **to King's Mills**, Hamilton Township, Warren County, Ohio." *Office of The Secretary of State of Ohio.*
1917, April	U.S. enters WWI
1917, mid-May	**The Third Ohio Regiment sent to Kings Mills** area to protect the munitions plants there. *How the Great World War Came to the Queen of the West* (Cincinnati), Koch, Felix J. Myers Engraving Company, Cincinnati, 1917, pp 23.
1917, Aug. 20	**Blast** of ton of powder at **Kings** Mills **kills four**: Alvie Joseph, Cin, Ohio; T. M. McDonald, New Albany, Ind.; Frank Howell, Gracy, Alabama; Rudolf Augst, alien; James H. Owens, Athens, Alabama severely injured. *Cincinnati Enquirer 8/21/17.*
1917, Aug. 22	**Blast at Kings Mills claims another** victim, James H. Owens, Athens, Alabama. *Cincinnati Enquirer 8/22/17.*
1917, Oct. 23	**Patent #1243857, Muenzenmaier**, for jacketed bullet. *TDS.*
1917/1918	The Peters Cartridge Company produces **84,169,800** rounds of "our **caliber .30** service ammunition [this would have been in addition to contracts for caliber .45 ACP cartridges produced for the government]. *America's Munitions 1917-1918, report of Benedict Crowell, Assistant Secretary of War, Director of Munitions, pp193.*
1918	**Building R-2** (metallic cartridge loading) **constructed**. *Remington real estate listing, 1944. George Kass.*
1918, Nov. 11	WWI over.
1919, Jan. 21	The **King** Powder Company **capitalization increased** from $ 750,00.00 to $950,000.00 (probably to finance the new operation at Wurtland, Kentucky). *Office of the Secretary of State of Ohio.*
1919	**Building R-23 (ballistics and indoor shooting range) constructed**. *Remington real estate offering, 1944. George Kass.*
1919	**Building R-9 (primer assembly) constructed**. *Remington real estate listing, 1944. George Kass.*
1919	Between 400 and 500 acres of **land** were **purchased** at **Wurtland**, Ky. by the King Powder Company to build a new powder plant. *The Russell (Ky.) Times, September 1942, pp 5.*
1919, Oct. 5	**G. M. Peters died.** *Hist. of Exp. Ind.,* pp 276; Apoplexy. Honorary degree Denison, 1913. *Cincinnati Enquirer obituary Oct 6, 1919.*
1919	**King Powder Co.** starts **KICO** plant at Wurtland, Kentucky to make black and, ultimately, Detonite explosives. *Undated newspaper article from David Spencer.* (Note: The Russell Times issue of September, 1942, says construction actually started in 1920.)
1920, May 18	Harley T. Peck, **Patent # 1340245**, assignor to Peters; addition of non-combustible material to shotshell to prevent cutoffs (lead, mica, asbestos, etc). *Sones.*
1920	**Geo. King**, president - **Institute of Makers of Explosives** (vice pres. since 1916). *Hist. of Exp. Ind., pp 280.*
1920, (early)	Outside **flush toilets** furnished in **Kings Mills**. *Himes.*
1920, Aug. 24	**Harley T. Peck** assignor to Peters Cartridge Co. gets basic **patent** on non-corrosive primer. *TAR 6-1927 pp 39* (appears to be **Patent #1350465, primer** for small arms). *TDS.*

1920, July 1	The **Peters** Cartridge Company **amend its Articles of Incorporation** to read: "That the object shall be the manufacture and sale of cartridges for blasting purposes and use in fire arms, and also the manufacture and sale of material entering into the same, as well as the manufacture and sale of all articles capable of being manufactured and sold together with the transaction of any of any and all business incident thereto." *Office of the Secretary of State of Ohio.*
1920, July 1	The **Peters** Cartridge Company **increases its capitalization** from $1,500,000.00 **to $3,000,000.00**. *Office of the Secretary of State of Ohio.*
1921, May 16	Patent #1416121, **Peck**; primer for small arms. *TDS.*
1922, Feb 22	Harley T. **Peck**, **Patent #1407767**, assignor to Peters Cartridge Co, for **primer** for small arms (35% potassium chlorate, 35% fulminate of mercury, 30% antimony sulfide and 5% tri nitro resorcinol). For uniform ignition of smokeless powder. *TDS.*
1922, May 16	Harley T. **Peck**, **Patents #1416121, #1416122** and **#1416123** assignor to Peters Cartridge, for various **priming mixtures** containing differing amounts of potassium chlorate, lead sulfocyanate, di plumbic di tri-nitro resorcinol etc.–all mixtures corrosive). *TDS.*
1922	All service on the **Interurban** and Terminal's Rapid Division (Cincinnati to Lebanon through Kings Mills) **ceased**. *Cincinnati Streetcars Wagner and Wright, pp 210.*
1922, Oct.	The **first products** were completed **at** the new **KICO** plant of the King Powder Company at Wurtland Kentucky. *The Russell Times, September 1942, pp 5.*
1924, Aug. 26	Patent #1506084, Norman L. **Richmond**, for shotgun shell carton. *A two-piece, 25-count box with perforations along the sidewall. Sones.*
1924, Oct. 21	Patent #1512026, Charles Leroy **Holden** & William **Knedler**, for bullet. This was Peters "Protected Point Bullet" design, a jacketed bullet designed with metallic nose cap. *Sones.*
1924, Nov. 18	Patent #1516340, Charles Leroy **Holden**, for bullet. *TDS.*
1925, Oct. 20	Patent #1557695, Charles Leroy **Holden**, for loaded shot cartridge. This was for the .45 ACP riot shot loading. Design incorporated a cup around the base of the shot sabot; this and #1557696 were likely for the Thompson submachine gun. *Sones.*
1925, Oct. 20	Patent #1557696, **Holden**, for loaded shot cartridge. This is designed for the same cartridge as Patent #1557695 and had an inverted cup and wad at the base of the shot sabot. *Sones.*
1926, May 18	Patent # 1584993, Norman L. **Richmond**, for cartridge carton; patent claims perforations along the sides for easy opening. *Sones.*
1927	The **Peters** Cartridge Company, **50th anniversary** [began in 1887].
1927	**Peters** Cartridge Co. hires **Philip Quayle from U.S. Bureau of Standards** as chief physicist. Quayle subsequently introduces **Sparkography** (photographs at one millionth of a second, of projectiles in flight) to advertising and to quality control of cartridges. *Tuttle, 1932.*
1927, June	**Peters Cartridge Co.** announces **"Rustless"** feature. Peters says: "the chemicals (potassium chlorate) which cause pitting and corrosion… have already been eliminated since 1920" refers to a Peters 1920 patent (**see Patent 1350465**). *The American Rifleman, 6-1927.*
1927, June	Peters announces the introduction of an *"improved Semi-Smokeless Powder."* *The American Rifleman, 6-1927. Dale Hedlund.*
1927, Aug. 31	The **King** Powder Company **increases capitalization** from $750,000.00 **to $1,000,000.00**. *Office of the Secretary of State of Ohio.*
1927, Oct. 25	Patent #1646409, **Keplinger,** for oil cup. *TDS.*
1927, Nov.	**Townsend Whelen** writes about the new **Remington non-corrosive primer**, crediting J. E. Burns of Remington and H. C. Pritham with the development. *The American Rifleman, 11-1927.*
1928, Jan.	**Colonel George King elected president of the Peters Cartridge Company** [now president of both Peters and King]. *George King personal letter to Earl Thompson in author's files.*
1928, May	*TAR,* Quayle awarded Medal of Honor by Royal Photographic Society of Great Britain for advancing photographic art through spark photography.
1928	The **Peters** Cartridge Company: "…a number of **rim fire cartridges are now loaded with improved Semi-Smokeless powder** in which all the desirable qualities of the original Semi-Smokeless are retained and enhanced." Peters advertising booklet: *"What happens after the shot is fired" pp12.*
1928, Jan. 31	Patent #1657584, **Peck,** for manufacture of shotshells. *Sones.*
1928/1929	Business good for **Peters Cartridge Co.** *Himes, pp 122.*
1928	KICO plant adds **pellet powder** to the King Powder Company's line of blasting products. *This consisted of 2-inch long pellets of black blasting powder, either 2- or 1.25-inch diameter, packaged and used four to an 8-inch long cartridge. The Russell Times, September 1942, pp 5.*

Mason (Ohio) *Journal*, newspaper clipping *Killed in Explosion*, July 4, 1974

Morris, Jim, The Grand American, A Century of Trapshooting Tradition, 1900 - 1999, Amateur Trap Association, Vandalia, Ohio, 1999

Muzzle Blasts, journal of the National Muzzle Loading Rifle Association, Friendship, Indiana, 1939 to date

Naoum, Phokion, Phd, *Nitroglycerine and Nitroglycerine Explosives*, Baltimore, 1928

National Rifle Association, Journals of, *Arms and the Man* and *The American Rifleman,* Currently in Fairfax, Virginia, 1914 to date

National Rifle Association, *Reloading Ammunition, Volume No.1,* National Rifle Association, 1953

Nelson, S. B. (publisher*), History of Cincinnati and Hamilton County,*

Oakley, Annie (Mrs. Frank Butler), *Powders I Have Used,* Du Pont, 1914, courtesy of the Annie Oakley Foundation

Oakley, Annie (Mrs. Frank Butler), scrapbook of newspaper clippings and other memorabilia concerning both Annie Oakley and Frank Butler, unpublished, compiled by both Annie and Frank, courtesy of the Annie Oakley Foundation, (originals in the Cody Museum) 1880s to 1920s

Orr and Mills (publishers), *Directory of Warren County* (Ohio), January 1, 1900

Paso Del Norte Gun Collectors Inc. *History of the M1 Carbine*, El Paso, Texas, ~ 1990

Peters Cartridge Company, *The Primer*, various issues in the Warren County Historical Society Collection (courtesy of Edna Bowyer), 1930s to 1944

Peters Cartridge Company, catalogs and price lists, published by the Peters Cartridge Company, Cincinnati, Ohio and Kings Mills, Ohio, from 1889 through 1944, from files of Windy Klinect, Ted Bacyk, Bill Woodin (Woodin Laboratory), George Kass (Forensic Ammunition), Mick McLaughlin, Jim Eckler, Dale Hedlund, Cris Punnett and Ron Willoughby

Public Records Office, London, MUN 7/155, Ch III, Ch IV and Ch V, (Contracts through the Morgan Grenfel and J.P. Morgan Cos. for Mk VII ammunition in USA during WWI and cancellation thereof), courtesy of John Pople-Crump, for years1915 and 1916

Public Records Office, London, MUN 5/190/1440/6, (output of small arms ammunition from USA), courtesy of John Pople-Crump, for years 1915 and 1916

Rains, Colonel (General) George Washington, CSA, (West Point, 1842), *History of the Confederate Powder Works*, address delivered to the Confederate Survivors' Association, The Newburgh New York, 1882

Remington Arms Company, *In Abundance and On Time*, 1939 - 1943, published by Remington in 1944, photocopies furnished by Richard (Dick) Dietz of Remington Arms Company in the mid-1970s

Remington Arms, *Real Estate Listing of Peters Cartridge Company land* at Kings Mills, limited publication, George Kass collection, 1944

Roberts, Ned H., *The Muzzle - Loading Cap Lock Rifle,* The Granite State Press, 1940

Roberts, Major Ned H. and Waters, Kenneth L., *The Breech-Loading Single Shot Rifle*, Wolf Publishing Company, Inc. Prescott, Arizona, 1981

Robinson, *History of Greene County* (Ohio), 1902

Russell (Ky.) *Times*, newspaper article concerning *purchase of land*, September 1942

Sanford, P. Gerald, *Nitro Explosives, a Practical Treatise*, Crosby Lockwood and Son, London, 1906

Satterlee, L. D., *Fourteen Old Gun Catalogs* (Marlin 1888), fourth edition, Follett Publishing Company (Gun Digest Assn.), 1962

Schiffer, T. D., *The King Powder Company*, Muzzle Blasts, Friendship, Indiana, April and May issues, 1986

Scofield, John, *The Old Master*, the *American Rifleman*, 1941

Sharpe, Philip B., *The Rifle In America*, third edition, William Morrow and Company, 1938 and 1947

Sharpe, Philip B., *Complete Guide to Handloading*, third edition, Funk & Wagnalls Company, New York and London, 1942

Single Shot Journal, various issues, American Single Shot Rifle Association, Rudi Prusok editor, also, archives of the

Association (collected, organized and maintained by Rudi Prusok)

Smith, Captain F. M., Royal Artillery, *A Handbook of the Manufacture and Proof of Gunpowder*, as carried on at the Royal Gunpowder Factory, Waltham Abbey, Her Majesty's Stationery Office, London, ~1870

Smith, Ray M., *The Story of Pope's Barrels*, Stackpole Company, Harrisburg, Pa. 1960

Smith, William E*., History of Southwestern Ohio*, Vol III, Lewis Historical Publishing Co., New York and West Palm Beach

Stadt, Ronald W., *Winchester Shotguns and Shotshells,* Krause Publications, 1995

Stoeger, A. F. Inc. (catalog), *Arms and Ammunition*, 1929

Stuart, Jesse, *Head o' W-Hollow,* University Press of Kentucky, 1936 and 1979

U.S. Army Armament Research and Development Command, Ballistic Research Laboratory, *Relationship of Combustion Characteristics and Physical Properties of Black Powder,* by Kevin J. White and Ronald A. Sasse', Aberdeen Proving Ground, Maryland, November, 1982

U.S. Army Signal Corps, photo files, Library of Congress, Washington D.C. 1944

U.S. Bureau of Mines, *Technical Papers*, Washington, 1913

U.S. Circuit Court *Files*, (various)

U.S. Copyright files, Jim Sones, Denver Colorado, re Peters Cartridge Company

U.S. Geological Survey, *maps*, current and out of print

U.S. Government, Report of the Chief of Ordnance, Washington, D. C., 1918

U.S. Ordnance Department, correspondence records, National Archives, Washington D. C., 1890 to 1944

U.S. Patent Gazette, Cincinnati, Hamilton County Library, 1885 through 1945

U.S. Patent files of Jim Sones, Denver Colorado, re The Peters Cartridge Company

Van Gelder and Schlatter, *History of the Explosives Industry in America*, Columbia University Press, 1927

Various authors, *Forest and Stream, a weekly journal of the Rod and Gun*, Forest and Stream Publishing Company, New York, various issues 1885 -1906

Various authors, *International Ammunition Association Journal*, Lineboro, Maryland

Various authors, *Sportsman's Review*, Cincinnati Ohio, various issues, 1892-1944

Various authors, the *Gun Digest*, various editors, annual publication, 1946 to date

Various pieces of literature and promotional materials concerning The Peters Cartridge Company and the King Powder Company, too numerous to list, same sources as above

Wagner and Wright, *Cincinnati Streetcars*

Warren County (Ohio), Clerk's Office, *Deeds, Maps*, etc

Warren County Historical Society, Oral History, Unpublished manuscript in files of the, Lebanon Ohio, compiled under the direction of Ms. Phillips ~

Western Star (Lebanon, Ohio), newspaper articles (various) dealing with explosion of 1890

White, H. P. and Munhall, B. D., *Cartridge Headstamp Guide*, 1963

White, John, *Little Miami Railroad*, Bulletin of Cincinnati Historical Society, Volume 32, Winter, 1974

Wiggins & McKillop (publishers), *Directory of Warren County* (Ohio), 1878

Williamson, Harold E. *Winchester, the gun that won the west*, A. S. Barnes & Co. Inc., 1952

Witt, Constance, *Families*, Genealogical files of the Warren County Historical Society, 1981

Winchester Repeating Arms Co, *Winchester Arms and Ammunition Catalogs from 1865 to 1918*, Armory Publications, 1991

Worden, *Edward Chauncy, Nitrocellulose Industry*, D. Van Norstrand, New York, 1911

Xenia (Ohio) Daily Gazette (newspaper), *Interesting History, Goes Station*, May 6, 1986

Xenia Torchlight (newspaper), *Powder Mill Explosion*, March 13, 1867

Index

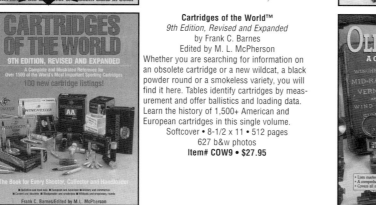